NO MAN'S WAR

Angela Ricketts

no man's war

A MEMOIR

Irreverent Confessions of an Infantry Wife

COUNTERPOINT
BERKELEY

Library of Congress Data Is Available

ISBN 978-1-61902-326-0

Cover design by Faceout Studio
Interior Design by Megan Jones Design

COUNTERPOINT
1919 Fifth Street
Berkeley, CA 94710
www.counterpointpress.com

Printed in the United States of America
Distributed by Publishers Group West

10 9 8 7 6 5 4 3 2 1

For my Mom and Dad.

"Know that you are not alone
And that this darkness has purpose;
Gradually it will scchool your eyes
To find the one gift your life requires
Hidden within this night-corner"

—"For Courage,"
from *To Bless the Space Between Us*
by John O'Donohue

part one

grey street

I dreamed myself a thousand times around the world,
But I can't get out of this place.

—DAVE MATTHEWS

NOVEMBER 21, 2010

SOMETIMES WHEN YOU wake in the middle of the night it's only for a slippery moment, a moment to re-cozy yourself, to remember with a flash of panic that forgotten appointment from the day before or to get up to potty. *Potty* is a word mothers begin using from the instant they give birth and never leaves their vocabulary until death. Sometimes what wakes you is a long-forgotten memory, the thing you tried to put behind you.

Once or twice in a lifetime you wake up and just know it: You are dying, even though three hours ago you were watching *Weeds* and fluffing pillows on the couch and wiping down the kitchen counter-tops because you never know what the night will bring. And because a perfectly neat home masks the other mess that spins beyond control.

I jerk awake and move the empty wine glass to see the time on the digital clock. Two something. I should remember the precise time on the clock, but I am a date person. Dates I remember; times, not so much.

In the silent house with a staring cat and three sleeping children and again without a husband present, I struggle through sleepy, disoriented

1

eyes to remember where I am. A sweet artificial stank hangs in the air; oh yeah, the Yankee Candle I blew out before I slammed the last gulp of wine. Nothing looks familiar as I go back and forth in my mind; which issue is more pressing, the crushing pain in my chest or where the hell I am? The glare of the streetlight shining into the window reminds me I'm home, home for now. This is our third house in less than two years, and it takes me a minute to remember where I am. Fort Campbell. Just across the Tennessee border, but with a Kentucky address, surely the result of a political fight over which state got to claim ownership of the home of the 101st Airborne. I'm back in the familiar zone I like to think of as Grey Street, a favorite Dave Matthews song about a woman who feels numbed and paralyzed by her life. Like her world has spiraled beyond her control. Where colors bleed and overlap into only gray. The vibrancy of each color not lost, just absorbed into a blanket of grayness. The gray of autopilot. The gray of another deployment, of a home with a man of the house who wouldn't know which drawer held the spoons. He's the man of the house in concept alone. He is three months into a yearlong deployment in Afghanistan, with no need to even own a house key.

But in this two-something wee hour, these ideas are just whispers under my blankets and inside my skin. My feet nudge around looking for the children, who sometimes wander half asleep into my bed. As soon as I move I feel it, the thing that startled me awake. It isn't a dream or a memory or a forgotten appointment. It's pain, the physical kind. What frightens me in that moment isn't the gripping pain in my chest, but a wave of incomprehensible terror for its newness and unfamiliar nature. A twisting stab in my back pushes me out of bed and to my feet. I feel sweat roll down the back of my neck, but it's almost Thanksgiving and I allow the chill from outside to come into our home at night. I prefer the insulation of blankets and flannel pajamas to warm air.

Oh hell. It's a panic attack. My body is at long last going on strike, revolting from the stress of eight long, intense deployments. That's what I've been warned of, anyway, in the "resiliency" workshops and briefings army wives sit through during deployments. Well, before deployments, during deployments, and after deployments. So all the time. Whatever you face or feel, surely it's addressed in a binder somewhere. The army's philosophy is that just by virtue of identifying and labeling an issue, it's 95 percent fixed. At each available opportunity, we are reminded to pace ourselves and manage stress. I picture the PowerPoint slide: "Panic attacks are a terrifying but normal reaction: It will feel like you are going to die, but here are coping tips . . . Remember, we are ARMY STRONG!" But what were the tips? Dammit. Breathe. That's surely one. I do feel like I'm going to die.

I grab my cell phone off the dresser and wander through the upstairs of our quiet house. Joe is almost a teenager, a stack of *Call of Duty: Black Ops* video games just inches from his sleeping head and a game controller teetering on the edge of the bed. The violent video games that Jack allowed because they are a reality of his job. Jack argued that the video games are disturbing with their accuracy and not gratuitous in their violence. The line between good guys and bad guys is clear, at least in the game.

Our two daughters, Bridget, who is ten, and Greta, five, are curled together in Bridget's room across the hall. Using the term *our* is an effort on my part. "My children" comes more naturally; I have to make an effort to remind myself that these are "our children." I'm not alone in parenting, at least not in theory. In reality, yes, I am alone.

In this moment of defining chest pain I am alone.

The blinding streetlight streams into the adjacent rooms and onto my sleeping babies. Sometimes, when morning comes, I find all three kids together in one bed, or all of us in my bed. But this is how they landed tonight.

My left shoulder pangs and I grip the wall without a sound. Just my palm on the ugly wall. For years the army painted the inside of our homes chalky white; then they decided to get all snazzy with the neutral tones.

At the bottom of the stairs, our wedding portrait hangs, and the light hits my neck in the photo just perfectly. I bought that double strand of mock pearls intending to wear them choker style with the wedding dress that I thought was so simple compared with the other dresses in the early 1990s. When my wedding day finally arrived, I was thankful beyond measure that the pearls were adjustable and could hang loosely around my neck instead of high on my throat. The latter would have been prettier, more chic. But I couldn't bear it. Couldn't bear to have anything choke me.

There's some warning signal about shoulder pain I should remember now. I flounder down the stairs. Calling 911 never enters my mind. Drama queens, attention whores, that's who calls 911 in the middle of the night in our neighborhood. According to post policy, Joe is officially old enough to babysit. It occurs to me to just drive to the hospital myself and no one would even know I was gone.

"Did you hear all that commotion last night was Angie Hawkins? She called 911 for a freaking panic attack at two a.m. Two fire trucks, an ambulance, and three MP cars. Woke up the whole block for a panic attack. And on a school night. She's just trying to get her husband sent home." Some roll their eyes and some shake their heads. The scenario of tomorrow's bus stop conversation fuels my confidence that I can drive the two miles to the hospital on my own and get back before the kids even wake for school. No one will know. I can save the story of my middle-of-the-night panic attack for a boring moment during Bunco or a punch line at the next coffee.

With too many symptoms to focus on them separately anymore, I grow weak and fight tears as the pain radiates back and forth from my spine to my left shoulder. One ugly green Croc lying by the door will have to do as I head to the car with one bare foot. Maybe I shouldn't leave the kids. What if they wander into my bed and I'm not there? The thought crosses my mind but dissipates in my brief hunt for the matching Croc. The hospital on post is two miles away, a straight shot without a single car on the road. I drive right past the emergency entrance and drive over the grass to turn around. Not even an MP on the empty roads that are usually peppered with at least one officer on each block, waiting to catch me blow through stop signs or drive on the grass. Just my luck. Not an MP in sight.

I don't bother to park, leaving my car running and the driver's door hanging open. I stumble into automatic ER doors and explode into tears. "I'm dying." I half expect a reprimand and an order to move my car before I die. My mask of strength is torn from my face.

"What's your name? Where is your ID card? Are you allergic to anything? Are you going to vomit? Where is the pain coming from? Rate your pain from one to ten. Ma'am, can you breathe?" But this ER tech says these words in a far-too-unaffected way. The workers behind the desk share glances, and a moment of embarrassment rushes over me and then past me. I want to scream at them that I was not stung by an imaginary bee and am not suffering from an imagined allergic reaction. They will realize it soon enough, and I will enjoy a moment of satisfaction, if I live that long. Somehow that's all preferable to a panic attack.

A heart attack leaves me in the ICU for a week. Not a cardiac event, but a full-fledged heart attack that leaves my heart compromised forever and leads to surreal discussions about a long-term prognosis. Cardiologists scratched their heads over what could have caused such an absurdity. Weeks earlier, I had jogged six miles up and down a mountain. I never touched a cigarette. I squeezed my size 8 ass into size 6 jeans. A heart attack?

Hours later in the cardiac catheterization lab, my last memory is the anesthesiologist reviewing my chart, reciting my age, weight, family history, general health information. He looks at me and shakes his head. A nurse in the frenzy of prepping the operating room flips on a CD player, AC/DC's "Hells Bells." I'd like to laugh at her ironic song choice. Even through my morphine stupor, I marvel, watching the fluidity of the staff's second-nature routine as a team. Not unlike army wives. Just before I drift into the bliss of anesthesia, my final memory is of the white-haired, jolly-looking anesthesiologist leaning close to my ear and asking me, "Why are *you* on this table? What broke your heart?"

smurf village

The cream of the crop, son. Bragging rights
and a year's vacation from the grit and spit.

THE STORY OF an army wife can't be told in a linear way; it
has to be written in reverse, with moments of back and forth. A
metaphor for how we live. Zigzagging, never in a straight line.

When we move away from Fort Drum, New York, and leave eight
years at the 10th Mountain Division behind us to become students at
the U.S. Army War College in Carlisle, Pennsylvania, on a cold and
rainy summer day in 2009, I can't quite absorb that this will be for
good. I refuse to glance in the rearview mirror as we drive away, telling
myself, *We will be back.* Most soldiers don't have the opportunity or
desire to homestead for eight years, especially in a place where they've
been stationed even before those eight years. Most soldiers aren't nuts
enough to *want* to stay in the isolated North Country so long. I spent
a total of fourteen years in the North Country of Watertown, New
York, give or take, over a twenty-two-year period. First with my parents when my father was stationed there, then again as a wife. The
second time, we came back just two months before 9/11, before the
game changed for everyone. Leaving now feels wrong, but our marriage is on a messy, poorly maintained autopilot, and Jack has convinced us that a year at the coveted war college will be great for our

family. So off we go and I tell myself we will come home to the North Country next summer.

A year at the war college is a gift, a gift of a year to unwind and reflect and take a look inward and also gain a perspective of the entire military system. Even more, it provides lifetime, hard-core bragging rights. Making or not making the war college cut is a big deal in our culture, and smugly working into conversation the phrase *war college* in a low and drawn-out voice is highly valued. Only one out of ten is selected to go, with a long alternate list of the folks almost but not quite selected to attend. The folks on the alternate list spend the entire year before the summer of war college waiting for an email or a phone call telling them they will have a spot. Some only find this out weeks before they need to report to Carlisle. So in addition to just having the simple bragging rights of war college, we have the added cachet of being selected first round and knowing a year in advance where we are headed. What's really sad in our little world is that we all know who is on whichever list, and who is not. Nothing is a secret. Not the successes or the misses.

I try very hard to talk myself into being happy about leaving Watertown, even if it is for the big-deal U.S. Army War College. Until now, the army has given us just about everything we've asked for. It's easy to take success for granted, and it could be swept away in a flash. Until now, we've always landed on our feet. Or at least given the appearance of it.

Fort Drum and surrounding Watertown are the only home our kids have known or remembered, so I reassure them with my hope that we will be back. A little trick I brought with me from my army brat childhood. I become as connected to places as I do people, maybe even more so. Saying good-bye and moving on to the next place never come naturally to me, it's always an agonizing process, and this is our kids' first taste of it. So I let them believe we will be back next summer, and hope it's true. Fort Drum is our home, our history.

After eighteen years of marriage, we finally have the double-edged sword of a year to hang out with each other and fall back in love. The shared nature of our infantry-focused lives equips us to function better alone than together. Now we drive away from our home and cross our fingers that this year will allow us to fill in the facade of happy smiles that mask exhaustion in family pictures—to share "essences," as our marriage therapist has told us. Gross. Tension we share; essences, no.

We soon discover that we don't just not know each other, but we possibly don't even like each other. The love is beyond question. What we lack is feeling natural together. We can't complete one another's sentences like other couples do. We don't have a plethora of inside jokes. Instead we have resentment and lost ground. Neither of us is willing or able to show our true self. Our interactions with each other are like the neighbor or coworker who you never can quite figure out, the one you choose your words around and hope the conversation doesn't stray beyond small talk. The desire to escape is mutual.

Simply saying there is a wall between us is an understatement. What we need to figure out is whether the wall is built of stones, which can be removed, or steel, which can't. I do know it's built by years of time apart and life decisions dictated by the pressure of the next looming deployment.

We married hastily on the eve of a deployment, young and foolish with a gut feeling of rightness—opposites attract and the other typical cliché nonsense. No matter what, marriage is a leap of faith. Even after the worst arguments or days of silence, I never questioned that I loved the idea of him. I never questioned his loyalty or his commitment to our family. Maybe this year we can find something to talk about, something that doesn't feel forced.

We planned our children around deployments. The army was and is his mistress, the one who holds our secrets, the third party in our marriage. We can't exhale until the mistress has her say. She is the one we each run to when we can't stand being with the other any longer. She is our safe place; we've never had the opportunity to become each other's haven. She keeps our lives inescapably intertwined. I blame our problems on him, and he blames them on me. Maybe in truth the blame lies with the mistress.

Our undeniable love for each other far outweighs the lack of natural interaction, though it is difficult to see sometimes. There is little indifference, and maybe the lack of indifference is what held us together in those years and the years since. Passion is never lacking in our marriage. Luckily we can thank the army for that gift. The army is our shared love far more than our shared enemy. Aside from our family of three children, our mutual investment in the army lifestyle is our glue.

One of the things I never quite grasp about couples who divorce is how they distance themselves from their identity as a family. How they untangle. No matter how low our moments get in the darkest times of our marriage, Jack is my family. Family stays. A life without him in it, though he is away more than he is here, is inconceivable.

While our year at the war college suffocates us with the shared realization of how far we've drifted from each other, it is liberating and magnificent in every other way. Life on Carlisle Barracks reminds me of one of those summer resorts with activities and leisure; picture the *Dirty Dancing* setting. There is no reason for stress. Every hour is happy hour. We take ballroom dance lessons and laugh at our power struggle, even on the dance floor.

Our tiny neighborhood of student housing in Carlisle is built for families the size of dolls and even bears the nickname Smurf Village. Somehow it works for our family of five, and despite the tension in our marriage, our Smurf house is the coziest of all our army houses. We are together, at least in our physical presence. Yes, if I happen to need to wash my hands or brush my teeth while Jack is on the john, then my butt practically touches his face. But somehow these are the good times, the moments we have a reason to laugh. I'm thankful for the levity provided by a tiny bathroom.

For an entire year, Jack wears a regular business suit to classes, but with his army backpack slung across his shoulders. He looks like a rogue Jehovah's Witness as he sets off each day. For an entire year we have the privilege of pretending that we aren't sandwiched between two long and lethal combat deployments.

The other students and their spouses come from parts of the world and military I don't even know exist. The word *spouse* is the new, politically correct term we are encouraged to use instead of *wife*. Somewhere in the late 1990s, wives' manuals became spouses' manuals, and then wives' clubs became spouses' clubs. The wives smile obediently and follow the herd on the shift from tradition, so that much of our predictable manual for how to operate is lost in the modern military. The truth for us is that there are no women in the infantry, thus no handful of husbands to insult with the use of the word *wife*. So I enjoy the freedom in our tiny culture of combat to use *wife* without a hint of hesitation and with a nice dose of indignation. Taking it one step further, most army family readiness manuals and media outlets further embrace the term *military spouse*. Double yuck. I am an army wife. I doubt my air force spouse neighbor wants to be lumped in with me any more than I want to share an umbrella title with her.

At the war college, I quickly learn to keep my infantry bravado in check. In the class of three hundred or so puffed-up American and international overachieving, type A personalities, only 5 percent are infantrymen. So not only am I amazed at the number of military jobs I never even knew existed, but female servicewomen, international students, and Department of Defense (DoD) civilian students attending the Army War College surround us. I'm outnumbered, and no one cares how many deployments we have or don't have. We are on an even playing field. And that weirds me out to an extent. I miss the familiarity of what we know.

Sure, our comrades at the 10th Mountain Division and other infantry divisions would pop back and forth to assignments for a few years at the Pentagon, but not us. We stayed, feet planted in infantry units, with the exception of two years Jack spent in a position as a small group instructor in the late 1990s. I hurried up and popped out two babies in those two years, because I knew it was the only guaranteed time he would be present for the births. Many wives have babies without regard to deployment schedules and possible Third World demands of their husbands, but not me. *Present for the birth* is my line in the sand, and one I've proudly predicted with accuracy. Jack experienced the heaven and hell of my labor right alongside me each time. In each of my pregnancies, I craved Jack's presence. The feeling of needing him so much both terrified me and reassured me that we were meant to be.

The collective Fort Drum years were focused on the comings and goings of deployments; I was unaware of the military jobs and positions beyond our tiny scope of infantry units. As the daughter of an infantry officer, I was, when I married my lieutenant in 1992, well aware of the cult of the infantry, the "queen of battle," the knuckle-draggers, the grunts. But somewhere along the way, I forgot that there are others, many others. The infantry is the gut and the fist, but we need the whole body and the brain to work. *But the gut and the fist are the coolest, right?* Don't tell the brain and the rest of the body we said that. One army, one team. That's our motto.

So for a year in our snug Smurf Village cottage on Carlisle Barracks, I embrace my identity as a military spouse. Most days, Jack seems like a haunted stranger who is unavoidable in such tight quarters. We do our best to not bump elbows in the minuscule kitchen. I learn to play bridge and attend self-growth seminars and team-building workshops. It becomes clear that focusing on personal, individual growth and learning will best facilitate the semblance of peace in the tiny house built for dolls. Jack and I quickly become experts at the Meyers-Briggs personality types and relish the excuse to blame our problems on our vastly different types. I make new friends, most of whom are married to combat officers and have been through many deployments. Birds of a feather. Most of my friends at the war college are reconnections with old friends from earlier duty stations, but I gain a few new ones. In the past, whenever we moved to a new duty station, I felt unsettled until I found "my people." Very quickly in Carlisle, I find my people.

I catch myself staring curiously at wives whose husbands have never deployed, and I try to wrap my mind around how that could possibly be true. Like a cow that has never crossed paths with a horse in the barn. We cows know the horses exist, but seeing them and munching grass alongside them for the first time are altogether titillating. There is no resentment or negativity, only curiosity.

In our home, we avoid topics like the kids and Jack's hypervigilant parenting style (compensating, hmm?) versus my laissez-faire style of picking my battles. Parenting is a volatile topic for Jack and me, so I cling to nonexplosive subjects as fodder for our conversations. One night I bring up how so many in the army and the rest of the military have never deployed, not even in a capacity beyond infantry units. Lots of guys deploy as part of a staff or joint team, higher than the division level. Those aren't terribly sexy deployments, but at least they come with deployment bragging rights. Where have these never-deployed guys been?

"Ang, it's not like that," Jack tells me. "Most aren't intentionally avoiding deployments. Everyone has a key role. Lots of guys would love to deploy, but it's timing and the needs of the army. They aren't in the right place at the right time. Other guys have no desire to deploy for their own reasons, and that's fine by me." He slides his reading glasses back on before returning to his required reading. He peers over the glasses for one last remark. "This is just my opinion, but my point of serving is to be in 'The Fight.' Otherwise, it would feel like going to practice every day without ever playing in the game. But not everyone sees it like that, which is great as far as I'm concerned. More room for me. Who cares what others do or don't. Everyone has a purpose. Quit keeping track."

Jack really speaks like that. In bullets from a manual. Bullets that sound an awful lot like propaganda bullshit sometimes. I'm the one who spits out the Kool-Aid when no one is looking. He gulps it. But this—this doesn't sound like propaganda-laced Kool-Aid.

I let his words sink in and listen to the voices of CNN playing softly in the background. March 2010. I hear the word *surge* tossed back and forth like a magic bullet. I don't watch the news on purpose, but it's hard to hide from where we are headed. I give up trying to pretend I'm not listening and turn my head to look at the screen of war-torn chaos with mountains in the background. Afghanistan. Iraq is the footnote of the news these days. I wonder if random folks from Podunk, Wisconsin, who have no one close to them going back and forth to war even know the vast differences between the two hells. The emphatic and wide-eyed war correspondent yammers about troop levels and a rising Taliban and high American casualties. Out of the corner of my eye, I see that Jack has closed his book and is watching, too. Like lonely crack addicts staring at a crack pipe on television. The war college is our rehab, but the addiction will jump onto our backs soon enough.

The cold truth is, we wouldn't have traded our deployments for anything; we love them. We love the thrill of our place in history, the thrill of having something bigger than us to steal our focus. When I say *we*, I mean Jack *and* me. The deployments are my bragging rights, too. I can play the role of the exhausted martyr when need be. I can climb on my high horse of sacrifice and mentally place the back of my hand against my forehead in feigned victimization. Half Scarlett O'Hara and half Jack Nicholson.

At the end of our war college year in Carlisle, I've become a semi-proficient bridge player and I've figured out that Norwegian "water of life" is too strong for even my liver. Meanwhile, our kids have exhaustedly explored museums and battlefields and run thousands of soccer drills with their tirelessly enthusiastic father, an attempt to cram in as many lasting memories as possible before the mistress calls him away again. Beyond war college classes, Jack focuses the rest of his restless energy toward a half dozen intramural team sports with his fellow students and realizes he missed his calling as a professional soccer or basketball player. Our marriage is not magically mended, and we are bored and missing the shared focus on The Fight. Which is a good thing, because halfway through the year, Jack's career is thrown an unexpected curveball that knocks both of us on our asses.

And we would never go back to Fort Drum after all.

a new screaming eagle
and his indecisive wife

OUR LAST MONTH at Carlisle in the spring of 2010 is nothing short of a comedy of errors, caused wholly by my indecisive nature. Jack graduates from the Army War College in June at a ceremony where the keynote speaker, Steve Forbes, drones on for a ridiculous amount of time. I try not to let my mind wander to what a perfect opportunity this would be for a terrorist strike. So many of the nation's and world's up-and-coming leaders, all in a beautiful outdoor garden on a quintessential June Saturday, held captive in folding chairs by an endless speech.

Will I stay in Carlisle with the kids for another year, or will I move to Fort Campbell with Jack? With a Jack who won't even live there, but is headed to Afghanistan for a year later in the summer. The decision I must make nauseates me. Army wives are *not* cut out to make decisions. We follow the herd; we follow orders, even if we argue and roll our eyes. But actively having a choice? Beyond comprehension. I am paralyzed. And I'm still seething that we aren't going back to Fort Drum. We have no history at Fort Campbell. Sure, we know people there, but it has its own mafia. There are off-the-record mafias in each of the infantry divisions, and we are a part of the 10th Mountain mafia. I feel too old and cranky to learn the shenanigans and interworking of a new mafia. The 101st Airborne mafia. The Screaming Eagles. Ugh. That

place is a whole new level of gritty energy and macho. But I'm not sure
I have the energy to keep up the perky, vacationing attitude in Carlisle.
I feel limp and depleted. But restless at the same time. Not unlike Jack.

"Ang! It will be great!" Jack says. "This is the 506th Regiment!
Remember when we watched *Band of Brothers*? This brigade is loaded
with history even better than 10th Mountain. Don't get me wrong,
10th Mountain is our home, but I can't let this opportunity pass us
by." Yes, he says "us," as if this is my opportunity as well. "I know,
I know," he continues. "I said I never wanted to go anywhere but the
10th Mountain, but you know I've always wanted to do some time
with the 101st. It's meant to be. This is my last hurrah. After this, I'm
done. I promise. After this, we will go wherever you want. But you
need to make up your mind, pros and cons on either side. I will deploy
just a couple weeks after I get there, and no guarantees the army will
let me stay there after we get back next summer. Who knows what will
happen. But if you come to Campbell, you will have the unit to lean
on. And you'll be three hours from your family in Indiana versus ten
hours here. But if you stay here, well, this is just not even the real army
at all. It's like a constant vacation. But you have to *choose*. And stick
with your decision!"

Jack is speaking in bullets again—a speech loaded with emphasis
and enthusiasm, but scary and a little intimidating too. Like I have to
decide rightthisverymoment. We had this one-way conversation two
weeks before being held hostage by Steve Forbes, and Jack was in the
middle of his own diatribe when I closed the kitchen door in his face.
He kept talking anyway.

By the time Forbes's unending speech blathers on, I have decided
to stay in Carlisle. At least, that's my party line. Inside I'm a disaster
of indecision.

I waffle for weeks, and I probably waste some good taxpayer money while I am at it. For that, I apologize. So for weeks I go back and forth, each time *certain* I have made the right choice. Yes, all of our war college friends will be moving on, but I already know people in the new class, so that isn't a big deal. I have one good friend at Fort Campbell, a general's wife, Melanie Evans. This connection will, of course, immediately put me into a category as a suck-up, but at least I won't have to ease my way in with no one familiar. I hesitantly accept a housing assignment at Fort Campbell and receive an address via email. This is it, the boat has sailed. Melanie takes pictures of the blue house, twice the size of our Smurf house, and texts them to me. Very cute but cookie-cutter. New. A tremendous departure from our minuscule and sweet Smurf house, but I like our Smurf house. It has character and a soul, along with the ghosts of at least fifty war college families before us—families that maybe fought the same battles within these same walls. Biding time between war zones. Also holding their breath and smiling polite smiles.

Melanie tells me I will like the new team at the 101st, comparable to the "10th Mountain of the South." She assures me our new Currahee team is incredible, no crazies that she can identify, and I will fit right in. Currahee is the moniker of the 506th Infantry, made famous by Dick Winters's Band of Brothers, the original paratroopers from World War II. The cool factor of this assignment definitely appeals to me.

Okay, Fort Campbell, here I come!

Wait. Deep breath.

I feel myself pick up the phone and dial the number to the transportation office. I hear myself cancel my pack-out dates from Carlisle. I watch my fingers email the housing office at Fort Campbell to take my name off the housing list. I give up my coveted number one slot in the housing wait list. Jack flips out, and flips the kitchen trash can. "Why can't you make a decision and *stick with it?*"

I just glare at him. I'm still pissed that we aren't going back home, to Fort Drum. To 10th Mountain. I didn't properly say good-bye. I blame him that I'm in this position at all. I had told the kids we would go back.

"Okay, this is all on you," he says. "I'm trying to track down my deployment gear and get ready to move out. You have two perfect options. Neither choice is wrong. But you make us both look weak because you can't decide. I'm out. This is all on you now."

Here's the big appeal of staying in Carlisle. I won't have to move and deal with broken dishes and boxes piled to the ceiling in every room and nailing a dozen holes into the wall to get each picture hung just right. No digging through my inventory of curtains to see which would fit this house and no weeks spent trying to create a home that would look like we'd lived there for years. Home is essential to me, and to Jack as well. We are on the same page with that. We both have a lot of stuff (okay, I have way more stuff), nonessential stuff. Sentimental stuff. The stuff that makes a house a home. Sometimes I envy those army folks who could move in and be established and ready to host a barbeque the next day. With the Carlisle option, I can stay put. Avoid that entire unpleasant dance altogether.

A few days later, Jack and I load the kids and the cat and head to spend a couple weeks at my parents' farm in Indiana before he signs in at Fort Campbell. Campbell is an easy drive from the farm, so Jack will go back and forth on the few weekends that remain before he deploys. The kids and I will just crash here, our every summer ritual in my parents' wonderful safe haven in the country, until a week before school starts and then head back to Carlisle and meet all the new neighbors who now surround our cozy Smurf house.

In the beginning of July, Jack reports to Fort Campbell to sign in with the Currahee Brigade and calls to tell me how cool it is and how great everyone is. The word *great* is Jack's favorite all-time word. He has that sound in his voice, the distant, little-kid excitement. "There's a huge black spade on my office door! The esprit de corps at this place is amazing. It feels awesome to be back with soldiers. I'm staying in the on-post billeting; it's a little gross by your standards, but come down and stay with me for a few days. You can visit Melanie."

So off I go, driving the three hours to Fort Campbell and trying to push thoughts of how convenient and comforting it would be to be so near my family for a deployment. *Stop! I made my decision. No dreadful packing and unpacking, remember?* I drive toward the Fort Campbell main gate, and the grittiness, the realness, of being back on a badass infantry post smacks me right across the face. Jack didn't quite capture the feeling in the air. This place reeks of adrenaline and hard-core war seekers. Even the post looks hard-bitten. No pristinely manicured rose bushes and quaint housing areas like Carlisle. This place was built for function, and no one stopped to consider that it might be a little ugly. Ugly is part of the charm. Carlisle is an illusion, a vacation; this place is reality.

All my life experiences and intricate training as an army wife have prepared me perfectly to forsake the ability to make a single decision for myself. I'm a perfect zombie.

I stop at the front gate and a soldier snaps my ID card back into my hand through the open window. "Welcome to the 101st Airbooooorne! The home of the Screaming Eagles, ma'am!" Even the gate guard is loaded with an almost pornographic amount of testosterone.

Melanie has given me her address and encouraged me to stay with her, giving me a welcome reprieve from the billeting Jack warned me about. Melanie's house is tucked in a hilled neighborhood with tall trees and long, curvy driveways—a clear indication of where the big dogs live. Her house is the oldest on Fort Campbell, a two-hundred-year-old log cabin rumored to be haunted. Melanie and I are long friends from my early Fort Drum years. We share a love for horror movies and cool boots, and she is also an astute people watcher, but quieter about it than me. Melanie doesn't fill silences with mindless chatter, and her silence doesn't mean she's plotting; it just means she has nothing to say. Thriving in her role as a senior wife, she does her best to be one of us, the midsized dogs. She pulls it off exceptionally well, but now that her husband is a general, her house reminds me that she is no longer one of us. Despite her tiny frame, to those who knew her best, she is Mighty Mo. Melanie considers herself a workout nazi and an exercise addict. Even the wives of the 101st emit badassery.

As Melanie and I sit at her kitchen table, I am overwhelmed with certainty that Carlisle is the wrong choice, and she must know it too. Instead of giving me an I-told-you-so speech, she smiles with reassurance and says, "Carlisle will be fine. The Currahee girls are a tight-knit group. Stephanie Roark is"—she pauses to choose just the right word—"quirky. But in a good way. She's fresh and full of excitement. She and Aaron haven't been married long, less than ten years probably. She's loaded with energy. You two would have made a good team. The rest of the ladies are so much fun to be around; I can't really publicly admit to a favorite brigade, but it's the Currahees." I'll bet she says that to all the brigades.

I'm not sure if she's trying to make me feel better or twist the knife. Stephanie Roark is the wife of Jack's new boss. Jack is now second in command of the Currahee Brigade, only one heartbeat behind Stephanie's husband, Aaron.

I drop my head with a heavy thump on her kitchen table and feel the tears well up. She sees it and tries to lighten the mood. "Hey, you made a decision. I know it's hard for us to make decisions. But you'll be *fine*. No sweat. You can come to visit." She draws out the last word with her Georgia drawl that tells me my error is catastrophic. I belong here. What was I thinking?

"So hey, where is the housing office?" I ask. "I'm just going to go talk to them."

Melanie smiles and gives me a map with directions to an office five minutes down the road. I sign in at the reception area and wait my turn to speak to someone about the housing list. "Hi, I'm Angie Hawkins. I turned down a house about two weeks ago, and I realize I lost my ranking on the list. But I wondered if, well, if maybe there's any way I can . . . um . . ."

The Tennessee woman working at the desk interrupts my stammer. "No problem, Mrs. Hawkins. We knew you'd get here and realize you wanted to stay. We have a house for you. It's just across the courtyard from the one you were assigned before. It doesn't have a sweeping front porch, but it's the same layout otherwise."

My punishment for being a dumbass. No sweeping porch.

And after all, I will spend the year waiting for Jack in Fort Campbell, among my people, instead of insulated in Carlisle's cozy escape from the Real Army.

Jack does not take the news well. I carefully plot that telling him at a crowded Chinese buffet is the best option to avoid another tantrum; I think the audience of buffet foragers will force him to keep his cool.

His foot taps vigorously under the table, and the muscles in his jaw bulge. His blue eyes drill into me. But by his third overflowing plate of kung pao, I plead my case in the most pathetic way I can muster and convince him that this is it. This is right.

Through shovels of steamed broccoli, he says, "All right, Ang. All right. But this is all on you. You have to set up the movers and handle the move on your own. I don't have time for this."

He will be gone in less than two weeks, and I have two weeks to haul my ass back to Carlisle and move out in the most inconspicuous and stealthy way possible, hanging my head and avoiding the judgmental consequences of my indecision.

currahee

What kind of husband and father volunteers for an eighth combat tour? One who can't turn down the opportunity to join the historic ranks of a Band of Brothers. One who thinks it will save his ass. But possibly deep down, one who just can't stand not being in The Fight. And one whose wife doesn't lift a finger to stop him.

THREE MONTHS BEFORE my disoriented search for my other green Croc in the middle of the night, my front door has another reason to open in the wee hours. Each time Jack and I plan the good-bye scenario for a deployment, we think we've come up with a magical way to make the process of good-bye anything less than brutal and horrific. Even if we keep the brutal and horrific under the guise of a scripted scene, with firm hugs and confident words, the wailing agony is right under the surface. Every single time. This time he needs to be at the brigade headquarters in the middle of the night to manifest and draw his weapon, so he arranges for someone to pick him up from the house, sparing me a drive in the middle of the night. He has considered driving his Jeep and just leaving it in his office parking lot for me to pick up later, but we are so new to Fort Campbell, and my unfamiliarity with the straggly and spindly layout of this post takes that option off the table. Navigating my way to his office seems overwhelming; it's the small things that overwhelm at these times, so Jack knows arranging a pickup is best. This plan will be a piece of cake. He can tuck the kids into bed, then sleep a few hours before he has to go. His rucksack waits packed by the door. His uniform is draped over the closet door.

Jack never unpacks any of his personal items after the movers carried in load after load of boxes from Carlisle. I made sure his boxes had an enormous letter J scrawled on them in black Sharpie and had the movers carry them straight to the garage. There they will sit for a year, piled and waiting neatly in a corner. So aside from the rucksack by the door, he doesn't have a place in this house. It won't be his home, at least not for the next year.

The last few hours of the Sunday night before he leaves, Jack tucks each of the kids into bed and reminds them to be good and help Mom out. Words he says each time. I stay in my bedroom and try to block out the wrenching scene, wanting to leave this one to him—the rest of the year will be all mine—but I can hear the sobs and the pleading. Doing this at home was a terrible idea. A public good-bye at least forces us to maintain some degree of dignity. I feel the bitter tears well in my eyes as I hear Jack choke back his own gasps at each of our three children's bedsides. The children separately weep as he slips from one bedroom to the next, but I feel spared that I can't hear their actual words. Somehow the notion that this is anything but our regular routine escapes them, which is a blessing. When Jack finally makes his way back into our bedroom over an hour later and with the muffled sobs of at least two kids still audible from their beds, he falls on the bed and his back heaves. He weeps, though *weep* seems like such a strange word to use for someone who is the polar opposite of any mental image the word might conjure. I stare at him and allow the hot tears to drip from my cheeks and onto the neatly folded Martha Stewart quilt on the bed, but I also feel numb. Not even angry or devastated; this moment is too familiar to feel much of anything except numbness. I hover in a weird limbo of just needing this part to be over and wanting to soak in the last remaining hours. Mostly I need it to be over. The eighth time we've danced this ritual, and the first time he has wept. His eyes have filled with tears before and he's been unable to speak, but this outward display of emotion is altogether new.

I feel myself detach.

I learned to detach sometime around the third deployment. It must have been the Macedonia or Bosnia deployment, when we were stationed in Germany. We were married six years before we had kids, because he was deployed back to back in various peacekeeping missions, ranging anywhere from six to eight months. There are only so many times you can give in to that desperate feeling of sending your better half off to a potential combat zone. Even though Macedonia and Bosnia weren't war zones as we see them today, at the time it was a big deal. Looking back, it was a piece of cake. If I could go back in time, I would warn the younger, softer me. I would shake my head and say, "Girl, just you wait. This is the easy part." At the time, there was nothing for me to compare it to except Somalia—which was a complete nightmare and meltdown.

Of all eight, the good-bye for Somalia makes the other seven look effortless. Jack had to pry himself from me when he boarded the bus that would take him to the plane and then to Somalia in December 1992 in the middle of heavy falling snow. As he took his seat and looked at me through the window, the bus closed its doors and started to slowly pull away. Not even waiting until he was out of eyeshot, I flopped facedown into the snow and fake vomited. I wailed and sobbed and didn't give a shit that everyone around me was staring or that Jack was mortified from his seat on the bus. He waved as the bus pulled away, and instead of waving back, I retched and dry heaved again. Zero dignity, or anything even resembling dignity. Looking back on that scene, I'm embarrassed, but also amazed that I used to have such a capacity for emotion.

For each moment of good-bye after that, I became increasingly hardened. Army wives refer to this phenomenon as the "black soul." It's my coping style; it's not for everyone, but it works for many others and for me. Each of us figures out her own, and for those who don't figure it out, well, those are the wives who don't stay army wives for long. Sappy, clingy marriages just don't last in this world.

For the next three hours on that sweltering Sunday night in August, we lie awake together on the bed, not touching. I'm afraid if I touch him it will start the wave of emotions over again. I hope he is sleeping, and he probably hopes the same of me. Neither of us even closes our eyes. Without an alarm clock needing to wake us, he gets up a couple hours after midnight and dresses silently, and I follow him down the stairs and hug him. Tell him to be safe, which is just rhetoric at this point. The meaning and novelty of those words long worn off. Both our voices crack in our final good-bye, my face buried in his steeled chest. I try to pull in his scent, but it's gone. Masked by the mistress. She's taken him again. All I smell is her, metallic and industrial. Gritty.

"The last one, girl. The last one."

I close and lock the front door, and the heavy aroma of his army gear still lingers on the staircase as I begin making my way back up to the bedroom minutes later. Well, that was ugly. There really is no good way. But we continue to try.

As I pause at the top of the stairs, I hear no sound from the kids. I peer into Joe's room first, and there are all three of them, sleeping crisscross and overlapping in a pile of blankets and pillows on the floor. Sound asleep, finally. They must have found solace in each other. I lean down and smother each of their faces with light kisses, careful not to wake them. I take in the warm, cozy smell of each of the children, ridding my nostrils of the fading memory of army gear.

With that last step out the door too late or too early for anyone else to be awake, Jack Hawkins officially becomes Currahee 8, heading for his third tour to Afghanistan, this time in the precarious mountains of eastern Afghanistan backed against the border of Pakistan. In each of these moments, I never know if the worst is ahead or if I will look back and think, "That wasn't so rough after all." The mistress keeps this secret closely guarded.

In all likelihood, this will be the last deployment and we both know it, somewhere deep down. We need it, though, both of us. We need to see this final deployment through to the end to know if we fit together beyond the scope of the chaotic canvas of the war. Everything about war feels permanent, even though we know this moment will pass, like every moment does eventually. When it does eventually pass, there will be parts of the war that are forever permanent.

These are the things wives don't talk about directly. The anger. Rage, even. Sure, we discuss the surface frustrations at never being able to plan a future vacation with accuracy. All the husbands in our circle seem cut from the same cloth, stand with their hands on their hips wearing vacant but polite smiles at social events. Like they try too hard to seem carefree and in the moment. Somehow we never talk about much more than the mission in front of us. Instead we talk about SOPs (standard operating procedures) for how to deal with every scenario in our lives. Even free thought is taken out of the equation. We are a well-oiled machine. Built for war, not for introspection or anything even remotely touchy-feely. The U.S. Army War College was the first opportunity for introspection Jack and I experienced in the army, but we were careful to keep it in a neat little box we put away. Scratching at the surface might start an unstoppable ooze of emotion. Emotions and thoughts we certainly share, but never discuss. Because discussing it makes it too real and reminds us that we can't change any of it, anyway. Walking any path other than this one is unfathomable.

Sadness is expected, and we have a protocol to handle sadness. Fury is hidden away and later displaced on each other or other petty issues. Next week maybe a dog will shit in my yard, and the perfect venue for me to flip out will present itself on a gorgeous platter. *Here, this is where the rage goes. This is a perfect excuse for the tantrum you've been holding in.* Until then, the sadness waxes and wanes, and the anger crouches and waits.

The morning after Jack leaves, I drive the girls to school and come home to a bouquet of pink balloons tied to my front door. Left by my new battle buddies, the CurraShees, a wordless reminder of solidarity. Joe took last night's good-bye the hardest, and I offer for him stay home from school with me. Maybe we can find a good movie on cable and eat chips all day. Be slugs, indulge in laziness. There are never any tears after the initial good-bye. The day after isn't about sadness; it's about relief and a lingering bruised feeling. Like the actual beating is over and this is recovery.

Sometimes, not often, but sometimes, I think about the overall scope of the war. Surprisingly, no one in our circle ever talks about the war as a whole. Only that we are doing great things over there and should be filled with pride. We are filled with pride, but I wonder if we secretly all wonder what the point is. If it's worth it. We fight an ultimately losing war, but that little nugget of truth never works its way into the conversations of our inner circle of warriors and their wives. Somehow whether or not the war is winnable is beyond our scope, an irrelevant detail. We don't do it to win anymore; we do it because it's what we know how to do. Get ready to go. Get ready to come back. And the moments in between we mark on the calendar. It's our battle rhythm.

I doubt Jack learned our new zip code before he was gone.

The deployment this time is voluntary. Barely home from a fifteen-month tour in Iraq, he'd been home just under two years. I suppose that was long enough. I was blown away for a moment when he volunteered to leave us again, but quickly accepted that the action of a combat zone was his drug of choice. A part of me was ashamed at my sense of relief to have an excuse not to deal with our marriage. I could exhale. Back to his mistress. Jack is addicted to being in The Fight and the adrenaline rush of battle. He doesn't drink, smoke, or swear; his vice is far more subtle and insidious. And I'm the sicko codependent, hitched along for the ride.

currashee

I've got my sisters; keep your ass over there.

—ANI DIFRANCO

THE CHOICE TO move to Fort Campbell was right. Being here in the same boat with my new batch of army sisters is a comfort. A yearlong deployment lies ahead, and there's no time to waste with polite getting-to-know-you dances. Our familiar template for how we operate gives us the foundation and structure to become a family even before I've finished unpacking and nailing curtains to the wall, because sometimes curtain rods are just too much work.

Being with the CurraShees is a refreshing departure from our eight long years at 10th Mountain, before the war college. Where is their bitterness? These women are full of vigor and energy. Feisty. There are six battalion commanders' wives in the Currahee Brigade. Each has her own talent and contribution to the total overall package of the team—so unlike our brigade at Fort Drum. The CurraShees have their issues, but we keep them in our house. We don't air our dirty laundry. So, as far as anyone from the outside can tell, we are the ideal brigade.

I live in the same neighborhood with the battalion commanders' wives not just from our brigade, but from the whole division. We aren't spread over two neighborhoods like at Fort Drum, and the togetherness in one place creates a refreshing dynamic. At Fort Drum, we identified

more with our neighborhoods; here the esprit de corps comes from the
unit or brigade. There is a competition between the brigades, and it's
very clear who belongs where. But it's a healthy, mostly humor-based
competition. Not backstabbing or plotting. Never those things.

A week after I move in, I'm still surrounded by boxes and melting
in the August Tennessee heat and humidity. Melanie calls to ask if I
want to go to Harper Village Bunco. Melanie knows I loathe Bunco.
Bunco is one of those games that a few women take entirely too seriously, as if their fates depend on the rolls of the dice. The thought of
enduring such a heinous activity with people I don't yet know sounds
even worse. I glance around at the disarray in my house. Every room
looks like a giant monster has picked it up, shaken it upside down, and
plopped it back in its place. "Okay," I reply, "I'm in. I can be ready
whenever you pick me up."

I walk into the front door behind Melanie and take in the colorful,
put-together home. For a second I want to back out and run back to
my own house to dig into those boxes with renewed determination.
I have too much work to do to be playing Bunco. But then I see the
line of wine bottles and neatly arranged platters of lady snacks and
desserts and abandon any idea of escaping. On the short drive over,
Melanie has confided with pride that she is included in the Harper
Bunco because she is still hip and approachable. Down with her people. Which is a complete departure from the perception of the other
women in her neighborhood of the rolling hills and long driveways.
Somewhere along the way, most of the wives of the big dogs lose the
ability to have fun. Melanie grips tightly to that quality, enjoying being
among this group more, in a looser crowd.

Melanie introduces me to everyone I've already met at the
CurraShees' barbeque the weekend before, but this is my first

introduction to many of the other Harper ladies. Twenty women talking over each other, cackling with wild laughter, singing and dancing. Within thirty minutes, I am overwhelmed and overstimulated, but fascinated. This is a twist on unwinding. I don't even know that I'd call it unwinding. These women feed off the energy of each other. At Fort Drum, we played reindeer games. We endured the people we could no longer stand and left the party at the first available opportunity. Then we each cloistered into our smaller groups and sneaked into one of our homes to finish the night with a bottle of wine and the people whose company we could bear.

One woman in particular intrigues me. She looks like a butchy phys-ed teacher, crazy but with cool, rooster-like hair. Carefree and wild. She is far and above the loudest and most obnoxious one in the group. Later, I won't even remember playing Bunco that night, won't recall being bored senseless by the rolling dice and number counting, the awkward intensity of women overly driven by a competitive desire to win a ten-dollar Starbucks gift card. These women don't really give two shits whether they win; they only want to scream and throw the fuzzy Bunco dice across the room. The tedious nature of the game takes a backseat to the swirl of energy and chaos from my new crowd of people. My new social circle. The 101st mafia. Back in Carlisle, I would be playing a quiet game of bridge on this Saturday night.

"It's my diiiiickkk! 'My Dick in a Box'! Who's got that song on their iPhone?" The rooster-haired, dubiously boyish one wants to perform. I'm not in Kansas anymore.

In the car on the way home, with the ringing in my ears from hours of noise equal to a post-AC/DC concert, I blurt out to Melanie before I even close my car door, "What the hell!?"

Melanie laughs and starts in with her Georgia drawl. "You'll be fine. The one with the spiked hair, the loud one, you will love her. I saw you trying to figure her out. She's actually very likable and easy to be around. Everyone in there is at a different stage in their deployments, and they get together to let loose. They were certainly a little wilder tonight than normal."

"Someone asked me to come to one of those murder-mystery parties next week," I say. "I think I'm supposed to wear some sort of Texas beauty queen costume. Really? Me? I guess I need to dig out some kind of Anna Nicole Smith getup."

"Here's the best news. You'll be so busy this year that you won't even notice the year has flown by. In Carlisle, time would have crawled."

The next Friday night, I host the first Pizza Friday for our neighborhood. I haul folding tables and chairs to the large courtyard our homes share, right next to the playground and under a huge spreading tree. I invite the six CurraShee battalion commanders' wives and our brigade commander's wife, Stephanie Roark. I also mention it to the other neighbors and ask them to spread the word. Each Friday night that late summer and early fall, and then again the following spring and summer, we gather on Friday nights for pizza and drinks. Each mother pitches in drinks and snacks for the kids, and ten bucks toward pizza. The worst part is, I open my house for potty privileges, and some of the younger kids have poor aim. Small price for camaraderie.

The impetus of Pizza Fridays is something I heard from the six CurraShee commanders' wives. Before my arrival, they interacted very little with Stephanie Roark, who lives in Melanie's neighborhood. I wonder if the logistics of living in another neighborhood keep Stephanie and the other women at arm's length from one another. Why doesn't Stephanie invite the CurraShees over for drinks or even

a potluck dinner? She never hosts anything informal at her house—
a house that is made for entertaining. Each echelon of command
comes with a progressively more fabulous house, whose purpose is to
entertain. Considering Stephanie's young children, possibly she's just
too overwhelmed. Most brigade commanders have children who are
grown and off at college, but Aaron and Stephanie Roark married later
in life and thus still have rug rats. Very mischievous, but redeemingly
cute rug rats.

With Jack only second in command, Pizza Friday will be my little
contribution to the team. My role requires little of me, really, but I
want to bring Stephanie closer to the group. The rest of our brigade
team has been in place for a year already, and Jack's position was
only added for the deployment. The team has a year jump-start on
the dynamics of their relationships. Maybe Stephanie feels left out by
the group members' closeness and clear, deep connections with one
another. I can relate to that sense in this group but I quickly overcome
it. I marvel at their banter and natural way of relating. They tease each
other ruthlessly, but no one ever gets pissed off or bursts into a fit of
tears. It never seems mean-spirited. Possibly I can be a bridge between
the six CurraShees and Stephanie.

Stephanie Roark can seem awkward and has a kinetic energy that
makes her fun and fascinating, if a little superficial. Melanie has a mas-
terful way of framing her words and descriptions in a positive way,
and shame on me for swallowing her descriptions without a grain of
salt. When Melanie said "quirky," she meant straight-up cartoonish.
But beneath Stephanie's *quirkiness* I find something very vulnerable
and relatable about her.

By the time Aaron Roark reached his brigade command, Stephanie
had clocked less than ten years as an army wife. The six battalion

commanders' wives under her, and I, each married our husbands while they were lieutenants; we have the street cred. Instead of acknowledging the experience of the other CurraShees, which would earn her a sympathetic pass and an embrace from our group, she plays the role of wise mentor. But she doesn't get the nuances and lacks the army wife finesse that has taken the rest of us two decades to perfect.

Stephanie has some entertaining quirks, such as dancing while engaged in regular conversation. Literally, she boogies with no music. It must be a nervous tic. This is her first long deployment, and Stephanie tries a little too hard to take it all in stride. I would hug her if she would let me, but I have to remember that she thinks she is mentoring me.

Before Jack and I arrived in the unit, Stephanie gave a famous speech to the six CurraShee battalion commanders' wives at a social event, and the speech defined the rest of her existence in their eyes. Again playing the sage, she said, "You must have your close friends outside of the army. These are business relationships, not friendships."

Oh man. What a rookie-ass move. When the famous speech is retold to me, I am sympathetic to her clear naïveté. Stephanie underestimates how vital to each other's survival our bonds are. These are sisterhoods, not even friendships. We don't choose each other like normal friends do. We're plopped here in this boat regardless of how our personalities fit. Just like a family.

Outside of these circumstances, though, we would be great friends. I am attracted to Stephanie's free-spirited vibe, and she has great style and taste in clothing. Her house is filled with eclectic and refined pieces of artwork collected from around the world—not the typical, sterile army family home that looks as if a folksy Americana craft store had exploded inside. Because of my sympathy toward her, I consider pulling her aside and telling her to knock off the pretenses, but I know it won't go well in my favor. She will react defensively. These women don't need a mentor, anyway. Every single one of them is gutsy and levelheaded. Stephanie can learn from them, if she lets her guard down long enough to realize it. Even in her quirkiness, Stephanie is galvanizing. And it could be much worse.

The slight void she leaves as a mentor is fine by me; I enjoy filling in as the unscary big sister to the other CurraShees for a change. Jack isn't a threat to their husbands; he's not their competitor or their boss. Jack and I are a sidestep to the left of the storm for a change. It's nice to be nonthreatening to these women; my position in the middle feels just right.

Three months after that first CurraShee party, in the predawn after my blind drive to the ER, they will be the ones helping me stay afloat. Right at my bedside, as if we've known each other a lifetime instead of three months.

Somehow, my three favorite CurraShees, Julia Ortega, Sarah Gray, and Kim Dunn, appear in the ER less than an hour after I leave my car running in the ambulance bay. Nothing is kept quiet for long in our neighborhood.

That early morning in the ER, before the words *heart attack* are even spoken, these women form an instinctive, protective cocoon on both sides of me. They mask our worries with snarky jokes about the lengths I will take to score a morphine drip. I hear Julia, the sensible one with a limitless amount of well-directed energy, make a hushed phone call to arrange for a neighbor to help my kids get ready for the school bus, and to be sure to tell the kids that I have food poisoning. Sarah, the nurturer, leaves to tidy my home by making the bed I left and hiding the box with the still-packaged pink vibrator from the "passion party" we attended together as a group (sex toy parties are a rite of passage for combat wives, marking the beginning of a long deployment). Kim, the benevolent and compliant soul, rubs my feet even after I ask her to stop. Through my morphine stupor, I remember an awareness of how fluidly we fell into our get-shit-done roles during a crisis. They bring the book that was on my bedside table, my old pink bathrobe that they make fun of for my wearing it over my clothes in the middle of the day, and lime LaCroix. I remind myself again that I've known them only three months.

My CurraShee sisters at the 101st, whose husbands are deployed with Jack, are with me each step of my heart attack ordeal. It could have happened to any one of them, the fear and realization evident on their faces. They've known me for only three months. Somehow this fact bears repetition.

Jack is a quarter of the way into his deployment in the mountains in eastern Afghanistan as I lie in the ICU, and an option for him to come home is never presented to me. The Currahee Brigade engages almost daily in heavy combat; we've lost half a dozen soldiers that week alone. I have plenty of support here from my parents, and as much from my army sisters, so asking for him to come home would be redundant to the support system I already have in place. Unlike my family, my army sisters are in the same boat of deployment with me. They walk the same walk. Our neighborhoods are like giant dormitories. We leave our front doors open and wander from house to house. We are just that present in each other's everyday lives. Yes, we delicately balance that iron bond through the filter of competition and politics as our husbands are brothers in arms, but we also jockey for the top position when ratings time rolls around. I'm sure these political plays were made here, but since I was an outsider to the 101st mafia, I wasn't yet wise to the intricate playing style. And anyway, Jack isn't competing against his fellow Currahees this time. He's competing against himself.

Regardless of their own hectic schedules as battalion commanders' wives, their daily flurries of meetings and phone calls and putting out fires and doing their best to be the voice of reason and an ambassador of calm wisdom for the wives in their husband's commands, it is those wives who stand at my side immediately following my heart attack and who stay there for weeks while I slowly recover. Even in their exhaustion from treading the waters of war themselves, they reach out and hold me up when I need it. Not for a second do I think they'll let me drown.

Jack and I speak on the phone in my ICU room after surgery, and I insist that I will be fine. I'm not sure yet if that's completely true. I'm in no mood to reassure him. No mood to deal with the delay, echo, and static from the crummy phone connection. My parents are here now, my whole family. My army sisters float in and out of the room, ignoring ICU protocol. Jack doesn't argue with my insistence. Dealing with illness is not Jack's strong suit, and the thought of his impatient presence is stressful. I'm not sure if this is something he can quickly "fix." Before I even leave the hospital, it's already decided that Jack will stay in Afghanistan, where he has a clear mission. Back here? The mission isn't quite as clear.

a heart too steeled to break

Squint your eyes and look closer,
I'm not between you and your ambition.

—ANI DIFRANCO

E VEN THOUGH I am numb to my surroundings—think I am tough and can handle the stress of a roller-coaster marriage, three children I too often procrastinate mothering, and the constant backdrop of the war—my body has taken a quiet inventory of each thing I have ignored. The long evenings of wine drinking and laughter that I tell myself are the catharsis I need aren't enough.

In my long weeks of recovery that winter, I have quiet and a reprieve from the vigilance of minding the flock during deployment, even though I play second fiddle to Stephanie this go-around. My busy world of year after year of running-the-war-behind-the-real-war that has taken so much of my sweat, time, and energy maybe doesn't need me as much as I think or hope it does. Our year at the war college wasn't really a time to reflect. Yes, it was a time to unwind, but no, not to reflect. We used that year to recharge. The period of physical recuperation from an out-of-the-blue heart attack is finally my time of introspective reflection and taking stock. What have these two decades of life as an army wife cost me, and have I gained more than I lost? I am reminded of Tori Amos lyrics: *These precious things let them break their hold over me.*

Between Tori and Dave Matthews, they've unknowingly written the perfect soundtrack of an army wife's life during wartime.

Our three children were toddlers and barely school age throughout the decade after 9/11. The impact that the rotation of deployments will have on them remains to be seen. They've spent their entire lives inside the wire, just as I have. While the kids seem resilient, I can't deny how deeply they must be affected. Over the years, their ears have aimed at me while I hid behind closed doors on the phone, discussing in a hushed voice funeral arrangements for soldiers liquefied by IEDs. Funerals when there is nothing left to bury. Or hearing me talk a mother out of giving her children over to foster care because she can't bear single parenting for another day. In many ways, my kids aren't just robbed of their father's presence, but are deprived of mine as well. I am here in body, but my mind is overwhelmed. On overdrive. Too preoccupied to play Chutes and Ladders.

I find myself almost embarrassed by the countless questions from friends and peers about why I had a heart attack. They're probably also worried for themselves; what has happened to me could happen to them unless I can cough up a succinct answer. *"Can you believe I had a congenital defect all these years and never knew it? I sure did get lucky that they caught it when they did!"* The simple explanation I would like to have doesn't exist.

A month before the heart attack, I rode with Julia, Sarah, and Kim to Toccoa, Georgia, to participate in a reenactment of the original Band of Brothers weekend. We dressed like Rosie the Riveter (Rosie the Riveter is now a lesbian icon, but I let that detail slide) and attended an old-fashioned dance in an airplane hangar. It was clear that this town reveled in its Currahee heritage and took the role very seriously. The people's costumes flawlessly reflected the early 1940s wartime. We looked almost silly in our T-shirts with rolled-up sleeves, red bandanas on our heads and in Old Navy jeans. Oh well. The town welcomed us with a red carpet: the wives of the current Band of Brothers, battling the Taliban in Afghanistan.

I never had had so much fun on a road trip. We stuffed ourselves with junk food, laughed at nothing in particular, stopped for potty breaks, got lost, argued over directions, and quickly began laughing again, surely at something between Kim (the Korean American wife) and Sarah (the Japanese American wife), who jockeyed for leadership in the front seat. I sat in the back with Julia and enjoyed the laughter. Those two crazy Asians were an endless source of entertainment, mocking each other's heritage and bickering over who was the "angrier Asian." We never discussed the heaviest pressures of the deployment or the casualties. We'd become our own family unit, hunkered down until that storm passed. I liked their approach.

Stephanie had driven to Toccoa separately with our brigade command sergeant major's wife, an innocuous, relaxed, and seasoned woman with grown children. I knew Jill from the Fort Drum years, knew she'd been around the block with deployments and was far more natural at the army wife game than Stephanie. But Jill was older and less feisty, so she let Stephanie be—didn't even try to teach her the ropes. But looking back, I wonder if Jill's unaffected attitude stemmed more from what we would all learn soon enough. Maybe Jill already had wind of what was coming. Just a couple weeks after we returned to Fort Campbell, Jill's husband of nearly thirty years, the top enlisted man in our brigade, would be labeled a sexual predator in an investigation and removed from his position, sent back to the States right after

Halloween, and allowed to quietly retire. I wonder if Jill knew this then, and that's why she was quieter than usual.

On Saturday morning, we rolled out of our rooms at the Holiday Inn and stood ready and waiting at dawn to ascend and descend Currahee Mountain, "three miles up, three miles down," just like in *Band of Brothers*. We were supposed to have eaten a big spaghetti dinner the night before, but we were still lost at dinnertime and the Angry Asians were bickering. We arrived late and only made it to the dance. On the upside, there would be no barfed spaghetti this morning.

Stephanie held court with a local news crew and made an impassioned speech about the brave fight being led by her husband. I cringed and hid my face in my hands, wanting her to stop talking in that weird voice. It wasn't her words; it was her delivery. So staged and overly sincere.

The mountain climb wasn't as bad as I had expected. I tried my best to ignore how out of shape I was, soak in the atmosphere, and imagine Dick Winters and his men training on this very trail for World War II. Such a different war than the one we fight now. I wondered where their wives were now, if any were still living. This weekend honored the soldiers, and I wondered about their families.

On Saturday night, the final evening of the two-day celebration, we attended a formal dinner. With seat assignments. Of course, Stephanie was at the head table, along with me, our rear detachment commander, and Jill. The other CurraShees had to scramble for seats. They were in the back of the room. Kim was fighting tears, and this broke my heart. Surely Stephanie at least helped dictate who sat at the head table; at least that was the perception. Stephanie often went out of her way to belittle Kim in subversive ways like this. Why? Because Kim is adored by the women in her battalion, because Kim has a natural grace and a considerate, quiet, and unassuming nature. Kim reminds me of a Korean version of Snow White. These are qualities Stephanie possibly envies. Also, Kim deserved a seat at the head table, above all the rest of us.

Why did Kim deserve a seat at the head table? Because her husband was the battalion commander of the actual unit we were there to commemorate. Stephanie's husband was not the commander of the unit as it was in 1942. That was Kim's husband. No one attending the weekend would have picked up on that slight technicality by the way Stephanie took over.

Finally we ended up in our seats, hoping the geezer Currahees around us hadn't noticed the pissing contest over seating. Our group might have been the only people under the age of seventy in this entire banquet hall. I leaned over to Joel, Stephanie's rear detachment fella, and asked, "Where is the bar? I need a drink, like an hour ago."

He smiled at me, his cheeks bright red. "This is a dry town," he said. "No booze at all here. Anywhere. But see that guy over there? The good-ol'-boy-lookin' guy? He gave me this." And he nudged my leg under the table. I looked at the mason jar of clear liquid. Desperate times call for desperate measures, and I was thankful for the moonshine and didn't allow myself to contemplate how unsanitary it might be. I poured some into my empty water glass and gagged it down.

Stephanie was the opening speaker. Once again we sat through an even more amped-up version of the rousing speech she gave for the media show this morning. It was a spectacle. It ended in her wiping the tears from her cheeks, a gorgeous touch of dramatic flair. The audience seemed to love it. Or maybe half of them were asleep because we were hours past their likely bedtimes. Maybe we needed to take pulses. I looked around the room and wondered again. *Is this me in fifty years? Still focusing on this one period in my life? Still defining myself through war? Still aching for that time in a sick way, because even though it was the hardest and most painful, it was when I felt the most alive? Would I do everything I could to recapture that feeling in fifty years, still grasping for that exhilaration?*

cadence of a culture

THERE ISN'T ALWAYS enough time for a slow getting-to-know-you build of relationships in army culture, so jumping into the middle suits me. Army culture and protocol are second nature to me— the only life I've ever known. So I've earned the right to practice a little irreverence, as far as I'm concerned. I've learned that irreverence puts people at ease far better than polite formalities. Protocol freaks out new wives—those who didn't grow up with it. They assume it's some complicated secret code. Here's the secret: Protocol is just good manners. Some knowledge of more specific protocol is required of an officer's wife, and since I grew up surrounded by it, the nuances of protocol come easily to me. I understand the protocol well enough to differentiate between the subtleties of what can be blown off and what is nonnegotiable. Wearing a name tag on the upper right chest is non-negotiable. Discreetly ducking out of a boring ceremony is totally open for debate, as long as the exit is stealthy and unnoticed.

There isn't much about army life I don't love, but that's a bold statement to make since I don't have a framework for any other kind of living. From the time I can remember, I lived on post. Not on base. Other branches of the military live on base. Army has posts.

I met Jack on a hot summer's night in a seedy dance bar in 1991, when I was home from Indiana University for the summer in Watertown and working as a bartender and teaching aerobics classes. *Yes, how 1991.* I had one year of college left, mediocre grades, a major

49

that refused to settle, and no idea what I wanted to be when I grew up. I loved shopping and wearing Doc Martens combat boots with dresses. I wanted to be a rock DJ. Or a fashion something-or-other. But no concrete ambition. Just ideas.

Fort Drum, where the 10th Mountain Division had uncased its colors and which the division had named as its new home in 1985, backed up to an interesting but also rundown factory town called Watertown. Before the 10th Mountain arrived, Fort Drum was just a quiet little training post used mostly in the summer. The arrival of the 10th Mountain shook the North Country awake and created jobs, establishing an infrastructure to maintain an entire infantry division. Most of the infantry posts I grew up in were adjacent to seedy towns with rows of strip clubs, tattoo parlors, cheap motels, and Joe bars. (*Joes* is the slang word we use for younger enlisted soldiers. "Stay away from the row of gross strip malls outside the main gate. Only Joes go there. And hookers.")

Watertown was still unspoiled and unaware of what had hit it in 1991. It still held its innocent charm. Local, family-owned restaurants lined the downtown area instead of chain restaurants. It would be another ten or fifteen years before Watertown bore the slight resemblance to an infantry town. Watertown is surrounded by lakes and rivers, and everywhere I looked, it was green and fresh. Quiet and sleepy in the most lovely way. My parents moved to Watertown in 1987, the day after I graduated from high school. I pouted and refused to speak for the duration of the 1,100-mile drive from Alabama to Watertown.

But within a week, Watertown felt like home, more so than any other place we had lived. I loved the rural Northern accent of the natives. Only twenty minutes south of the Canadian border, Watertown residents didn't say "yeah" or "yes." They said "yup." Within a month, I was yupping like a native and working as a waitress in a quaint little family restaurant on the outskirts of town. Before long I was working in the mall, at The Limited, which was the height of fashion in 1988, and going to a local college. After two years in Watertown, I transferred to Indiana University but came home to Watertown on every break and every opportunity, even if it meant driving my dilapidated Dodge Omni the eight hundred miles from Bloomington to Watertown. My parents loved Watertown and the 10th Mountain Division as much as I did, and we all dreaded moving. After four years, we knew it was coming.

My parents must have been a nervous wreck that I, an only child, would never find my way out in the big, bad, real civilian world on my own. My mother was right to assume I needed dates, even though she was the rare army wife with a career of her own and she wanted me to be equally independent. But she also knew that I hadn't figured out what I wanted to be when I grew up. I wanted to be everything, but nothing. I can't recall how many blind dates she sent me on, most of them dreadful but marginally entertaining. Her only criteria as far as I could tell was "lieutenant" and "Catholic." It seems every time I left the house that summer, I recall my mother saying, "You might meet your husband today!" I wasn't even twenty-two years old yet, but my parents knew what I have since discovered: Army brats grow up to become soldiers or army wives. We are a culture that perpetuates. My father was an infantry officer stationed at the 10th Mountain in Fort Drum, New York, and Watertown was not exactly a hot bed for available women.

On that July night, I can't even remember my date's name. Only that he never stopped bragging about being a West Point graduate. We'd gone out as a group, thankfully, to Alexandria Bay, a tourist village north of Watertown, and wound up in a dance joint with a dirt floor and lots of strobe lights. The music was loud, and I could see his lips flapping as he continued to brag about something or other, and I looked around the dance floor and bar, my eyes pleading for an escape route. I remember what I was wearing. A short white tube skirt and a white T-shirt. It was too hot for Doc Martens, and thankfully so. My white-bread husband-to-be might not have given my try-hard alternative self a second glance if I hadn't been dressed so . . . so 1991 mall-esque.

Sometimes the cheesy clichés in life are true. Like love at first sight. I am here to say that it definitely exists. Jack walked past the guy checking IDs at the door, and I saw him immediately. In the snapshot I carry in my memory, a light from heaven actually shone on him as he stood just inside the doorway of the bar. My date must have noticed the look on my face, because his eyes went to where mine had landed.

"Hey! That's Jack Hawkins! I graduated from Air Assault School with him yesterday! He's a butter bar like me, but he's not a West Pointer." *He had to toss in that detail, didn't he?*

On a regular night, I would have come up with a thinly veiled retort to make my awareness of his cocky attitude clear, but I didn't want to wreck an introduction to this man I already knew would be my husband. Before Jack ever opened his mouth, I knew what his voice would sound like: Midwestern with a hint of a Southern accent. I knew what he would smell like: soap and hopefully not man-perfume, though the early 1990s were a cesspool of stanky men's cologne.

Jack somehow saw my eager date waving his arms across the bar and made his way to our table. I don't remember the introductions; the music blared and conversation was impossible. C+C Music Factory's "Gonna Make You Sweat" began, and Jack about-faced from our table and made a beeline for the dance floor. Little did I expect this would be an ever-present theme in our future life together. Jack making a beeline to the dance floor. He loves to dance, and he's good. While his moves haven't necessarily progressed past the mid-1990s, he still has the soul and moves of one of the New Edition, not quite Michael Jackson but definitely Bobby Brown.

I can move on the dance floor myself, and before the second chorus of that atrocious song, I was dancing with Jack. His date eventually gave up and huffed off, and I tried not to notice my date's eyes boring into me. After five or six songs, the date started tugging on the back of my shirt and mouthing the words, "We're leaving!" He was pouting, and it made him even less appealing.

"Okay!" I shouted back. "I have to go to the bathroom! I will meet you outside in five minutes!" In the short time it took me to say those words, Jack's date had moved back in. I went to the ladies' room and asked frantically for a pen. Of course no one had a pen. In a bar. On a Saturday night. Their looks told me how unlikely I was to locate a pen. So I tore a huge paper towel from the roll and used my Clinique Black Honey lipstick to write "Angie 788-2152." I left the restroom and saw Jack way on the other side of the dance floor, clearly in the grips of his date again. It would take me ten minutes to make my way through the crowd, and huffy stuff was standing in the exit glaring at me and waving his arms again. That's when I saw Jack's buddy, who was hammered. I'd seen them walk in together.

"Are you Jack's friend?" I asked. "Will you give him this?"

A drunken nod, a thumbs-up, and the paper towel got shoved into his khaki shorts. Hmm. That wasn't very reassuring. As I walked out and was led to the car by my now-silent date, I wondered what had come over me. I never gave out my number like that. Ever. For all I knew, that woman he was with was his wife.

The next afternoon, the phone rang and I heard my dad answer in his rough and tough infantry voice, the voice that reeked of disdain for his only daughter's gentleman callers. "You want to talk to Angie? Well, here ya go." And he scowled but passed me the phone.

"Hello?"

"Hey! It's Jack. From last night? Tom gave me your note. Are you available tomorrow night? Can I take you to dinner?"

"Sure, I don't have plans tomorrow night." Yes I did. I was supposed to work; I could feel a sick day coming on already. I couldn't turn the date down. There wasn't time to waste.

The next night, he pulled into the driveway in his jet black Bronco truck right on time. Punctual to the minute, as if he'd been sitting down the road killing a few seconds to time his arrival perfectly. My parents were standing in the kitchen, and as I ran out the front door, I heard my mother call out, "Let him come to the door! Play hard to get!"

Jack took me to a little restaurant in Sackets Harbor, a picturesque little village right on Lake Ontario. I wanted to stare at him, soak in his perfection. He looked like a Ken doll, but the badass variety. Not a GI Joe, because he was too pretty for that. He wore a gritty, tough exterior that didn't naturally suit him. *His features and radiant coloring and blue eyes will be gorgeous on our daughters, and our sons will be built like Adonis,* I caught myself thinking. What the hell possessed me? I was gone. Gone and in love. All of a sudden, my future was clear.

We had two weeks together, and one of those weeks, he was in the field. Not exactly an ideal amount of time to make a boy fall in love. Jack was an army brat too, but left home at age seventeen to enlist in the army and then was later commissioned after graduating from college. He was a child of divorce and the eldest of three boys whose lives revolved around Ohio football, and aside from his happy-go-lucky personality, he wasn't terribly interested in a girlfriend. He was serious about his career—no time for a relationship. My work was cut out for me.

Jack was a brand-new, hungry infantry lieutenant. He'd just graduated from Ranger School and had no intention of falling in love. His true loves were the army and the hope of finding battle. The first Gulf War had just ended. He'd regretted missing it by weeks. He was the complete opposite of me: focused, hyperorganized, and almost humorless—well, not humorless, but just not my kind of humor. But oh so cheerful. His gumption and drive amused and intrigued me. He was the most endearing and child-like person I'd ever known. While we had opposite personalities, the chemistry between us was intense and undeniable. When he kissed me, I forgot my name for a few seconds. He even had a recording of his voice, which he used as his alarm clock in place of the typical beep-beep. He played it for me, completely unaware of how hilarious it was. His bright and clipped voice cried out, "Wake up, Ranger Hawkins! It's a *great day!* Make something *happen!*"

I cooked for him, and he devoured every morsel like it was the greatest thing he'd ever put in his mouth. That man could eat like I'd never seen. A dish called baked hamburgers, which, looking back, is borderline revolting, is still a favorite of his. It's ground beef baked in a ketchup sauce, and I was so proud of my domestic skills, considering my room at home was a disaster area. Suddenly I knew what I wanted and where I wanted to be. The Doc Martens boots were given to a friend.

Two weeks later, my parents left after four years at Fort Drum and headed to my dad's next assignment, in Korea. I was headed back to Bloomington to finish college. Jack came to say good-bye, and I knew he wouldn't ask me to stay. He was a man with a plan, and I knew enough of him to be certain he wouldn't stray from a goal once it had been set. I drove away with my parents that Sunday afternoon in August, with no reason to ever come back to Watertown, broken-hearted and sobbing like a fool.

He wrote me letters from the field, short and to the point. Factual information. He deals in facts. The letters almost made me smile, and it would be much later before I grasped that his pragmatic approach to life would cause many future moments of restraining myself from slapping his head. He called once in a while. Twice during my senior year, he bought plane tickets for me to visit for the weekend. Each time, we had an amazing time together, laughing and eating and watching movies and having dance parties in the little apartment he shared with another single lieutenant, and making out for hours. And each time he sent me back to Indiana, he gave me the speech. The speech broke my heart, but by then I suspected it was a mantra more than a non-negotiable fact.

"We have a great time together, and you are the most beautiful woman I've ever seen. I think about your smile nonstop, but I can't get serious right now. Not until after my company command. My goals are mapped out, and my priority is the army. The army is all I ever wanted." His company command was a handful of years and duty sta-tions away; if I waited that long, I would be a late-twenties spinster. Hell no was I waiting that long, though beyond question he was the love of my life.

The following summer, I graduated from Indiana University, then eventually loaded the new black Acura Integra my parents had given me for graduation, and headed back to Watertown. Jack had called a month earlier and simply said, "Hey girl! Did you get a job yet? What are your plans? So hey, I talked to my roommate, and he said you could live here with us if you want. I mean, if you want to look for a job here in Watertown." That was as close as I would come to an admission that he'd retyped the goals he kept on a frame in his wall. He must have added "Take a Wife" to that list of externally focused goals. Does that sound incredibly unromantic? It wasn't at all. It was sublime. I arrived at our shared apartment in Watertown, and a couple weeks later, he proposed on a whale watch in Maine. He'd bought a sterling dolphin ring at a gift shop for twenty bucks and knelt next to a puddle. Eventually I got a big, fat diamond, but the rock has never had the sentimental value of the cheap dolphin ring.

Jack and I shared a love of army life. He didn't have to spend time assimilating me to the culture; in fact, I taught him about the intricacies of protocol and political nuance. Army life was the only life I'd known. I had been bored by college. I missed the military cocoon I'd been raised in. So I jumped right back in without a second of hesitation.

After spending an accumulated five weeks dating, Jack and I eloped one Monday night, with only a few hours' notice. Just enough time to get the paperwork and then meet him at his battalion chapel for a quick, no-shit marriage ceremony. It was the eve of his deployment to Somalia in 1992. His unit was the first U.S. Army battalion on the ground in Mogadishu, in December 1992. It would be many years before I could look back on the Somalia deployment and realize the resolve and determination it gave us. Somalia was our litmus test, one that laid the floor of many deployments to come, and how we would each operate.

Before we married, Jack told me that one of the things he found most attractive about me was that I spoke army lingo. Isn't that romantic?

He didn't have to translate acronyms or explain the complex politics of rank; I knew them better than him at that point. In turn, I trusted he would be a lifer in the military, and that I could remain safely in the only world I knew. We fit well in the life the army carved out for us.

Back then his sole thirst was for the gritty life of a badass infantry officer. I was hungry for the sisterhood and safety of a culture I knew well. I was eager to start at the bottom of the food chain with him and hoped he would ascend the ranks, even though I knew that with each rank and promotion, the level of competition and politics would grow and that our peer group would grow smaller and smaller. I understood the intricacies of fraternization; although our peers were our competition, they were also the ones we were expected to buddy up with. We'd maintain a congenial closeness with those at echelons above and below us. I knew the chess game well. Even better, I could play it without showing that I was familiar with the game. I didn't make the game seem as awkward as it was, because the politics were second nature. In a strange way, they were a genuine part of who I was.

Many around me didn't have the same fluid way of navigating that part of our lives, and I cringed at their bumbles. Especially their attempts to buddy up to senior wives. Bumbles like laying on compliments too thick, feigning fascination at boring chitchat, and making facial expressions far too exaggerated to be real. Now we're getting into *perfumed-turd* territory, my pet name for senior officers' wives. Back then, in the decade before 9/11, I looked up to the perfumed turds. I just knew they had an inside track on information, a special key or password that would suddenly be passed to me when Jack made his way to that level. But that was a decade and a half away.

From the day we met, I've loved the cadence of Jack's footsteps. Our marriage has somehow survived two decades of the darkest of times, and I always cling to the familiar, fast pace of the *clop thud clop thud* of those boots on linoleum, or hardwood floors if we were lucky enough to score housing with hardwood. I realized a few years into our marriage that I married a stranger. A five-week courtship, not even enough time to pee with the door open in front of each other. We hadn't let our guards down long enough to see who we each were behind our polite masks. Yet I was too proud to admit I might have made a mistake and maybe jumped in too soon, and I suspect that he felt similarly. But the deployments saved us. They were galvanizing and gave us a shared focus of the lifestyle we both loved. In that regard, we have always been perfectly matched. Distant enough from each other to survive the years spent apart, but close enough to share a common purpose. We were built for war. Autonomous enough for survival.

part two

before the worst

IN THE DOZEN-PLUS years since that perfect-turned-tragic Tuesday morning in September 2001, "What were you doing on 9/11?" has become this generation's question of solidarity. On the twelfth anniversary of 9/11, we sit down to eat dinner, and Jack starts the family conversation (he loves prearranged dinner topics, keeps everyone on their toes) with a broad opener of, "So how do you kids think America has changed since 9/11?" And we look at each other for a long, uncomfortable moment.

"Dad, I was like, three, then." Joe is the first to answer. Bridget had been a year old, and Greta hadn't even been remotely on our horizon.

I won't dig into the horror of that day in 2001, because it's been written about over and over. I am watching the *Today* show and getting Joe ready for his first day of preschool in Watertown, New York. We'd arrived at the 10th Mountain again two months earlier, and Jack is at a training center on the other side of the country. On his way to Kosovo. With the news and gravity of that day, suddenly a deployment to Kosovo seems superfluous. We can't read the future and see then that there will be a plethora of other opportunities to join in the hunt for bin Laden. Afghanistan looks like a quick, easy, and almost fun victory. Like a really badass camping trip, but with a vengeance.

So I spend that winter after 9/11 with Jack on a completely ignored deployment, with the other half of 10th Mountain in Afghanistan. Families of soldiers in Afghanistan are suddenly offered free child care.

This is my first wake-up call about the hierarchy of deployments. In our world, gone is not gone. All deployments are not created equal.

I cluster with my Kosovo-deployed girlfriends and listen to the Afghanistan wives rattle about whether they've heard from their husbands and how proud they are. Each of them wears sweaters with huge American flags knitted into them every chance they get. The presence of a flag on an outfit is a pretty good indication of where a husband is deployed. I endure a Longaberger party (no one loves a friggin' Longasucker party like an army wife) hosted by my attention-seeking neighbor Virginia Hickman and hear her talk about the mini press conference she has set up outside the gate. She's taken her wedding album and her daughter gussied up with red, white, and blue bows in her hair. I intentionally turn my head to appear not to listen. But I listen. And as soon as I get home on my 2002 dial-up internet, I look up the interview and shake my head. Virginia is exactly what army wives do not want to look like. A bossy, entitled glory hound who defines herself solely through her husband's position as an army logistician. A self-promoter.

While it is considered gross to seek media coverage for ourselves, we revel in seeing our men on the news and in print. It shows us that what we do matters. In those immediate months after 9/11, of course Kosovo is wholly overlooked by the media. It's old news.

It's not that the first five years after 9/11 won't be painful and won't have a huge suck factor, but the gravity of the war life hasn't set in yet. The weariness and the numbness. The straight-up bitter. Most of us will white-knuckle the first five or so years, and only the weakest will go batshit crazy or bail completely. Deployment Darwinism, dahling. In 2002 it is still an exciting novelty.

Afghanistan seems like a cinch. Sure, there are some high-adventure moments in those first few years and the length of deployments stretches from six months to nine months, but it still appears manageable. Especially for me. Deployments have a strange peace and predictability that always appeal to me. Jack has deployed three times before 9/11, and we fall naturally into a rhythm. The shittiest part of a deployment is the month before it begins, and the month before it ends. The months in the middle are mostly peaceful, fueled by routine. We live in a comfortable but rundown duplex on Bassett Street in Fort Drum, New York. A thirty-minute drive to Lake Ontario and the Thousand Islands, and an hour's drive to the edge of the Adirondacks. Where snow is measured in feet, not inches. I relish the winters there, relish the excuse to hibernate with my kids and measure time between Tuesday pizza nights at the Commons with the other deployed mamas and their broods. We bond over star-shaped chicken nuggets while our kids eat cheese pizza and watch cartoons on the big screen. Plopping my kids in front of cartoons for some mommy time comes so easily. The subzero temperatures and mountains of snow don't exactly make outdoor play very accessible. It's one thing to build a snowman in six inches of snow, but in six feet of snow, it's altogether impossible.

Somehow it feels like the kids will be little forever, like we have all the time in the world and that the time we sacrifice with Jack deployed won't matter in the larger picture of their lives. This is an arrogant and naive assumption. It doesn't yet occur to us that we might blink our eyes and realize that Jack missed years and that I was too distracted by playing reindeer games with other wives to soak up my time with our children.

Jack is still as hungry as ever, a new major now. During his lieutenant and then captain years, majors' wives seemed so authoritative to me. They drive minivans and organize bake sales and call to remind me to clear the date of this month's coffee with the battalion wife's calendar before sending out invitations. In 2002, we still do paper invitations. Evites are new and surrounded with long discussions about their validity and break from tradition. Somehow, taking a stand against wasted paper defines an army wife as a pot stirrer.

So finally here I am, the one with a minivan, planning coffees and volunteering to help the time pass. Child care is free for volunteers, and I am all over that like white on rice. In the early years, I want to be right in the center of activity. Can't bear the thought of missing something, anything. I believe the fund-raisers and luncheons and newsletters and team-building workshops and mentoring matter. It will be years before I see those activities as Kool-Aid. In retrospect, whether these flossy activities themselves matter in the grand scheme is open to debate, but they certainly keep our time occupied and prevent wives from sitting still while the men are gone. What does matter is that an adherence to these shenanigans fosters a sisterhood while also carrying on tradition. But more importantly, it hasn't occurred to me yet to question the overall meaning of anything about my role. And that's the difference between then and later, attitude and awareness. Perhaps the focus on being a solid mentor also keeps me afloat, helps me even more than the wives I think I am molding.

Those strictly protocol-driven activities keep my hands from lying idle during long winters and longer deployments. Something within me easily lures me into mischief, catches me up in an impulsive moment of pouring glitter into a carefully selected set of invitations for the monthly coffee. Both creative and passive-aggressive, all at the same time. Brilliance on my part. Glitter is festive! An impeccable excuse! If pressed, I can feign ignorance at what a calculated, bitchy move the glitter was. My greatest hope and delight are that the recipient of the glitter-filled invitation will open the envelope in her minivan, sending glitter cascading into every nook and cranny, then walk around for months with sparkly, pesky, unrelenting glitter strewn haphazardly on her black capri pants. I perfect my technique early. No one tries harder or believes with more passion that she matters than a newly anointed major's wife. And I do not disappoint.

I am aware that this is Jack's dues-paying time, and mine, too. The politics at Fort Drum are thick and heavy. Obvious. How an infantry officer performs as a major dictates the rest of his career. While I am cognizant of this fact, it doesn't prevent me from harassing Jack and berating him for the nights he spends working in his office and napping on a cot next to his desk. So yes, deployed is better sometimes. At least then the kids and I don't wait for him to come home, don't hope he might make it in time for dinner. It's easiest to just tell the kids Dad is at work. Even if he's deployed. Whether he is gone or home, they don't notice the difference.

We, the soldiers and their families, are fueled by the momentum and patriotism of the entire country and the media focus. Those things might seem insignificant, but they matter to us as a culture. Yellow ribbon magnets are displayed in their newness on vehicles, before the tags are faded and forgotten. Walking with my husband into a gas station to pay for gas and having the attendant tell us it is already taken care of. The eventual waning of public support of the war isn't what eventually takes a toll on us. The first two years after 9/11 seem easy almost, in and out and the Taliban taken care of. Still no bin Laden head on a plate, but the public rage and need for revenge over the attacks on our soil appear to be satiated. Deployments at 10th Mountain the first couple of years are six months, nine at the most. We can handle that. Piece of cake. Our army spent the 1990s in various Third World dumping grounds acting as police and peacekeepers, kind of like the older brother who saunters in and tells everyone that it will all be okay because he's arrived, but nothing really changes. But 9/11 changes everything. Then, two and a half years later, Iraq is added to our army plate. Very different wars on vastly different soil for vastly different reasons. But it's all called the War on Terrorism, so the public falls right into line. It happens so fast that it confuses even us in the U.S. military and our families at first. We drink the Kool-Aid, can't gulp it quick enough on the way out the door to rid the world of bad guys. We have the power, and we are in control. A swagger that only an American can master.

It takes a few years to notice that the same soldiers go back to both war fronts, Afghanistan and Iraq, over and over. I look for 10th Mountain patches on the shoulders that whiz by on the nightly news screen. Privately I wonder if we are a large-enough force to spread out and sustain a long war, but I'm just a wife—surely someone bigger has this covered? None of us in the thick of it has the time or energy to stop and really take a broad look yet. Only a handful of guys are tagged "it" for back-to-back deployments. Infantry divisions like the 10th Mountain, 101st Airborne, and 82nd Airborne—they're the real workhorses. The light infantry divisions. Easy to move and quick to be ready. And a handful of heavy armored divisions are back and forth as well.

Yeah, there are things about those first years after 9/11 that suck, but they're mainly inconveniences. Missed births of babies, weakened marriages that can't go the distance, too many missed holidays to count. The loss of soldiers, mostly young enlisted men and a handful of young, junior-grade officers. Senior leaders? No way. Maybe a close call or two, but those were and are likely to be exaggerated. In the early years, at our level we feel impenetrable.

Then sometime a few years in, someone in Washington decides that one-year deployments will be more efficient. A promise of at least a year dwell time between deployments is made, on paper, but it doesn't always hold. So there we are, a year gone, a year home. Sometimes Iraq, usually Afghanistan. At least for the 10th Mountain. Our main presence until 2004 is Afghanistan. Then Iraq is added to our now overflowing plate.

a taste of this side of war

May 2004. Jack spends a year minding the flock, which gives him an appreciation of the bedlam during deployments.

"I'M PREGNANT!" I blurt out this news to Jack at his office at the brigade headquarters building. I called ahead to make sure he isn't in a meeting with his commander, Colonel Douglas O'Malley. This brigade commander works Jack harder than he's worked since the lieutenant years, but Jack doesn't mind. He respects Colonel O'Malley and uses this time under him to watch and learn; Jack is never one to shy away from the toughest jobs. This attitude is both a blessing and a curse for me, the one waiting at home for him. Which is exactly why I just went to his office that day. Secrets are not my thing.

Jack is exhausted but smiles as he leans back in the chair at his desk in the corner office where the primary staff works, just within shouting distance from O'Malley, and looks at me, not surprised by my statement, but summoning some enthusiasm through his work distractions, for the sake of the moment. I've clung to the images Jack paints in stories about O'Malley, who keeps a framed piece of artwork on the wall in the conference room and points to it with his laser pointer during endless staff meetings. Well, calling it artwork might be a stretch. Inside the frame on the wall are the words A FIELD GRADE OFFICER MUST BE PUT TO DEATH ONCE IN A WHILE TO ENCOURAGE THE OTHERS.

That sums up O'Malley to a T. Being here is risky, not because we're not allowed to visit, but because he intimidates the crap out of me; no one wants to be the silly wife hanging around the office.

"That's awesome, Ang! Will the housing office at Fort Knox take a pregnancy as enough to get us on the four-bedroom list?"

"Yep. I checked the website. I remember exactly where the houses are; it's those historic redbrick ones. I used to take my morning walks over in that neighborhood around the parade field with Joe in his stroller. I secretly hoped I would get to live there someday. How cool is this? They have fireplaces, and it's walking distance to the pool. Do you remember the place with the—"

"Hey, can we talk about this tonight? I might be late getting home because we've got a lot going on. I have a meeting starting in five minutes, and I have to prep these slides." Everything in his world when he's not deployed revolves around PowerPoint slides. How exactly that works in combat, I'm not sure.

"All right," I say, disappointed that I can't squeeze in just a moment to congratulate myself for timing another pregnancy just right. "Want me to bring you something to eat?" He doesn't even get to answer me before someone from another office calls impatiently for him and he feigns a light hug on his way out the door. No PDA in uniform. It's a bummer that my pregnancy isn't more thrilling news, but we're not surprised. With each of our three children, we've been blessed that babies came easily. With the deployments, it would suck to try and try and then put it on hold. Plotting and planning our babies' arrivals around projected deployments are my small victory.

This is the spring of 2004, Jack has been home from his first tour in Afghanistan for barely a handful of months, and we have slipped back into our family routine pretty seamlessly. Deployments are still six months long, maybe slipping to nine months here and there, but manageable. Jack is still working with relentless focus toward his goal of his own battalion command, and I stay busy spinning my wheels as the Officers' Spouses Club vice president.

We're finishing up our third year at 10th Mountain now, which is our second tour since we were married here before Somalia. We have orders to move back to Fort Knox, Kentucky, to spend a couple years in a relaxing job away from an infantry division, a couple years to recuperate before, hopefully, returning to the 10th Mountain for battalion command. That's Jack's grand plan, anyway, and his branch manager assures him he is a lock for it. The 10th Mountain is Jack's first choice, and we haven't yet reached a time when he doesn't get his first choice in anything—which is easy to take for granted, but can end at any moment. The army is a fickle beast. Anyway, only a handful of folks wanted to stay in the frozen tundra of 10th Mountain year after year. So it wasn't exactly like we had to fight too hard to stay.

Joe and Bridget were born at Fort Knox, where Jack was an instructor in the late 1990s. We were only two hours from my parents, and those were wonderful years, having my parents close by to dote on the kids and take the endless videos of them—videos that I was too tired to take. I look forward to going back, and most of all, I look forward to qualifying for a four-bedroom house. The army gives one bedroom per child, sometimes fewer if the kids are the same gender and close in age. I hope I've sidestepped that policy with baby number three.

Just weeks before our packers come to move us out of our ranch duplex in May, six and a half years before I lie in a cardiac cath lab, Jack calls home on a Wednesday afternoon with the news that our orders for Fort Knox have been pulled. My pregnancy with Greta planted just enough to qualify us for another bedroom on post at our presumed destination of Fort Knox. His whole brigade is headed to Iraq for a year.

The brigade is leaving for Baghdad in three weeks. Jack is still a major and has barely been home four months from his first deployment to Afghanistan. Long enough to knock me up, per our plan for baby number three. I got pregnant knowing we were leaving Fort Drum and knowing he would be present for her birth. After I hang up, I lie in the hallway and sob on the floor. Joe comes out of his bedroom where he was playing with his Playmobil set. He asks me if I fell and need ice or a Band-Aid.

Jack quickly brainstorms and presents Colonel O'Malley with an idea. He volunteers himself to Colonel O'Malley to stay back to be the *sheepdog for the flock of families* as the rear detachment commander. He has an idea to develop an army-wide system for rear detachments, to fill a huge, unplanned-for void left by a constant rotation of deploying units—and now deployments are a year long, which is unprecedented. It's one thing to white-knuckle it through a six- or nine-month deployment, but a year at that point feels like an eternity. A few months earlier, the wife of a deployed soldier at another army post killed herself in her home, and the death went undiscovered for weeks. Finally it's time for the army to notice that its families are desperate for an infrastructure to help them during deployments. It's too soon for us to comprehend that this might be the beginning of a generation of self-entitled military families. No time to think of the long-term effects.

Until this time, units typically left their weakest behind for rear detachments. But this deployment will be different. New policy lengthens deployments to a year each—this is the first of those at 10th Mountain. In Iraq casualties are expected to be high. So Colonel

O'Malley buys into Jack's revolutionary idea, and I am nothing short of relieved. Score another win for me for accurately planning a pregnancy after all, but barely.

The next week, at a standing-room-only brigade-wide meeting for the thirty-five hundred families who still reel from the announcement of the sudden deployment, Colonel O'Malley shows slides and maps of where the soldiers will spend the next year. Gives details about their living conditions. Babies cry and wives look around, bewildered and disinterested in operational details. The walls of the auditorium swell with tension and frustration.

Colonel O'Malley leans into the microphone and asks, "Is Major Hawkins here? Please stand up, Jack. Major Hawkins is the best major in the brigade. He's currently my brigade S3, the operations officer. The top one percent of the army today. And that's why I selected him to serve as my new rear detachment commander. He will be available day and night to ensure our families are well cared for." For a second, there is complete silence.

Then the wives stomp and cheer. I feel pride well in my chest. *That's my man.* The robust and barrel-chested Colonel O'Malley steps back from the mike, smiles, and points to Jack: *You da man.* I smile too, anticipating the year ahead. Being the only man on our block of husbandless wives will be the least of his worries.

I've never seen Jack in a more beautiful light than I do over the following year. In the thirteen years we've been married, I've known him as tough and determined in his career. Approachable but not exactly relatable. That year, I see him become a human, and it sounds weird to hear myself say I didn't see him as human until then. Of course I did. Maybe what I mean is I see him in a different light once he gets a taste of the chaos and restlessness we go through on this side during deployments. Even with his army BlackBerry constantly at his ear and the juggling of the unpredictable nature of rear detachment responsibilities, he has time to organize massive nature hikes for up to twenty of our neighborhood's kids—kids who are temporarily fatherless because of the war. The kids love him and follow him like the Pied Piper. He treats them like miniature soldiers on these epic hikes, gives them all packing lists for what to bring in their backpacks to sustain them through five hours of humping through swamps and thick forests. Inevitably he returns with at least one kid on his shoulders and another tapped-out mini-adventurer wrapped around his waist. He's always had a connection with children that I don't quite feel. I have trouble thinking of what to say to kids, how to speak to them. For him, it comes as second nature.

I can't wait to see the look of contentment on Joe's six-year-old face when they return from their long hikes. He beams at Jack over his glasses and grins, loves the opportunity to share his dad. The dad who in the past has had such little time for him now has time for everyone.

My own appreciation for him develops far beyond his simple presence with us as a family, because we see him so little that I'm dying to say the words "He might as well be deployed." *But God forbid an army wife complains about the amount of hours her husband spends at the office when everyone around her is deployed. She could lose an eye or a limb or an ovary. And I am smarter than that.*

What I watch that year is a gradual appreciation grow in him, an awareness for the amount of shit families go through on this side. Most guys who served previously in rear detachment positions saw their job as a smack in the face and spent their time absently minding the flock, ticking off days until it ended, just squeaking by. Jack is the first to see a huge void in the way the army handles deployments. He ends up on the cover of the *Association of the United States Army* newspaper that year, hailed for the systems he put in place to handle just about any sort of shitty situation that could arise during deployment. He creates something called the Soldier Readiness Contract, which ends up being used army-wide by deploying units. Each soldier must complete a two-page form, kept by the rear detachment, which outlines where his family lives, how they wish to be contacted, anticipated funeral details in the case he should be killed, everything short of what his wife's favorite color is. I helped Jack brainstorm that contract, and it feels awfully close to Big Brother territory. But in 2004, we need this added protection and change in the way we conduct rear detachment procedures. Things are escalating quickly in terms of casualties and frequency and length of deployment. Wives panic more easily, expect more support from the army system than ever before.

Luckily, Jack and Colonel O'Malley's wife, Kate, have an excellent relationship, even friendship. They click. I've seen other commanders' wives go to battle with their rear detachment commander, and their symbiotic relationship is a nice added bonus. Kate and Jack are two peas, in a strange way. Unlike her husband, Kate is nurturing and infinitely generous with her time and her energy. Even-keeled and an excellent listener, she doesn't play games with the wives. She is a grown-up. Although she's mildly intimidating in her own way, it isn't because she needs to be the center of attention or craves recognition. She just wants things to be right. Yes, she and Jack are a perfect duo, and I love that she adores him for his exhausting energy and his work ethic.

Jack becomes a rock star that year. But the coolest part for me is that he *gets it* now at a gut level. I appreciate how engaged he is with the other wives, how he never has a bad day, never is without a reassuring smile. The wives feel safe with him, and beyond that, he gets an invaluable glimpse at what my life is like during deployment. It's nothing like the extended slumber party complete with pillow fights that he likely imagined. I will never have a true grasp of his secret world during deployment, but now he has a real picture of my world.

prophetic dream

January 2006. The dreams we want to dismiss
are the ones we should remember.

WHAT IS THAT sound? It's 5:00 on Sunday morning, and Jack isn't in bed. This is when he still slept in a bed. The clunking and thumping of things moving around is coming from our garage. Luckily the noise hasn't woken the children, or else I'd be heading down the hallways to the garage not just curious, but pissed.

I walk to the garage anyway. "Honey? What are you doing? It's freezing out here. And it's really early. It's still technically nighttime by my definition." Our garage is tiny and not heated. January temperatures in Fort Drum rarely make it out of the negatives. The cement garage has black industrial storage containers from ground to ceiling. In the rafters are my far-too-many holiday decorations, stored in color-coded containers. On the other side of the garage are neatly organized storage chests holding Jack's plethora of "hobby" gear: enough hunting, fishing, and sporting equipment to entertain a small village of testosterone-loaded dudes. Unfortunately most of it is rarely used, but he loves it nonetheless. Jack thinks it is important to have a vast array of interests and hobbies outside the army, even if the army rarely allows him to engage in these hobbies.

He turns from where he's digging deeply into one of the containers, and I can see his breath hang in the air. For a second, he stares blankly at me, like he's not quite sure what he's doing there himself and even less sure how to say it. "I'm packing some more gear to send on the next pallet. I had the weirdest dream. I dreamt Rob Macklin was killed, and he's a Cav commander, the same kind of battalion I'm slated to take in the fall after I get back. It occurred to me that I need to be prepared and take enough gear to stay for the whole deployment. If one of the commanders gets killed, I'm next in line. It would make sense to just keep me there. My dream was so detailed, so real, I mean, of course it's not going to happen, but I need to be prepared. Afghanistan could go to hell any second."

It's three days before his second deployment to Afghanistan. I can't help but picture the Macklins. Her swollen belly pregnant with their first child in a twenty-year marriage.

Jack comes back inside. The kids, who are seven, five, and one at the time, are awake now and demanding pancakes. Pancakes on the weekend are Jack's thing. He makes breakfast, and the dream is easily dismissed among the bedlam of spilled syrup and our three young children vying for Daddy's undivided attention. It lingers in my mind, though, the dream and my mental image of the Macklins. But we don't speak of the dream again.

Rob Macklin's wife, Laura, who seems a little too deadpan and guarded for me to fully call a friend, at forty-one is older than most first-time mothers. Their baby is due a few months after Rob deploys. As I eat my pancakes, an eerie but clear snapshot from a recent conference snaps into mind. Rob and Laura leaning forward in their seats. Rob, who normally appears too stiff and serious for any kind of real PDA, not unlike his entire peer group, rests his hand in an uncharacteristic and intimate gesture on his wife's swollen belly and Laura's face contorts in concentration as she takes frantic notes. I remember my curiosity about the notes, but from community information meetings, I've seen that the woman can be an intense note-taker. She is aware of details that seem irrelevant in my mind and slip past me in meetings. Getting caught up in trying to figure people out causes me to miss an awful lot of substance in those meetings.

Community leader information meetings, also known as CLIF. The grand stage for perfumed-turd posturing. This meeting is held by the division on the first Wednesday morning of each month. The purpose is for various on-post agencies and organizations to give updates and pass out information for the perfumed turds to pass down their food chains and into the hands of the wives under their umbrella. Mostly battalion commanders' wives attend, but also other senior staff wives and, of course, the brigade commanders' wives and the three generals' wives on post. It is an event. But it bores me senseless. I am the president of a volunteer organization this year, which makes my attendance a requirement—though I sit in the back and can slither out if the *tedious* becomes too much. I don't even remember the organization I presided over, which is bizarre. The clubs and organizations run together and seem to overlap in their redundancies. But their existence keeps the machine moving, keeps us busily taking notes.

CLIF meetings are the Kool-Aid factory. Only a select few make it into the doors to see how it's made and hear how it should be driveled out. But the meetings are also an excellent opportunity to people-watch and provided fodder for weeks' worth of playground discussions. And it's far preferred to have endured the meeting and be able to participate in later rehashing than to be a nonattendee and have to just listen to the others.

I haven't witnessed Laura's levity, never heard her laugh, and I have no reason to force a friendship between us. But she is a close friend of my close friend Elizabeth, which tells me that Laura is a good egg. Laura is one of those people who I probably would become friends with if she lived in my neighborhood, but I have no real motivation to dig past her exterior to find a possible shared sense of humor or shared enjoyment in issuing silent fashion violations.

The battalion commanders and field grade officers at Fort Drum live in two neighborhoods separated by maybe a mile and a half. So if our husbands don't work directly together and we aren't in the same neighborhood, the only time we cross paths is for officers' spouses luncheons or Bunco. I doubt Laura participates in either of those perfumed-turd venues.

the butt boy and earl grey tea

Having a general on your side is never a bad thing.

I CAN'T REMEMBER IF Jack leaves for his second tour in Afghanistan a few days before or after Greta's birthday in the end of January, but we eat birthday cake and celebrate hurriedly before he goes. This particular day-of-deployment ritual is relatively painless because he will return at the end of June to prepare for his nearing battalion command in another of the division's brigades, which is halfway through a year in Iraq. So how long will Jack be gone? Five months. No one has a right to moan about a five-month deployment. I drive him unceremoniously to the division headquarters on a frigid Saturday morning, anticipating the restful weekend stretched ahead with movies and pajamas and lots of unhealthy snacks. We hug, and he climbs out of the car with his rucksack and waves over his shoulder. Bridget sees my tears and reminds me, "Mommy, don't cry. Daddy will be home from Ass-damn-stan when the leaves turn green on the trees." I cry anyway the entire duration of the ten-minute drive home, but by the time I pull into the driveway, I am done.

By this time in early 2006, almost all units are deploying for a year at a time. If you have a special circumstance like Jack does this time, you phase back or forth, but the vast majority of soldiers will face a year deployment. Troop levels in Afghanistan are low, I think only a handful of brigades. The 10th Mountain sends one infantry brigade, a support element, and their division staff. Another 10th Mountain brigade is in Iraq, and the other brigade is preparing to go. Our neighborhood is filled with families at varying stages of the deployment process, and at varying levels of frustration and exhaustion. Watching the soldier across the street come home when I've just begun has a special kind of sting.

Jack's job in Afghanistan this go-around is a division staff position, and his larger-than-life boss is more of a perfectionist than Jack. As the secretary general staff to the commanding general of 10th Mountain, Jack is the general's whipping boy. Or the funnier job nickname, "butt boy." I like that one better, too.

General Stewart is an impassioned, demanding leader who wears his emotions on his sleeve, a rare quality for someone of his rank. By this point, most generals are emotionally awkward and void of personality. Feelings slowly trained out of them. As army generals go, this guy is all heart and a lot of gut.

Years devoted to a black-and-white, non-nuanced infantry life slowly bleed the personality and color from a weathered soldier and steal his ability to relate to others—a common trait of senior officers. Stoic, a transparent mask of exuberant friendliness that barely covers a desperate desire to be anywhere but in a conversation with a civilian or wife, and always with his immaculately ironed shirt tucked in. Jack and those like him are the kings of small talk, glancing around the room and plotting an escape. Conversations that exchange information but don't dwell on the meaning between the lines. No time for nuance, only time for the mission. Navigating nuance is my job, to fill in the gaps in Jack's inability to connect with people on a deeper level. I hate minutia and small talk, but my irreverent nature catches people off guard and has always been one of my greatest assets in relating with others. Irreverence puts people at ease. Somehow Jack can't seem to soak in this exquisite concept. But again, he doesn't feel the primal need to connect with others the way I do. He's content to maintain a protective distance, stand a cordial but stiff guard over people, protecting himself and us in his own unique manner.

Nothing I said in the above paragraph applies to General Stewart. He certainly is not irreverent or at ease, but he is a natural communicator. He oozes charisma. Tears well in his eyes when he talks about soldiers and their families in his speeches.

His wife, Linda, ranks among the top five scariest senior wives I've ever encountered. Linda is a strong-minded, serious infantry wife who has raised five boys while her husband was climbing the ranks. She wears her experience in a sturdy set of convictions that show on her face and she sports a mop of gray hair that she seems uninterested in coloring. Linda's intimidating appearance could be countered with a pleasing, demure personality—but it isn't. We are thankful for her at the helm because there is never a time that we burgeoning perfumed turds need a firm leader more. Linda spells it out to the wives of the 10th Mountain that she's not here to be our buddy. She is our mentor and our leader. And I better be quick with a fucking RSVP to her social, or she will call my ass and ask if my phone is broken or if I just have no manners. Of course I toe the line with her and never earn that humiliating scolding, but I witness other not-so-lucky wives being left stunned in Linda's wake of reprimand. In a sick and secret way, I adore her. I love that she does what's right and doesn't care what anyone thinks. Linda is revered by wives who count, by the ones who also work their asses off and aren't concerned with being loved or even liked. Linda is present; she is with me. She might scare the shit out of me, but at least she doesn't play games or just show up to make pretentious gestures, unlike her predecessor. Linda earns respect.

Behind the scenes, Stewart maintains nearly impossible-to-meet standards. To say that he is simply *particular* is a gross understatement. Flags for receptions and ceremonies need to be ironed until not even a memory of a wrinkle remains. There will be hell to pay if his Earl Grey tea isn't on his desk at the precise moment he expects it. While it isn't Jack's job to fetch tea, it is Jack's job to make sure the tea fetchers are efficient and on time. On the other side of the planet, I scramble to manually make corrections in 450 "Tour of Homes" brochures that were printed with a mistake in someone's rank, before Linda notices. I wish I had Jack's tea fetchers.

Jack calls home maybe once a week, and we talk for exactly ten stilted minutes on the free morale line. There is a delay of a few seconds, and it makes talking painful and frustrating. We end up talking over each other, and I'm almost relieved when the call ends.

"Ang, stop talking and listen. When you are done talking, say the word 'over'; that means you're done. Then, we won't be speaking over each other. Got it?"

"Okay, that's a good plan. Greta has been sick and I'm trying to get her an appointment, but I might just take her to the Urgent Care. I hate going there, though. It's packed and everyone is sick. I feel like we're just going to get sicker by being there. Over. Oh, and I think there's something wrong with the Jeep again. The stupid check engine light is on. Should I just quit driving it, or do you think it's okay, over? I can drive the van to Indiana for spring break—"

"*Ang!*" He's laughing as he interrupts me, that boyish chuckle of his, but I can tell he's frustrated. I miss him. I don't want to miss him. "This only works if you shut your piehole after you say 'over.'"

"Oh yeah. Sorry, I forgot. Should I say 'over and out' instead?"

"Nobody says 'over and out.' It doesn't exist. That's some kind of movie thing. It's just 'out' when we're done talking."

I should know this. It has taken me almost ten years of marriage to train him not to say "out" when he ends a phone call with his mother, who was an army wife for a short time, but was confused by all things army, anyway. Then I hear the recorded woman's voice that reminds me our call will end in thirty seconds. We are still talking over each other when the voice returns and says in a passive-aggressive, overly polite tone, "Your call has ended. Good-byeeee."

Then the line goes dead. I hear the tiredness in his voice, but he doesn't complain. Email is a more reliable method of communication, something that younger wives take for granted. They weren't around during the Somalia days, when I heard nothing from Jack for months, then got twenty-six letters delivered all on one day. Email, though, can be our angel and our devil. It can complicate the coping patterns we fall into during deployments. Too much communication isn't always a good thing.

This is going to sound pretentious, but I have to get it out of the way and just say it: Jack was born to be a soldier. *But all the perfumed turds think their husband is the biggest badass of all; I am no different in that regard.* He is perhaps brilliant, in a very myopic way, at military tactics and strategy. His far greatest asset, though, is his tirelessness and determination toward a goal or mission. He is laser focused in an almost scary way, like a wild animal. Jack isn't scattered and introspective like me. Being married to him makes me a better person. There's a reason opposites attract.

But as my longtime best friend from the early years in Germany used to say, "We all think our husbands are the best. That's why we married them. Because we keep them on a pedestal. No one is going to admit her husband is a dud, for Pete's sake. So don't go telling me how great your husband is at soldiering, because I think mine is better." I admire her for addressing so plainly what we all danced around.

So I try to remember her words. The army has told Jack time and again what a super stud he is, and it's hard not to start believing it. It's hard not to drink that Kool-Aid. I'm both lucky and cursed in that Jack is a 10th Mountain Division golden boy and has maintained his precarious position at the top of the heap for years, though he worked his ass off to get there and we do not take it for granted. He's been promoted twice ahead of his peers, was an honor graduate from each of his army schools up the echelons, including Ranger School. Slowly pronouncing the acronym BZ is an enormous perk of being married to him. BZ is shorthand for "below the zone." Only the tiniest fractions of officers are promoted below the zone, so this comes with a similar swagger to U.S. Army War College selection. I never talk about any of this with my army wife friends, and I feel icky doing it now. We know who the braggadocios are. Jack would be horrified. It's not something he would ever mention, because he's only competing against himself. Those are his accomplishments, and he doesn't need to brag about them. It's hard not to jump on that horse and ride the shit out of it. We want to brag about our husbands, but the wise ones don't make this transparent, rookie move. It always comes off as desperate. Try hard. Most of us have a keen awareness of where we each stand in the pecking order, though.

But it's different for the wives. Our husband's accomplishments define us in a weird way. Most of us have passed up our own careers to support theirs. So we cling to his accomplishments and achievements as if they are our own, because somehow, doing so makes it worth our having given up ourselves for his career. The same goes for failures. Wives feel those even harder than the men.

There's a smug satisfaction that comes with being married to someone with a golden reputation. It gives me a quiet confidence, and I don't have to try so desperately to make up for shortcomings in his career. I'm not the "please love me" girl, which I'll admit is only partly my nature. The other part is a quiet confidence that I didn't have to try so arduously to prove myself and overcompensate for my husband's beer belly or his lack of deployments.

My social standing among our peers is comfortable around the others who feel the need to wait for opportunities to one-up each other. The position of occupying the top of the heap is coveted. So in essence there's an invisible target on our backs, Jack's and mine. In contrast to the culture of constant competition, these one-uppers are also our lifeline and closest allies. A delicate dynamic and dance that we can't avoid.

stillness

When there is nothing to do but wait,
nothing to do but hope it isn't you.

O N A F RIDAY in May 2006 in the remote mountains of Kunar province, a Chinook helicopter crashes while picking up an infantry squad on a mission and careens down a mountain in flames, killing ten soldiers inside. Difficulty in accessing the wreckage site and confusion about who exactly was on the helicopter create a hush of silent chaos following the crash. Fort Drum families of soldiers who are in Afghanistan hold their breath for two solid days until notifications of KIA (killed in action) are confirmed and complete.

Before I hear of the crash, I shop for groceries early Saturday morning in what is usually a crowded commissary. Not even the cashiers are their chatty selves; no whines about empty carts not returned to the trolley. No cars enter or leave my neighborhood; everyone with a husband in Afghanistan hunkers in her home watching CNN with the curtains drawn on the beautiful spring day. Playgrounds are devoid of children and the usual mayhem of activities.

No messages on my machine, and I flip on the news. Thanks to the ticker scrolling across the bottom, I learn only that it was a 10th Mountain Chinook. A transport helicopter intended to carry up to fifty soldiers. While the media spend the day freely hypothesizing the details of the crash, back here we endure an immediate, mandatory blackout of communication between Fort Drum and Afghanistan. No calls, no emails. Nothing. Strict protocol to ensure that word of mouth doesn't spread a soldier's death before the unaware widow has the privilege, honor, and dignity of hearing per regulation, from a gussied-up chaplain and officer who knock at her door. From the news, it must be us. We just don't know *who*. Sometimes information finds its way through commo blackouts.

The soldiers aboard the crashed helicopter were incinerated to the point of requiring dental records for identification, according to CNN. I make sure my kids are in their rooms playing. Sometimes, oftentimes, the media get facts wrong. They forget we are watching, the families of those who might have been incinerated. The CNN anchor smoothly moves on to a story about Britney Spears.

I look outside again to see if anyone is standing in the street talking. On our street of about thirty families, maybe five homes have a husband who isn't deployed. Most men are in Iraq, though, so I would think some neighbors would be outside. News from Iraq seems mild today. No reason for my neighbors to hunker down in their hovels. I say hovels, because these houses are hovels. One-story duplexes slapped together in a big, bad hurry in the late 1980s, when Fort Drum expanded with the arrival of the 10th Mountain. The linoleum floors were patched with whatever kind of linoleum the housing warehouse had stocked. No one even bothered to make it match. The vent for our dryers blows directly into the front door and covers the entryway with lint, no matter how often we step outside with a broom to clean it up. The heating vents are in the ceiling, even though we live in the coldest part of the country besides Alaska. So the story went, when the houses were slapped up, they borrowed blueprints from houses in Fort Bragg,

North Carolina, and didn't bother to make even slight adjustments for climate. The floors are colder than a witch's titty in winter, as my dad liked to say when he visited. Summers could be blistering, and the houses weren't built with air conditioners. In the summer of 2005, the powers that be decided we needed air conditioners. The residents of Bassett Street were tickled with relief and waited impatiently for theirs to be installed, each of us keeping track of who got hers first, and wondered if there was rhyme or reason. For two weeks no one talked about anything except the air conditioners. We assumed it would be an outside unit, one of those little boxes in the backyard. Nope. They came and carved a huge hole in the living room wall, dead in the center, and installed the loudest, ugliest window unit I've ever seen. Surely it was cheap, and that's why we got it.

But all of that changed the next year, when the army decided we all needed better "quality of life." They threw grandiose (but when you look really closely, cheaply made, not unlike Bassett Street, just grander and newer) new homes at us. Hopefully to take our minds away from two wars with no end in sight.

Bassett Street is probably ugly and rundown, but nearly every resident keeps an immaculate lawn and does her best to decorate the facade of her home. Army wives really are masters of making even the hugest dump seem like it's not so crummy after all. Life on Bassett Street is about the camaraderie, not about the aesthetics of the gross duplexes, though the gross duplexes give us a galvanizing and always-available topic of discussion. When we run out of things to talk about, we can always bitch about the housing.

Bassett Street is usually overflowing with gangs of kids of all ages. They spend their days going back and forth to and from the woods behind our street and creating worlds and games on the playground. Saturdays are normally a flurry of noise and a cascade of wagons, Big Wheels, and bikes left in the center of the street; cars had to stop and move the toys just to maneuver into their driveways. Today there are no bikes and no water wars with hoses. And it is probably the warmest, most gorgeous spring day we've had so far this year. But it's a ghost town.

I think I will drag the kids to Mass this afternoon.

I wrack my brain to remember the last time I heard from Jack. Was it Monday? He's in a staff position and spends his days in the headquarters, the JOC, right? It's impossible he was aboard that Chinook. But I allow my mind to go there, to imagine the nondescript sedan pulling up in front of my house and the formally dressed notification team of soldiers walking to my front door. Would I open the door? Would I scream like the women in movies? Or would I reach deep into my black soul to allow myself to hover from above and feel nothing? I am tremendously unruffled in crises; it's the little things that push me over the edge. But that scenario doesn't even qualify as a crisis situation; it would be the end of the only life I've known.

As an only-when-I-need-it Catholic, I drag the kids in the afternoon to a standing-room-only Mass. Crowds of families pray their asses off in silence. Again, the weight of the stillness is crushing, smothering, and sickening. On the way to my car after Mass, I see a woman heave through her sobs and vomit into a trash can.

"eyes on the prize, violet."
wait. is that too cliché?

What, me? I'm the power-hungry one? No way. Okay, it's maybe true.

THIS SATURDAY MORNING, I'm nursing a hangover and trying to keep my mind away from conjuring images of the helicopter crash.

Jack is due home in two menstrual periods. It's sorta sick, but that's how I measure time between deployments. He is due home in late June 2006, two periods from now. For him, this deployment is curtailed to only five months, because in June, we begin preparations for his new gig as the "command team" of his own battalion at 10th Mountain.

Planning for a goal so far in the distance is incomprehensible to me, but I admire his gumption. Everything he's done in the years between then and now—the six deployments, the missed dinners and birthday parties, his absence from our three babies' nightly baths and diaper rashes, my countless angry phone calls to his office because I watched the other men on our street pull into their driveways after work while he worked through the night and instead napped on a cot stored behind his desk in his office, his indifferent but indulgent hugs of reassurance when I cried tears of frustration, my ultimatums and empty threats that I was fed up, fed up to *here*, the years he missed out on being a present father, the years that our family took the backseat to his ambition—all of it was with that one goal in mind. Battalion command. "Eyes on the prize, Violet." I can almost picture that ambition-crazed mother from *Charlie and the Chocolate Factory*. And here it is, a decade and a half later: our prize. His prize for making the army his first and only priority.

Jack's command will call on me to sling an awful lot of Kool-Aid, but deep down I am delighted with the three years ahead of us. It's my prize as much as it is his. I like to think of myself as a traditionalist, with a twist. I'm a closet liberal, and sometimes I wonder if I should have wound up living in artsy-fartsy Seattle. Maybe I should have been a Foo Fighters groupie. Doing yoga and talking about my chakras. Engaging in pretentious and ignorant but deeply concerned debates about the plight of Third World refugees. Maybe writing the fashion dos and don'ts for the back page of a women's magazine, snapping stealthy pictures of fashion horrors and blacking out the eyes of the perpetrators before print. Eating authentic Asian-fusion dinners instead of lukewarm Swedish meatballs at my third mundane reception this week, which bore no difference from the previous two receptions, and the same reheated Swedish meatballs. And at these receptions, I make mental notes of the fashion violations, the room overflowing with fanny packs because nobody loves a frigging fanny pack like an army wife.

Most senior army wives are dorky. Old and nerdy before their time. Small-town, athletic nerds. Their sense of fashion goes down the toilet with their husband's personality. Navy or khaki pants and a cream, not white, mock turtleneck sweater. A sensible bob topped with a sun visor. The same lipstick shade they picked out at the PX Clinique counter in 1995. It works, so why change it? I'd like to think I'm one of the anomalies in my group; some of us do try to stay current. On the days when I work my ass off selling Frito pies at a fund-raiser for the troops, nothing makes me happier than an out-of-the-blue compliment from a young wife or soldier: "Ma'am, you're kinda hip. I hope it's okay that I say that to you. You aren't like the other older wives"—I was barely thirty-six years old—"I hope I can stay relevant and un-nerdy someday." The use of the word *relevant* refers to my fashion sense, but I allow myself to take it at a deeper meaning. That I matter. Although I wrestle with angst about the perception of irrelevance as "just a wife," the little compliment reminds me that I do stand my place in the line of army wives in history. We are relevant. Even if my interpretation isn't the original context of the compliment, I let myself believe it is the intent. I like that better. We wives read deeply into the littlest, most innocuous compliments and criticisms. They are all we have to go on. Everything else about us is a reflection of our husbands. So little of "us" left to make us unique.

But aside from the nerdiness and forced pretention of so many in my crowd, I love them. They are my people. When you share a common thread like ours, we don't let a poor fashion sense stand in the way of our sisterhood. There is no rhyme or reason to what creates a friendship or a connection. I've never chosen my people for political or strategic reasons.

I'm judgmental as hell, and a little mischievous. Maybe even borderline devious. It's probably my biggest flaw. I have an answer for everything. I think I can fix everyone. I dislike people until I like them. I think that if my house is chosen for enough tours of homes, and if I prepare the best meal or throw the coolest party, my flaws will be hidden. But they are transparent to all who know me, and I don't even fool myself.

Army brats turned army wives wear the lifestyle with the most grace and fluidity. We aren't daunted by the political games and can navigate the waters with more ease and finesse than those who weren't brought up here. We don't overdress or call a senior wife "Mrs. Senior-Wife" but call her by her first name. Most of us wouldn't dream of handing out calling cards, and we don't obsess over wearing white after Labor Day. It's instinct for brats turned wives to know which exact moment of the national anthem to place our hand over our heart. We don't have to read the back of the program to be reminded of the lyrics to the army song. It's emblazoned on our very beings as a person. We haven't watched *Army Wives* and don't base our knowledge of the intricacies of our lifestyle on a one-dimensional dramatized image. I can spot a new army wife from a mile away and can pick a relaxed army brat turned army wife out of the same crowd. The two groups are different animals altogether.

I jumped into life as an army wife with both feet, and aside from fleeting patchouli fantasies, there isn't much I would change. This moment in Jack's career, in *our* career, does feel like we have arrived. Finally a seat at the adult table. The possibility that Jack could eventually become a general crosses my mind on occasion, but I never let that idea linger. Half because I've seen how easy it is to slide from grace and lose everything, and half because the idea overwhelms me with giddy excitement. But I wouldn't dream of saying this in my outside voice. Jack isn't the one with stars in his eyes. His brass ring is a battalion command in combat. It's me who covets the big house that Mrs. Stewart occupies.

But only the most obnoxious wives dare say this aloud, and many of them do, which is just tacky. Showing visible ambition only makes that woman a target. Best to stay nonthreatening and do the best in one's current position. The plotting ambition is left for each couple behind closed doors, and it is obvious that many couples do plot and plan their future climb of the ranks. We do to an extent, but mostly take for granted that Jack will succeed because he always has. He doesn't need to call in favors from generals or pull strings. We are naive in that regard.

buoyancy

Finding a friend who digs beyond banal conversations about volunteer meetings, late-arriving school buses, and family readiness trainings is a rare and beautiful gift. The cunning of the oppressed.

THE NIGHT OF the Chinook crash, May 5, 2006, before we see the Saturday morning scroll of the ticker on CNN, Elizabeth Bianci and I share a quiet dinner at her house with our kids parked in front of a Disney movie and holding overflowing bowls of popcorn to keep them busy. Elizabeth is a trusted friend who enjoys a bottle of wine or two and deep, philosophical conversations about the intricacies of our vicarious bags of bullshit as leaders' wives. Elizabeth is savvy and clever, a sharp-witted girl. Possibly the smartest person I've ever known. I envy her ability to read situations. I read people, but she reads situations. The adult conversations she carries on with her two small children amaze and confuse me, and in turn her children have impressive vocabularies. Talking to my kids does not come naturally for me. I'm that "because I said so" mother.

I've known her for months before I realize she has an impressive job. Most army wives, the few who actually work beyond volunteer shenanigans, are teachers or nurses. Practical jobs, rarely *careers*, which are flexible enough to accommodate our nomadic lifestyles. Not Elizabeth. I googled her once, as I do with most people who intrigue me, both good and bad. Elizabeth researches and writes government engineering documents and contracts from home. I've asked her about it, and she shrugs it off. I want to ask her to explain to me exactly what she does, because it seems so incomprehensible to me, but I don't want her to think I'm a sheltered idiot. Elizabeth is levelheaded; she feels no need to get caught up in the hamster wheel of wives' drama. Once or twice I've dragged her to Bunco, and she's barely forgiven me for putting her through the excruciating torture.

Elizabeth is easily dismissed as aloof and arrogant because of her introverted nature. She doesn't seek the center of attention and uses words like *ubiquitous* and *apoplectic*, not because she has a word-of-the-day calendar to increase her vocabulary. She is a people-watcher, the more absurd the better. Elizabeth wouldn't be caught dead wearing a fanny pack. Elizabeth is an army brat like me, but I would never guess it. She has a very refined, East Coast quality to her voice and demeanor. A sly smile that belies nothing of what she's thinking. She is content in her own skin, could give two shits about impressing anyone. I want to be her when I grow up.

Elizabeth's husband is a hard-charging fast-tracker in his career. He is articulate and politically savvy while many other infantrymen struggle for words—a combination that is a recipe for success. The Biancis have two curly-headed boys who are clever, cute, and witty, like their mother. Elizabeth and I share a taste in obscure music, bizarre death metal that would embarrass us if we were to die on a long run and be judged by the playlist left behind on our iPods. She sees her role as the mentor and caretaker for large groups of women as ridiculous, believing that they are all adults and should be accountable for themselves and their actions. She does not take shit, but she also does not preach. She defines herself through thought and ideas, not through her husband's position. I love her for this. She is one whose company I would choose, not one who I am forced to spend time with.

I look at Elizabeth while she's telling a story, and I wish there were more Elizabeths in our world and fewer Regina Sweeneys. Regina is a whiner and a bore. Heaven forbid you get trapped in the commissary in a one-way inescapable conversation with her. Dull and lackluster, she is probably just an unhappy person by nature, regardless of the details and circumstances of life or the presence of war. She reminds me of the sad donkey from *Winnie-the-Pooh*. Eeyore. Her stories drone, she is without color or clear distinction, yet her presence is undeniable. She smells like scalp and burned toast, all the time. She finds entirely too much pleasure in winning at a mundane Tuesday morning of bowling league, perhaps a symptom of a deeper issue. Her husband is equally awkward and nondynamic, but he at least bears a glint of wisdom, humor, and maybe even cunning behind his wildly undergroomed eyebrows. Their children are brats, ill-mannered and disrespectful. Entitled. This does not go unnoticed.

Earlier in the week, I had to call Regina about something piddly regarding an invitation for a reception for a general's wife. I dreaded making the call, prayed I could just leave a message. I tried to send her an email, but her email address was nowhere to be found. I spent two days looking. Finally I called. She picked up on the fourth ring, just shy of my goal of leaving a voicemail. So tonight while I revel in Elizabeth's presence, I'm still wearing the icky juju of a depleting conversation with Regina days earlier. Obviously I need to practice the art of not allowing others to infiltrate my psyche quite so much.

I have a laminated, dog-eared picture of the fat and happy Kool-Aid man, and Elizabeth and I take turns hiding it in each other's homes. A surprise waits in the kitchen junk drawer to remind us that politics, games, and power plays of other wives are just a bunch of Kool-Aid: our predictable, mind-numbing minutiae; the wives with a sense of entitlement simply because their husband is deployed; the martyrs; the victims; the power hungry. Don't drink the Kool-Aid, sista. Spit that shit out. Don't listen to the man. Don't follow the scripts they give us. The army has turned brainwashing into a fine, sinister art. Think for yourself! *Yeah, right. As if it's that simple.*

We vent to each other on nights like this, but when Wednesday mornings roll around, there we sit, in our mandatory community leaders' meetings. CLIF meetings. Gathering the Kool-Aid to dispense to the waiting wives. Antiestablishment behind closed doors and behind the veil of several glasses of wine, but playing nicely by the rules when we must. Walking and talking contradictions. With Elizabeth, I pretend to care less than I actually do, and she doesn't call my bluff. She's got my number. She knows that I bowl in the Officers' Wives Club Tuesday morning league, the cream of the crop for perfumed turds.

There are a handful of our peers who I'd love to discuss with Elizabeth, but if she doesn't have to deal with people as a neighbor or in her direct unit, chances are they aren't on her radar. Which frustrates and impresses me about her. I thrust myself into situations with these people, only so I can come home and complain about them, but she's not like that. She doesn't feel like she's missing anything by not participating in Tuesday bowling. So I don't get to tell her about my woeful phone call with Regina. It's easy to not notice Regina unless you have to.

Anyway, even if she did know Regina, Elizabeth wouldn't want to talk about the woman. Elizabeth would want to discuss the institution that perpetuated Regina's place in our system and put Eeyore in the position to be a droning time burglar to begin with. Elizabeth is far more evolved than me, clearly. More mature. Spending time with her reminds me I need to up my game.

Or maybe the truth lies in a combination of the two perspectives. It's the wide variation of women in our little shared petri dish that makes our lives never boring. Really all that we have in common is we each fell in love with a dude in a uniform. The rest of it is a wild card. So we have the Eeyores, the dramatic Stephanies, and the rest of us. Each of us trying to get through the day, the deployment, and the time in between.

Elizabeth and I feel safe to let our guards down and discuss the other wives, the ones who wear their obnoxiousness with blind pride. The ones who pontificate at meetings about reserved parking for VIPs, the ones I could swear use a fake, vaguely British accent when speaking to groups, and the ones who initiate protest petitions because they suspect the organic produce in the commissary isn't really organic at all. Like my neighbor Tammy Crocker, the one who called 911 for an imagined bee sting and is famous for using the phrase, "Madam, you have impugned my integrity! You must cease and desist immediately, or I shall report you to the MPs!" Seriously, I heard her use various phrasings of this statement on at least three separate occasions. With a hint of shame, I admit that I live for those moments.

Finding "my people" is critical when living on post; they are the ones who will keep me afloat, the ones who don't care if I take my bra off in front of them and pee during phone conversations. Elizabeth is even choosier about her people than me, and I'm curious about her closeness to Laura Macklin. I assume the attraction is because they're both brainiacs. I doubt they pee on the phone with each other, though.

That night—the night before we find out about the Chinook crash—our kids are content to watch *Finding Nemo* for the fifty-ninth time while we enjoy our solace in each other, our words, pasta, and our slow, cathartic boozing. I am relaxed that Jack's butt-boy job doesn't come with responsibilities for me beyond social coffees and luncheons, but also eager to be a battalion commander's wife and enjoy the pizzazz that comes with it. Battalion command is the pinnacle and undeniable statement of arrival as a senior spouse. Even Elizabeth secretly revels in it. Well, maybe . . .

"Just you wait," she says. "These young wives are adults, but we treat them like children. Tell me a single place in the real world that provides *free* child care seven days a week. Then when child care is full just one time, or they miss out on the free pizza night, they flip out. We spoon-feed them rhetorical information like they're imbeciles, and in turn they behave like imbeciles. If we lived in Bumfuck, Wisconsin, and their husbands worked for IBM, how would they cope? No one there would call once a week just to check in like we do. I have one young wife who knows which fast-food chains give free food to deployed families on which night."

"Elizabeth, c'mon. Some of those wives are still teenagers without driver's licenses, and from Texas, for Christ's sake. *Texas.* Those wives are babies who have babies of their own, and we live in the goddamn tundra. Oh, and their husbands are deployed constantly. In the real world, they would have their families around them for support, I guess. I agree that hissy fits will be pitched when the extra freebies stop, but for now, they need it."

Elizabeth looks at me with her intense gaze that makes me feel both a little nervous and a little childish. She swirls the thick red wine in her glass. "I'm also sick of hearing my wives complain that no one on the news even mentions Afghanistan anymore. Iraq, Iraq, Iraq. But they're right. It's demoralizing. At any rate, I'm certain I'm a crushing disappointment to the majors' and captains' wives in Eric's battalion." She doesn't say "our battalion," a small nuance of word choice but one loaded with meaning. It's his job, not hers. "I don't show up at Steering Committee meetings with seasonally colored M&Ms and little birthday gifts for every yahoo. I just can't. It's exhausting. We're all volunteers. Why are we constantly congratulating and rewarding ourselves? Just get it done, for Christ's sake. The cycle of ass kissing only gives them more of an entitled swagger."

Elizabeth and her husband, Eric, are longtime friends of Rob and Laura Macklin. Eric is the commander of an infantry battalion, falling into the same brigade with Rob Macklin's reconnaissance "scout" battalion. The Biancis are godparents of the Macklins' newborn daughter, who was born a month after Rob deployed. By the time Rob meets his daughter, she will be sitting up and maybe crawling. No longer a cuddly newborn by then, but a squirmy baby.

At the end of our second bottle of wine, Elizabeth confides her worry over postpartum Laura. Worry that Laura might experience an extra oomph of difficulty as a new mother because of her age, Rob's absence, and her generally high-maintenance disposition. I remember those first weeks after my first child was born, the exhausted and emotional wreck I was. And I was twenty-seven, not forty-one, and Jack wasn't deployed. I tell Elizabeth that I've made a little baby gift for Laura, just a simple, tiny onesie that I hand-embroidered with a yellow ribbon and DADDY'S LITTLE GIRL in pink. My standard baby gift. Laura and I only know each other peripherally, so Elizabeth offers to pass the gift on my behalf, sparing me an awkward conversation of small talk.

We are half drunk, emptied of the week's frustrations, and it's time to corral the kids and head home. Walk down the street to my empty duplex with the freezing linoleum floors. One last question. I ask Elizabeth to describe army wives in one word. Just *one* word. She thinks, pushing her curly, wild black hair away from her pale and freckled face, slams back the remaining wine in her glass, and belly flops onto her couch with a thud.

"Elizabeth? Dude, did you just pass out?"

"No, Hawkins, I'm thinking. Shut up for a second."

"Don't hurt yourself." I laugh and wait.

She rolls onto her side and looks at me. "Buoyancy. We are buoyant."

chinook, down

Smacked in the face with the memory of the dream
we shouldn't have dismissed, but how could we know?

O N T H A T V E R Y Friday night on the other side of the world, Jack is standing with the 10th Mountain command group in the Joint Operations Center (JOC) in Afghanistan when over the radio comes word of a Chinook crash in Kunar province, as Elizabeth and I guzzle a bottle of merlot and shred parmesan cheese and wax philosophical about the intricacies of our roles thousands of miles and oceans away. Blissfully unaware of how our world is about to be rocked. Jack feels the tension on the command center floor increase as they wait for word from the scene of the crash, hoping it was just a hard landing. The Chinook CH-47 was attempting a complicated landing to exfiltrate soldiers from a precarious mountain location.

In a moment, the group in the JOC hears a series of explosions as the aircraft tumbles down the side of the mountain, and everyone standing in the command center realizes it's the worst-case scenario.

That moment syncs nearly to the hour with the lazy dinner I share with Elizabeth and the indulgent discussion of our buoyancy. The army wife's ability to float, tread water. Not sink. Laura is probably nursing her newborn and tucking her in, nursing her one last time before mother grabs a few hours of sleep.

A cruel synchronicity and the universe's test of Elizabeth's definition. Jack stands in the command center, remote from the crash site with another of his bosses, the chief of staff. General Stewart is there, too. Not quite absorbing what happened, they look back and forth at video screens, trying to figure out what just happened, voices around them a pandemonium that quickly turns to the stony, robotic voices of controlled, trained chaos. Later I learn that within minutes after the crash, a soldier in the JOC turned to where he stood with Stewart and reports, "Sir, we think Titan 6 was onboard! He's not on the manifest, but he was on board. Reports coming in from the site that he got on previously. Men on the ground had eyes on him in the Chinook as it went down. Didn't have time to manifest." A manifest is a strict roster that maintains accountability for every soldier in case of a mass casualty like this. A correct manifest will speed the casualty notifications; an incorrect manifest will hold the process in limbo for days.

The chief of staff turns to Jack and says, "Jack, pack your gear. Be prepared to take that command ASAP. Commo blackout effective immediately. Call Ang before you get out to the field, and tell her you aren't coming home next month. Tell her close hold." The term *close hold* means "shut the fuck up with this information."

Titan 6 is Rob Macklin's call sign.

impulse and instinct

Can a dream cause tragedy?
This isn't how our glory day is supposed to happen.

CLOISTERED AND WHISPERING in our baby's room, the far-thest room from the kitchen in our tiny ranch-style duplex, just twenty-four hours after Elizabeth and I decided we could float and not sink, I try to absorb Jack's words when he calls Saturday night. When the phone rings, I recognize the number. Military line from Afghanistan.

Elizabeth and her two boys have walked up the street to share a pizza inside. She is busy cutting the barely cooked cheese pizza into bite-sized pieces with kitchen scissors, a little trick I taught her for the kids, when the phone rings.

Earlier that afternoon, I had spoken with Elizabeth and she had lamented that Laura was beyond furious that her rear detachment commander would not return her avalanche of phone calls asking for intel. Laura was on edge more than normal, according to Elizabeth, probably due to the roller coaster of hormones following the birth of a baby. Laura wanted answers, dammit! I can't say that I blame her. Jack is in a staff position, so I don't have anyone to call to demand answers from, or I would probably be doing the same. My point of contact is scary Linda Stewart, and no way in hell am I going to breach protocol about seven hundred different ways by calling her. We are supposed to wait for news to arrive through official channels. Even if the waiting goes on for an entire day and then a little longer.

"Laura told me that she heard footsteps in the baby's room late last night," Elizabeth said. "She went to look, and of course, the baby was sleeping. I hope she's not losing it. This is her first deployment with a baby. She is sleep-deprived."

Elizabeth said her own phone rang off the hook all day, as she fielded calls from freaked-out wives and mothers who saw the ticker on CNN all the way in Montana. I encouraged her to bring the boys to my house and wait it out. My phone hadn't rung once.

With five children arguing over pizza in the background, coupled with the delay and echo of a phone call from Afghanistan, when my phone finally rings I scurry away from everyone else to answer. I move with the phone into the living room, still within earshot of Elizabeth and the kids and the pizza festivities.

"Hello? Jack? What's going on? Are you all right?" Please let it be his voice on the other end. I push away visions of the woman retching after Mass hours earlier.

He starts to answer, and I can barely hear him over the static on the line and the kids. I notice Elizabeth standing in the kitchen doorway looking at me, trying to read my face for clues. I don't realize this until later. I don't stop to consider how she perceives this phone call from Afghanistan, how it could apply to her.

I take the phone and quickly walk down the long hallway in Greta's room, the baby's room. Isolating myself in a separate room is instinct. And also necessity; I couldn't hear a word he was trying to say out there in the kitchen.

Jack doesn't begin with hello. "What have you heard back there?"

"I've heard nothing, D, commo blackout. No one has any idea; it's deadly silent here. What the fuck is going on? Wives are losing their minds. Some woman barfed in the chapel parking lot."

"Ang, I can't talk long. Getting ready to head out to an FOB [Forward Operating Base], where there are no comms [communication: email or phones]. The chief of staff ordered me to call you and tell you I may not be coming home. I could command here now. Well, that's what it looks like now. We're in crisis mode. I was directed to call and tell you, and only you."

And with those words . . . I remember. Jack's dream flooded back to me. The dream and the pancakes that followed. "Was it Rob?"

A silence. Maybe it's the delay, or maybe he can't speak for a second. "Yes. Rob jumped on the Chinook at the last minute and didn't manifest. We haven't made notifications, because we can't get a team down the side of the mountain to the wreckage, and anyway, it completely torched. General Stewart wants to do all notifications at once, even though the rest of the manifest is clear. He expects that by tomorrow morning, the casualty notification teams will be in place."

"Jack. That dream. It was a premonition."

"Can't talk anymore. Don't tell anyone what I just told you, got it? Very close hold."

"Shit. Elizabeth Bianci is here, in the next room!" Now I hear myself whispering loud enough to meet the criteria of a shout, if that's possible. A shrill hiss is a better description.

"Oh Jesus, Ang. Cover it up. She can't know yet. I wish you told me she was there before I started talking."

As if I'm going to think to interject that little nugget of the scenario right off the bat, under the circumstances.

"I will call you when I get more information," he says. "I hope the chief's reaction was just a possibility. I love you." And the line is dead.

I stare at Greta's crib. Too stunned to hyperventilate or cry. What just happened? I need to get my shit straight, walk unscathed back to the kitchen, grab a piece of cold pizza, and announce that Jack and Eric are okay. That the whole crash is a confusing mess, and, no, he didn't say anything else.

I will never be able to pull this off. She knows me too well. I can't stay in this bedroom forever.

I open the door of Greta's room to find Elizabeth, whose legs have given out, sliding down the hallway wall to the floor. She heard bits of my end of the conversation and thinks Eric, her husband, is dead. She is certain he is dead, as our children eat pizza and laugh at *Finding Nemo*, viewing number sixty, just at the end of the long bowling-alley-like hallway in the kitchen.

"It was Eric," she says. Her back is against the wall and she falls to her side. Her voice sounds hollow, nothing like her regular voice.

I drop next to Elizabeth. "No. No. It wasn't Eric. It was Rob. Rob is dead." Less than a minute after hanging up with Jack, I've spit out what I was supposed to keep secret.

Elizabeth and I lie together there in the hall, crumpled in awkward positions, not touching—she is not the hugging type—both of us laboring our breath and occasional mutterings, "Holy Fuck" and "Oh God." I can't remember who cries first, and I don't remember how long we stay there that way. I don't remember anything of our collection of five children just at the end of the hall. Do they stay away because they sense they should? I don't remember putting my children to bed that night; I don't remember anything after that time in the hallway with Elizabeth. The politics and posturing and shenanigans of our external world and personality conflicts are gone in that moment. Of course they will come screaming back all too soon, but in that dark hallway, we breathe together and absorb the shock as the intimacy of death hits our group for the first time. How did Elizabeth have the intuitive sense to choose the word *buoyant*?

I remember pulling ourselves to our feet, together and without a word. We stand and know we have to put our game faces on, our war faces.

"I'm Laura's person on her Soldier Readiness Contract," Elizabeth says. "I can't go home. What if she calls me? I can't just sit there while she talks into my answering machine. We're going to have to stay here until ten o'clock. Casualty teams can't make notifications past ten. What's the earliest they can visit? I think it's something like six in the morning. Did Jack say when they're going to do this?" Her voice is shaking, but she has moved into tactical mode.

"Umm, I think he said tomorrow, but it's tomorrow there already. I would assume, yes, by first thing in the morning. I can't remember what he said exactly. But no one can ever learn that we both knew before she did. Why don't you leave the boys here? You stay too; you can go home early and be ready when they call."

We are fooling ourselves for thinking no one else already knows, that maybe that's why everyone has stayed hunkered at home all day long. Nothing is secret in our circle for long, and this happened twenty-four hours ago.

"We'll stay until ten," she says, "then go home and sleep there. Eric might try to call me. I'll bring the boys back here early, or whenever they call me. Okay. That's a good plan. Oh my God. This isn't happening."

We make a pact that neither of us will ever tell a soul about that night, the phone call she overheard, and the details we learned about

Rob's death while his own widow stewed at home that her rear detachment commander hadn't called her yet.

The next morning, Sunday, she brings her sleepy boys to my front door before dawn. I can tell she hasn't slept, and neither have I. She looks at me and says simply, "They called. I have to go be with her. I think they're doing the notification now."

"I've got the boys. No worries about them."

I don't think we had a name for it yet, but a new phenomenon was swirling up from between us and would manifest in the coming weeks into an exhaustion, an exhaustion that bled from the members of Laura's inner circle into the inner circles of those members, and on and on. It wouldn't be long before the army had a name for it: caregiver fatigue. The energy it took to hold up one of us taxed the rest of us. Meals poured into Laura's house, meals that weren't being eaten by anyone in her home. But the women who stood vigil by Laura in the coming weeks had passed their own children on to their own circles of support. Within a year, we would have systems in place for this; we would realize that the caregivers needed care themselves, and so on down the chain. But this was the first one in our group. This is the one that wrote the script for what to do, and what not to do, for tragedies to come.

dodged bullet

If he hadn't told me about the dream on the morning of the pancakes,
I might have suspected he exaggerated—not his nature to
dramatize or emphasize reality. The weight of that dream and
the avoidance of taking Rob's place bring him home a month later.

THAT SUMMER OF 2006, I bring Jack home from another deployment. In the several days that followed Rob Macklin's death, the command group scrambled to figure out who would fill his place. The possibility of Jack's filling the vacant command was only one possibility. When asked his preference, Jack diplomatically stated to his command that he would prefer to take command of the battalion he'd planned on, build his team from the beginning, and deploy to combat together. Beneath his logical response was the lingering memory of his dream.

The division command group is given Phil Schneider as an option. He has already finished his battalion command, but hasn't been selected for war college. Rob Macklin's command thus falls into the hands of Martha Schneider's gaunt, somber-looking husband. The command's reaction that it would fall to Jack was only a possibility. For Schneider, the second command does end up helping his career, but turns Martha into the pariah of Fort Drum.

Back to Jack's homecoming from Afghanistan: Considering he has dodged an entire additional year in Afghanistan, we should be walking on air. Our marriage begins to unravel beyond the typical redeployment awkwardness and resentment. He is brooding. He criticizes the way I handled the kids while he was gone. The adjustment to an extra person living in my home is harder than the deployment itself, but this time even more so. And the nature of his obsessiveness embarrasses me. He asks me if I ever really loved him or just married him for comfort. Really? Like he makes so much money that it's worthy of gold digging? What an insult. Maybe the dream messed him up. Would this just fix itself? I can't exactly go to my girlfriends and share that my normally cheery husband now thinks I'm a gold digger. They would look at me like I had a penis growing out of my forehead. Nightmares about Afghanistan, that's what I can handle. That's a nice and normal reaction to combat. Not this. Not at all.

After confessing his assumptions and delusions about me to a stunned army chaplain, Jack seeks help from a recommended therapist, Helen. The queen of the earthy, crunchy military skeptics. I love her. I would be her, had I not decided to take this path instead. In the three years ahead, Helen will be the one person outside our world who will steady us in the chaos. Helen is an outside touchstone for many in our world, possibly the only person outside who understands. She confides to me that Jack sees me like a fog that he can't pin on the wall. I love her analogy. He can't find an order in my disorder.

Both the army chaplain and Helen give Jack a warning: His words and accusations toward me will take an eventual toll. It might not show up right away, but the angry words will build a virtual brick wall between us. One that might never go away.

So instead I stand on the street with my friends and bitch about the time I wasted writing various volunteer organization newsletters that no one bothers to read. Or we talk about how Laura Macklin is coping, whether she's decided yet where to go. She can't stay on Fort Drum. Her life of details has slid down the side of the mountain with her husband. What would any of us do in her shoes? We talk about the pizza guy who drives entirely too fast down our street, and has anyone caught which pizza place he's from? Somebody needs to report him. One of the ladies stands on the street with a sloshy glass of wine and expresses outrage at not being able to find an adequate stock of hostess gifts in our tiny town. These moments of talking about things at arm's length are a relief. They carry me away from the images in my mind and force me to breathe, and more importantly, they remind me how good it feels to not just laugh, but also giggle. Safe outlets for unexpressed emotion. Juicy enough to keep me on the edge of my seat, but removed enough from my real terror.

We wives wear tremendous pride that outshines our private feelings of shame or inadequacy. We are a culture of self-entitlement— offered freebies and accolades to keep us in line and keep us quiet. Never forget, we *are* volunteers. Wives do not draw pay or wear rank. Our power is strictly vicarious. No matter if you bust your ass or not, we are all recognized pretty much the same. No rest for the weary. My schedule is full of meetings, fund-raisers, team-building social events, volunteer recognition ceremonies—all busy work designed to keep me just busy enough that I don't have time to stop and contemplate the big picture of what's going on around me. I just want to get through that day, that week, that month, that deployment, that reunion.

We use our savvy not only to take care of the families in our units, but also to posture before our peers. The worry for my husband's safety and the active mothering of my own children are secondary to my responsibility of keeping the families under his command tucked beneath my safe wing. And also making sure that my peer wives (perfumed turds) and the wives senior to me (mega perfumed turds) see what a breathtakingly fucking awesome job I'm doing and what a hardworking martyr I am.

it's more than just a bowling ball to a renegade bitch like me

*I feel better knowing that Jack and I aren't the only ones
acting like raging psychos, but I don't offer much insight
to anyone around me about how bad it's gotten in my marriage.
I can't even make eye contact with it myself. If I ignore the issues,
maybe they will go away. Or maybe he will go away. That's
the more likely outcome. Another deployment is inevitable.*

ONE EVENING, I smear a neighbor's blanket that has been left in my yard one too many times in a giant, steamy pile of dog crap. Each night, she leaves her piles of stuff strewn all over the neighborhood, never even thinking to clean up after her own kids' messes. Then after dark, I deposit it on her front porch. Her name is Pam Percy, and she reminds me of the mother from *Throw Mama from the Train*. She talks at a volume that should be considered criminal harassment. Her speaking voice is a yelling voice full of bravado. She also throws the expression "Good times, good times" into almost every conversation, even the ones that have nothing to do with good times at all. Thank heaven she isn't a close-talker, or I might have to plot her murder instead of smear her blanket in dog poop.

What's important is that my outrageous behavior really has little to do with Pam herself. Yes, she annoys me daily. But my impulsive act is motivated by collective frustration, not just her. Her blanket is simply my final straw on that particular day. It provides a perfect venue for my nasty, disgruntled, and pent-up anger at all the things that lie far beyond my control. This is before the weariness sets in. In 2006, I still have the energy to feel fury.

Now it doesn't take a master's in psych to mastermind shenanigans like a spur-of-the-moment, cathartic squish of a blanket in shit, but that's an example of the kind of pettiness I devolve into if pushed to the edge of frustration over and over, but too caught in the politics of living in tight quarters to just hash it out like a real woman. Of course I could feign ignorance after the fact, because the horror at my own behavior is probably worse than her horror at discovering the poopy blanket. Normally I plot my actions with a little more subtlety and thought, but on this night, the pile of poop is just too tempting. With the fresh smell of a soft and pungent-on-the-inside dog turd still in my nostrils, I cackle like a madman as I close my front door for the evening, delighted in my debauchery. After I tuck my own kids in bed, I can't look at myself in the mirror when I brush my teeth. How childish and lame. This isn't even a little coup I can be proud of. Poop smearing is for psychotic idiots, but damn, it felt awesome in the moment.

Our games of politics and posturing intensify, diversions and smoke screens to mask the fear and trauma that none of us could fully face or grasp. Ironically, the fear also brings us closer and more connected than we've ever been. More than before, we spend the evenings standing in the street, talking quietly as our kids whoop and holler on their skateboards and bikes. We crave the presence of one another.

Can't stand going alone into our own homes for the night to think about how close to us the war has finally gotten.

Helen also counsels my close friend Kat Dalisay's husband, who is an army dentist but spent his year in Afghanistan cleaning up and amputating fingers of bad guys who had botched IED attempts. At least once in Afghanistan, Kat's gentle-souled husband and a fellow dentist tried unsuccessfully to save a young boy who was blown to bits after playing with his uncle's stash of IEDs.

Kat Dalisay is a trusted, safe ally, maybe because her husband is a dentist and a mender of even the enemy. We judge each other by what our husbands do. Kat doesn't try to compete with infantry wives, and the absence of that tension is splendid. It's not everybody who would be my accomplice in stealing from the post alley a preferred bowling ball of one of our rivals, Donna Hooker. Hooker is a phony try-hard, a one-dimensional gulper of Kool-Aid. She hides her flaws. Doesn't she realize that everyone roots for the flawed person? No one wants to be friends with a flat mask of perfection. Ick. Tedious and boring. Each Tuesday morning, Donna ritualistically hunts down her favorite electric-blue ball tucked into the fifty-foot shelf of dozens of house balls. It's a wimpy eight pounds with tiny finger holes that would only allow Donna's thin, sinewy fingers and no one else's. It has the name JEANNIE engraved in script on the side. Everyone knows it's Donna's ball. One day, my purse is plenty roomy for that ball. I get to JEANNIE before Hooker does. It sits in my closet for the next year and a half. For weeks, Kat and I enjoy watching Donna obsess and scour the bowling alley for her ball. It takes her months before she moves on to a new ball. But her game suffers, without JEANNIE. We place far too much importance and we experience far too much pleasure in such silly, symbolic games. Symbolic because everything for us is symbolic; almost nothing is dealt with as it is. In a real and concrete manner.

A year earlier, the innocuous Hooker beat me by one vote in our race to be the Officers' Wives Club president. *Am I bitter? Nope. What makes you ask? Don't be an asshole.*

Stolen bowling balls and campaigns to be the queen of turds are a safe outlet for rage that we can't identify or place correctly. Maybe Kat forgot for an hour or so that her husband wasn't using his dentistry license to do root canals.

Outside of the unrest in our home, I find relief in the shenanigans and drama of the wives on our street. My next-door neighbor and across-the-street neighbor are at war over the current presidency of the wives' club, each believing that the other is not only unfit to rule the roost, but engaged in efforts to sabotage the other's credibility and reputation. They are both self-important loons, Tammy Crocker and Pam Percy. This is familiar territory. Pam leaves her kids' toys and towels and whatever-else in everyone's yard each night. The rest of us have the courtesy to go around the neighborhood and police our kids' piles of crap. Not Pam. This screams entitlement. Officially, I will never admit to the poop-smearing episode. Though I doubt I am the only one who feels driven to do something so stupid after a long day of mothering our flocks of children and mothering our flocks of wives.

I have my own issues with Tammy Crocker, who called 911 and wrecked Bridget's sixth birthday, something I'm still trying to forgive. It was just weeks before Jack came home this time and weeks after Macklin was killed. I was trying to mask my exhaustion with a rousing chorus of "Happy Birthday" and a few guilt gifts wrapped messily by my bitter and distracted hands. Tammy appeared red-faced and slovenly in my doorway with her toddler, insisting hysterically that she'd been stung by a bee and was going into some sort of dramatic and imagined shock and her throat was closing. She smelled like old spaghetti and perfume from the mid-1990s. I wanted to punch her and remind her that if she was standing there ranting about her throat closing, then it was not closing at all. But I didn't. I opened the door and allowed her to flop her dramatic ass on my sofa and wait for the ambulance and the MPs and the barrage of chaos that would come blazing into my dilapidated duplex within 180 seconds. Stealing my well-intentioned and exhaustive effort to recognize Bridget's birthday—Bridget, who was ever-polite, poised, and kind-hearted. Tammy's discarded toddler immediately stuck his hands into Bridget's pristine store-bought cake, and my gall seethed beneath my quiet mask of helpful neighbor. Tammy had broken a huge unspoken breech of army wife protocol.

"Your husband is hoooome!" I wanted to scream at her. He wasn't home literally, but figuratively. "Home" meant "not in a war zone." My moments of good intention were perpetually thwarted by someone else's drama. Something as simple as not answering the door in these tight quarters was just not possible. Her massive breech of protocol stung at me: The un-deployed wives *never* call on the help of the deployed wives. Unless it's to borrow an egg or a cup of sugar. That's totally within reason.

It's important to understand the echelons, from the wife of an infantry battalion commander to the handful of wives senior to me and down to the sea of wives under our chain of command. The entire wives' food chain. Most importantly, the complexities of dealing with peers. Our competitors.

Senior army wives, like me, are often underestimated and presumed to be innocuous and tired, a presumption that we use and take advantage of. Our political prowess and deep savvy allow us to exploit the assumptions of others, because in truth we are often the ones with the widest base of knowledge and information. I am privy to my husband's pillow talk, but also, over cocktails, I hear others' pillow talk. I carry on small talk with Belinda Beck in the commissary, not listening to her blathering story, but suspecting that her husband downloads porn to his government computer and noisily jerks off behind the door of his office. *Isn't that a government offense, Belinda? Hmm?*

One-upping about where our husbands are deployed is one of many unspoken games of the wives. Being in Iraq has street cred; Afghanistan, not so much at this point. Just like my husband's Kosovo mission was overlooked when Afghanistan was central in the media. Deployment locations go in and out of fashion quickly.

The death of Rob Macklin does something to our entire group that spring and early summer. It brings our crazy to right below the surface. It starts to show up like a disease spreading among the senior wives, displaced resentment and grief. Screaming profanities at snow plows that absently leave a trail of snow across the front of pristinely shoveled driveways. Yelling at housing personnel who don't move fast enough to fix a leaky faucet. In a fit of displaced rage, smacking our kids on the back of their heads for being too mouthy, when the kids are likely just trying to find someplace, any place, in the pecking order of mom's attention. Those on the edge take out their aggression on safe people, those on the periphery of our group. Direct fights among wives are rare, but juicy and cathartic on the few occasions that anger places itself where it belongs. I have a master's degree in a study close to social psychology—a degree I've never used for much besides mind games with the wives. Observing people and trying to figure them out, even playing with people's heads on occasion, I'll admit that I enjoy that talent a little too much once in a while. That's one of my little sins I will have to explain to Saint Peter someday. My cunning. My flaw. I can be both passive-aggressive and downright mean when provoked. I keep score. But at least I admit it. We can all be mean girls. Denying that there is, within each of us, a little mean girl to some extent is being dishonest with ourselves. The trick is to own that little mean girl and make her *your* bitch. Don't let the mean girl take over. Keep that little monster on a leash, and use her when you must. That's unfortunately where some of us go wrong. A lack of self-awareness.

Politics, friendships, and competition form naturally in the work environment. At the end of the day, those folks go home and escape until the next day. Many never meet their coworkers' families or know where they live. Now imagine that everyone in this workplace lives in one neighborhood, in close quarters. In addition to knowing how a work project is going, they've seen who slacked in cutting the grass. They've heard the screaming match with your wife or husband. They get pissed if you park a little too close to their driveway. They are a collection of type A control freaks who need to lead every situation and control its outcome. They've seen the pile of butts from the closet smokers. They wonder why some people always keep their blinds drawn. There is no line between work and life to balance; there is no escaping.

mountain mafia

Letting the days go by,
let the water hold me down.

—TALKING HEADS

I N T H E D A Y S and weeks following Rob's death in the late spring of 2006, Elizabeth is drained by caring for Laura, and I feel my own drain from caring for Elizabeth's spirit and her curly-haired boys, whom I adore. Women insert themselves into Laura's daily life to help her, to earn their own bragging rights. Nightly meals are delivered by volunteers for months, but Laura is rightfully needy and demanding about who and how. Some, like Martha Schneider, Laura's neighbor, go as far as to brag to newspapers about having inside knowledge of Rob's death before Laura was officially notified and the exaggerated enormous guilt Martha felt that her own husband was the casualty notification officer.

As time goes on, a full war between Laura and Martha develops, and there is a fine line between Team Martha and Team Laura. Planned interventions run by scary Linda Stewart are ineffective. While the idea of what goes on in those heated meetings is beyond intriguing, I am amazed that no one seems to notice that our intense focus on the ambiguous details and interpersonal discord is just a Band-Aid; we never deal with the real issue. One of our peers is dead, and now what? Who cares that Martha wants to hold court for the media?

Rob made his last wishes clear and left a detailed plan in his Soldier Readiness Contract for Laura to carry out his wishes. But one thing remains. Laura can't fathom where to go; should she move or stay? Her own family is not close; we are her family. She stays for one year, an unprecedented amount of time for a widow to stay on post. Her presence is a constant reminder of sadness. A reminder that we can't complain around her, because she has it so much worse. She becomes a martyr, the center of everyone's depleted energy, secretly dependent on the attention afforded a widow in our midst.

BELINDA AND LARRY Beck, part of the 10th Mountain mafia, have returned to Fort Drum that summer from two years in Hawaii. The most polarizing couple in all of army couple history.

It will take me until 2008 to finally see beneath Belinda's motives and also to have the justification to embrace my inner mean girl where Miss Belinda is concerned. For now, she seems harmless enough because she *gets shit done.* For now I choose to see the do-gooder in her, regardless of whether her good deeds are done for self-serving purposes. She is a spotlight ranger wife, and I figure her out early on. But while I don't fully trust her, I never see myself pulling her knife out of my own back. I never imagine her sinking to the depths that I will later see.

For years I have chosen to believe the best about Belinda, to defend her when others eventually see through her. Never believing I would also become one of her targets. Belinda's reputation as a manipulative, self-serving climber precedes her. But she is a tireless go-getter. Belinda and I have known each other for almost a decade. She was the divorced mother of two small children when she met her husband, Larry, at Fort Campbell, Kentucky, in 1993. She saw Larry as a ticket out and a ticket up. Belinda is older than Larry, who has an obsession with porn and an obvious drinking problem and who also treats Belinda with bitter resentment. This doesn't seem to faze Belinda as she caters to his every whim and focuses solely on his career and anything she can do to promote it. Eyes on the prize. We aren't the only ones, apparently. Physically, Belinda reminds me of Flo from that old television series *Alice*. She is a rural Tennessee gal, lacking a formal education past high school, with skin that has loved years of tanning, hair that's been teased and processed long past its endurance, and the kind of bone-thin body that comes from constant kinetic movement and lots of coffee, but I don't think she drinks coffee. She is the first to volunteer for everything and anything, and takes the lead on each project. Belinda is no follower. She aspires to eventually be the Officers' Wives Club president, but only after she has served every other dozen or so positions on the elected board.

Despite her generosity of time and energy to the community, Belinda is a backstabbing gossip hound who will twist any story in her own favor, and most everyone filters her words. She is full of shit and steam, but this is forgiven because she is such a valuable resource. Conversations with Belinda are patronizing and one-sided; she yaps and the other person is her hostage who has little hope of getting a single word in edgewise. If ever there is a sticky, complicated jam, Belinda is the person to call. Her motivation is strictly for self-promotion, and she is still revered for her effort. She has tabbed binders and notebooks meticulously maintained from every position and place that she and Larry lived. She can answer any question at lightning speed. Her primary concern is with her image and maintaining an appearance of selfless service, despite the deep family and marital dysfunction behind her own doors. Belinda must have no idea how transparent she is to the rest of us, but we are all so preoccupied, her presence is a selfish relief. Her husband is as lazy and apathetic as she is ambitious and relentless. Together they are amusing and cartoonish; she is hyper-aware of perceptions and he could not care less.

change of command

What goes perfectly with red patent pumps?
The answer is simple: No one is looking at your shoes.
No one gets the homage to cavalry red except you.

SEPTEMBER 23, 2006. A cold and windy, but sunny, Friday morning. The one we've waited fourteen years for is here. The cake was ordered; flowers should be there at the parade field. I am especially proud of my dress, and my red patent Kate Spade pumps brutalize my feet, but it's worth it. I need to get used to smiling through the pain. This is a good day to test my resolve in that regard. I look down at my feet and think of Dorothy and wonder what might happen if I click my heels together.

All our families are there for Jack's big day, my parents are here, and there are too many in-laws for me to keep track of. The change of command for an incoming commander is like being homecoming queen. He's the belle of the ball. We had a huge fight the night before, and I don't even remember what it was about, but I remember feeling emotionally bruised that morning. The snapshot of the day appears flawless, but under my smile I am terrified. This moment doesn't feel like I thought it would.

Before the ceremony, Jack stands wearing his cavalry Stetson awkwardly on his head and adjusts his spurs. This part of soldiering isn't

Jack's favorite. The pomp and circumstance are not his thing, or mine really. He just wants to get on with the show, get this part over with so he can finally look in the mirror and see himself as a bona fide battalion commander. Jack wants to get to the meat, wants to get dirty with his new soldiers, who are exhausted before they've even met the most exhausting man in history. Jack waits to take command of the battalion he was originally slated for, a reconnaissance unit made up of mostly infantry grunts and armor scout soldiers. The 1-71 Cavalry.

The kids and I have reserved seating on the raised bleachers right in front of the parade field full of the battalion's soldiers. I leave Greta, who is a squirmy toddler, with my parents and guide Joe and Bridget to our chairs with our names reserving the seats. I look out onto the field and think, *Here we go.* The soldiers on the parade field have just returned weeks earlier, bone-tired from a year in Iraq. Jack's reputation for being a hard-charging, organized, and motivated leader with unmatched combat experience has given us a sense of expected success. Not a sense of entitlement. We take for granted that things will go our way, because they always have.

I am lost in thought when I notice that Mrs. Stewart has climbed the steps and is standing in front of Joe, my fetching but nervous third-grader. Joe looks nothing short of completely horror-stricken, as his bright eyes peer over his glasses and dart back and forth between her and me. In that moment, I am relieved that Greta isn't here acting like the toddler that she is, dropping her binky repeatedly and pulling at my dress.

"Son, let me give you a lesson in etiquette," the woman says. "When an adult extends their hand to you, you reach out with your right hand and you shake it. With a firm grip, do you understand?" She glances at me with a look that says, *You dumbass. Why does he not know this already?* I am dismayed on his behalf. I instinctively pull him close to me and giggle. My simultaneous fear mixed with admiration of her deepens.

General Stewart is still in Afghanistan and doesn't preside over the ceremony. Jack's brigade commander, Vick Petty, probably appreciates the general's absence, as Petty has made his dislike for General Stewart clear. Jack told me Colonel Petty called Stewart the "division squad leader," which means that Stewart is a micromanager. There may be a nugget of truth to Petty's assessment, but it doesn't help Jack any. Colonel Petty knows that Jack is Stewart's boy, which doesn't get their relationship off on the right foot. I am reminded of the adage "People throw rocks at shiny things." I wonder how long before Petty started throwing rocks. I already don't like him. He is a close-talker, a personal-space-invader, and reminds me of a Neanderthal trying to assert dominance.

Joe sits perfectly still, probably on the verge of internal hysteria over his protocol reprimand. Bridget fidgets and looks around, like me. Poor girl is my mini-me. Life will be full of challenges. Meetings, ceremonies. All so painful for people like us.

The outgoing commander, John Morrow, has been talking for a really long freaking time. Aren't these speeches only supposed to be a few minutes? He grips the podium on the verge of tears as he recalls how proud he was of the squadron and its perseverance. Most outgoing commanders give pretty similar speeches, and no one loves the word "phenomenal" more than a high-ranking officer. But John is articulate and impassioned. It takes me by surprise, because I've never heard him speak. Usually, the outgoing command team has dinner with the incoming team prior to the change of command. An awkward but necessary dance we do, to facilitate a smooth transition. But in reality it's painful for both parties. The outgoing team members are usually depleted of enthusiasm and energy by two or three years in command, maybe disillusioned by what they expected the assignment to be, and maybe sad to be leaving, wondering if they should have played certain situations differently. The incoming team is full of energy and eager to get rid of the old team so the new one can take its place at the helm. John and Sandy Morrow have never even spoken a single word to us before today, and not even today. Aside from pleasantries during the ceremony, they ignore us. To this day I'm not sure why. Jack and I assume they are drained from two years in command and are simply ready to wash their hands of the unit. I also suspect Sandy Morrow was half in the bag that day.

I've seen the woman over the past two years around post and at meetings, and she has always looked and smelled hammered. She even leaned on chairs and walls, as if standing were just too taxing. Oh wait, she did speak to me once. Maybe six months ago. She stopped in the commissary and stared at me, then said in her lethargic, husky Southern drawl, "I liiiiike yer haaair." Then she stumbled away with her cart full of Stove Top stuffing and Hamburger Helper.

THE HICCUPS WE now prepare to face in the new squadron not only are unexpected by Jack, but later devolve into full-blown belches. My new role is luckily more fluid. The outgoing commander's wife, Sandy Morrow, is a train wreck who was dismissed by the spouses in the battalion/squadron. I'm more relatable than Jack. We wear masks of blissful enthusiasm for the benefit of the subordinate soldiers and their families, but we have business to do and more war to train for.

With his command upon us at last, I finally feel like the shit. Finally I have arrived and am invited to play with the big kids. Finally there's a seat with my name on it at events and ceremonies. But I make mistakes, I often speak without thinking, and I roll my eyes even more often. Whatever I say and do, though, is ultimately irrelevant; Jack is the commander and that fact alone puts his wife in charge of the battalion's families. Strong words? Yes. Did I wear rank? Probably. But did I work my ass off and earn respect? I hope so.

There are wives above me, with me, and below me who have no business trying to lead and support families through a war, but they still try. They sling Kool-Aid alongside me. They recite from the binders of scripts we are given at training sessions for how to manage families under the stress of war. *"How are you coping? Have you tried exercise or deep-breathing techniques? How about taking advantage of the free pizza dinner on post Tuesday night? There will be ice cream and bouncy houses for the kids!"* These wives, like me, don't earn their position through ratings and promotions; they married some guy who does. So whether the wife is slack-mouthed and stupid or quick and resourceful, it doesn't change her role. Mean or kind. Lazy or hardworking. Traditional or protocol-tossing. Sweet or downright evil. Whoever, whatever she was, she sets the tone for the families in that battalion.

On the flip side, many of the senior wives have earned a place of respect and a reputation for being mighty leaders in their own right. Many are as determined and wise as their husbands. Like Mrs. Stewart. I would hate to run into her on the battlefield.

a choice

"Which of those captains from the meeting do you want
to be your rear detachment commander, Ang? We both
know how important that dynamic is and how difficult you
are to deal with, so I'm leaving the choice to you." My man
knows what he is talking about. He knows that the relationship
could be a make-or-break situation in a deployment.

A COUPLE WEEKS OR so after the change of command, we have
our first steering committee meeting at the battalion headquarters.
Should I bring cookies? Or would that seem too eager? I wear cargo
pants and an easy T-shirt with Chuck Taylor sneakers. I don't want
to seem like I am trying too hard to be "down with the people," but I
also don't want to overdress and seem unapproachable. I must strike a
delicate balance. As I walk into battalion headquarters, I decide maybe
the sneakers are a little too much. But in the North Country, there is a
two-week period that divides flip-flop season from UGG season, and I
want to seize this moment before UGG boots become my only choice.

I've met many of the battalion's leaders at the change of command,
followed by our official welcome dinner a few days later, and then
yet again at my welcome given by the wives the following week. But
those were all social events; this is the first "work"-related activity.
Steering committee meetings are held monthly and are the opportunity

for Jack and me to disseminate information from the division down to the company-level commanders and the Family Readiness Group (FRG) leaders. A time for the links in the chain to share ideas, to plan events, and to posture. Always a time to posture. Eager to see the team in action, I can't wait to see what everyone has to bring to the table and dissect the dynamics and figure out how I will fit in.

Jack, who is always über-prepared, has laid out a detailed and strict agenda for the meeting, and I know that my place will be to interject a little humor and personality into the meeting. I am a great heckler. Maybe make us seem like real people, because Jack certainly gives a first impression of being mechanical, but also upbeat and approachable. It takes a while for people to realize he is earnest and endearing. With Jack, what you see is what you get. I come off as a smartass, and that might be an intriguing combination. Over the years, we've perfected our roles.

After the steering committee meeting in October 2006 with Jack and me reigning as the battalion command team, we committee members are already aware that our brigade is on the patch chart to deploy to Iraq the following summer. We have ten months to prepare and plan, even if none of us is ready to talk about it yet. Jack and I are hesitant to come into a battalion of war-weary folks who've just gotten back from a year in Iraq and start excitedly talking about the deployment we all know lies on the horizon. Both of us need to keep our thrill of being at the helm of a battalion during war in check, for now. But we are already plotting and scoping things out. My main mission for the day is to assess the captains in attendance at the meeting and choose one. Choose my rear detachment commander. After the meeting, I hang around and make chitchat with everyone as they gather their belongings to head back and go about their day. Some of the men exit immediately after the meeting, a few chat with each other away from me, and only one approaches me and talks to me like I am a person. As I talk with this relaxed, relatable soldier, I feel the click of knowing I've found one of *my people*. We have an easy conversation, and he tells me he's heard that I am also a Dave Matthews fan. *You had me at hello.*

I clean up the table with the empty cookie plate and head to Jack's office so we can rehash the meeting and its attendees while it's still fresh in our minds.

"Close the door," he says as soon as I enter. It feels as if the first day of school has just ended and it's milk and cookie time, time to rehash and analyze the new cast of characters.

When Jack asks me to choose, I don't hesitate. "The tall guy with the brown eyes. He stayed after the meeting ended and chatted with me. He looked me in the eye, didn't call me ma'am. Good social skills. Him. He likes Dave Matthews; it's a sign."

"Ouch. That's Ben Black. He's my best captain. Isn't there another choice?"

"Nope. Him. I thought the policy is the best stays in the rear to take care of families, right?" My retort is only half teasing. I want to make sure he remembers his own philosophy.

And with that simple exchange of sentences, Ben Black's fate as my future partner and battle buddy is sealed. When Ben learns of his new assignment, he fights it; he calls congressmen and pouts. Ben can be moody. He lacks Jack's tireless energy and focus, but makes up for it with his ability to relate to people, especially chicks. He doesn't think in black-and-white military terms, but on a more human level.

A year later, when Ben asks me what in the world made me choose him, he insists that he only stayed back after that first meeting because he had to get a paper signed by Jack and never would have hung around to talk to me otherwise. The very irreverence of this conversation convinces me again I'd made the right choice.

As I leave the headquarters in my try-hard sneakers on that first day, a group of women in a deep discussion lingers in the parking lot. They ooze frustration.

Wanting to be the resourceful problem solver, I approach. "Is everything okay? Anything I can help with?"

They look at each other, then their suspicious eyes land on me. "When are the afghans we ordered coming in?" one woman asks. "Our families paid for them, and they're annoyed that they aren't here yet. Sandy Morrow ordered them months ago."

My stomach lurches. During the transition, no one said a word to me about an afghan fund-raiser, where the money went, or where these friggin' afghans were—or even that they existed. Now I'll have to engage drunken Sandy in a dialogue and try to get to the bottom of this. My first real pain-in-the-ass command conundrum in Jack's coming three-year command. Not a very challenging one, but it offers a nice way to get my feet wet in the muddy waters of problem solving. Two years later, I will have spotted this kind of tense conversation from a room away, averted my eyes, and hoped to escape without getting involved. But at this early stage, I have the energy and chutzpah to attack with vigor. Make a great first impression.

It's well known that the most contentious of relationships in a battalion can be between the wife of the battalion commander and the wife of the battalion command sergeant major, the top officer's wife and the top enlisted soldier's wife. There are entire seminars offered to wives about navigating this complex relationship, perhaps making us look too hard for drama and power struggles that might not exist at all. But mine does exist.

Liesel Leonard, the wife of Jack's new command sergeant major, is an eccentric woman who has never participated in the army wife scene. It's fine to not participate all along the way, but to jump in with both feet as a newbie in a leadership position, well, that's just a recipe for disaster. Anyway, she never really does jump in with both feet. It's more like she tips her toe in the water when she feels like it. Liesel offers piano lessons in her nearly empty home, which strikes me as void of personality and warmth, and each time I speak to her I can only picture the mother from the movie *Carrie*. But there's also something gentle and thoughtful about her, and I hold on to high hopes that our opposite natures will be complementary. She refuses to call Jack by his first name and instead calls him "Colonel Hawwwwkins" in a singsong lilt. It isn't long before I realize that she will not be a strong teammate for me. The same is true of her husband, a self-admitted old and tired enlisted man who has never seen a day of combat, but is well liked for his easygoing, relaxed disposition. Pretty much the opposite of the stereotypical hard-ass, scary command sergeant major.

Had I met Liesel under different circumstances, I think I would appreciate her eccentricities and unique manner. She is so offbeat that it's hard not to find her amusing. Liesel is in her late forties at the time, but because of her long, gray, frizzy hair and frumpy, practical clothing, she looks much older. She has a slothlike way of moving and a witchy, shrill quality in her voice. Somehow I think she would be a perfect battle buddy for Regina Sweeney. They would get each other. Liesel makes her disdain for me clear with stares, sighs, eye rolling, and nitpicking at irrelevant details. She rarely even attempts to show up for meetings or other events, but when she does, the tension is clear.

As the wife of our battalion's top enlisted soldier, the command sergeant major, she is supposed to be my teammate and battle buddy.

Battle buddy is a cheesy term the army uses to describe the other half
of the command team, though more and more senior officers' wives
have grown to use the term with a solid dose of sarcasm, because it
almost never works out that our command sergeant major's wife is
a true battle buddy. In theory and under ideal circumstances, she is
supposed to be the one who galvanizes the enlisted wives and encour-
ages. The resourceful and wise one, not the weird and withdrawn
one. Instead, Liesel is ill equipped for deployments or, really, for
functioning in a combat unit at all. Passive-aggressive and lazy, she
offers zero commitment to her role, other than making occasional
appearances at her convenience. I resent this because I give so much
of myself to my role, while she gives so little. She blames her weakness on a lack of training through her husband's career and complains that enlisted wives are not "groomed" as officers' wives are.
As a natural introvert, she is overwhelmed by the deployment and
the demands of her role and she retreats, but refuses to relinquish
the title of "senior advisor" in the battalion. She plays the victim
and accuses me of intentionally leaving her out of decisions, but the
reality is that I am exhausted and sick of catering to her demands.
She does no entertaining at her home, probably because her only furniture is a card table, four folding chairs, one bookcase, and a piano.
No pictures on the walls. No computer or television. No warmth. I
want her house to at least smell like patchouli, but it just smells like
stale nothingness.

The lighter side of Liesel's presence is that she provides an endless
wealth of behind-the-scene chuckles. Nearly everyone has a spot-on
imitation of Liesel. In everyday civilian life, characters like Liesel can
be galvanizing because their very presence is anything but dull. I am
equally responsible for the tension between us. I'm sure I'm not as

good at restraining my inner mean girl as I should be, at least for the sake of appearances.

The other witchy one, but an oh-so-different witchy, Linda Stewart, pulls me aside about a month after the change of command, peers over her glasses at Liesel and then back at me, and squeezes my arm. "You've got your work cut out for you with that one."

a surge, some spin,
and a sucker punch

Isn't a one-year deployment enough? Elizabeth's husband and Rob's battalion, which is now led by Martha Schneider's husband, is en route home from a long, glory-less year in Afghanistan. Some men are already home; others are due back within days. The entire brigade, thirty-five hundred soldiers, is called back for a three-month extension. That's the second time my practical and buoyant friend Elizabeth winds up in a pile of tears on my hallway floor. She says, "We've been sucker punched again."

I REMEMBER THE PHONE call from Elizabeth Bianci so well. It's the middle of winter 2007, which in Upstate New York is the end of February. In many parts of the country, spring is right around the corner. For us, winter has months to go. March is the worst, April almost as sketchy and unpredictable. The snow and slush and cold and isolation only get worse. Elizabeth's husband drives a little VW Bug (no, not the norm for an infantry officer, unless he is secure in his manhood and has nothing to prove, something so respectable and almost hot about a man who doesn't need to prove his masculinity by his stupid vehicle, a quality shared by Jack). The VW is bright yellow. Only one piece of the hood remains visible under the piles of deep snow and ice. She gave up on keeping it cleared in January. By the end of February, he's supposed to be on his way home, and he could dig it out. She's ready for him to come, not just because she misses him, which of course she does. But more than that, she is exhausted by taking care of the families in her FRG on her own. They've lost dozens of soldiers, an unprecedented amount for one battalion, in the Korengal Valley. The same place Sebastian Junger would film *Restrepo* just months later. Elizabeth wants Eric back for many reasons, the greatest of which seems to be simply to relieve her of her duties. Those duties that have never come naturally to her to begin with.

Maybe it's Kat Dalisay who calls me first. Her husband is a dentist, and she has done her best to ride this deployment like a pro, keeping her whining to a minimum. Who thinks in a million years that marrying a dentist will wind up like this? Not Kat. But he's due home in just a week. So is Eric Bianci. So we think. Both Kat and Elizabeth call me within an hour. Both of them with quivering voices hovering on tears.

"Did you hear the news?" Elizabeth asks. "I can't fucking believe it. There's a town hall meeting in an hour, and these women are going to lose their shit. It's going to be a riot. Can you keep the boys for a while?"

When she drops the boys off, she doesn't come to the door. This must be serious. A few hours later, she returns to pick them up and it's maybe the worst I've seen her look. Even worse than nine months earlier during the Rob Macklin tragedy.

"I feel like we got sucker punched," she says. "Half the guys are already home; the other half are on their way. People have paid for cruises, vacations. Some of the women who left have moved back. It's a goddamn disaster. They extended us four more months. Maybe three. After the year we've had, this seems like an eternity. That meeting was straight-up anarchy from the outraged wives. I was waiting for them to start hurling tomatoes."

She stands there telling me this, and I am distracted by the knowledge that Jack's battalion is supposed to go for a year; they leave within six months. I wonder if this applies to us. Somehow it seems like a shitty time to ask.

Spring of 2007 brings an announcement from the Department of Defense. All Iraq deployments will become a minimum of fifteen months for combat brigades, as part of General David Petraeus's surge. Our brigade is scheduled to leave at the end of summer, and preparations for deployment begin. With this announcement, Jack makes an unpopular decision to replace several key members of his own senior staff, and I do my best to navigate the backlash from the wives. I lose the one levelheaded, helpful, and experienced major's wife, Patricia Reid. Low-key and direct, she reminds me of Peppermint Patty. Jack replaces her husband with a politically minded, driven (but never deployed) major who has been freshly hitched to Miss Audrey-Jill Jude Fontenot Sherwood of Someplace, Louisiana. Audrey-Jill is naive, sweet, and beloved by everyone, mostly because she is so innocent and helpless. I envy her airiness; it must be lovely to be so unaware. The Delicate Cajun has no idea what is about to fall in her lap in the next fifteen months, and maybe her oblivion will be her greatest asset.

Audrey-Jill makes even the youngest and greenest wives feel like they have their shit together. Her husband is a major, and so she falls into the mini-perfumed-turd category. I quickly realize that Audrey-Jill will not be the tough battle buddy I need, but she will also not be divisive and argumentative like Liesel Leonard. Audrey-Jill is determined to prove herself and volunteers to organize a chili dog fund-raiser for the battalion. She refuses my guidance, tells me to take this one off: "I've got it covered, Miss Angie! Frito pies are a Southern specialty!" The result? Twenty leftover gallon-sized cans of Hormel chili and a loss of $50. Audrey-Jill is galvanizing, though, thanks to her natural people skills and helpful nature. She is the kind of person who needs looking out for, and I worry how she will cope with the upcoming fifteen-month deployment and her first pregnancy.

I have identified the so-called problem children within the battalion, and I puzzle over how to handle them. With no viable experience from Liesel or Audrey-Jill, I establish an off-the-record group of younger wives in the battalion who've proven themselves to be steeled and reliable: Lindsey Grundy, Alicia Ramsey, Sophie Abbott, Abby Collins, and Anna Shaw, none of whom qualify anywhere on the spectrum of perfumed turds. They're wannabe perfumed turds at this point. Their husbands are not all in leadership positions, but these wives become the trusted backbone of our unit. Some married their husbands after 9/11, some before. All but Sophie have been through multiple deployments, but none of us for longer than a year. Three of them are pregnant. But they all have the intestinal fortitude and resiliency that both Liesel and Audrey-Jill lack. Liesel and Audrey-Jill haven't proven their buoyancy to me. Both strike me as fainthearted, and I can't see either of them going hip deep into the trenches with the families during deployment. Audrey-Jill knows her place in the pecking order and respects the experienced wives. Liesel does not. She challenges me at every opportunity, unwilling to work but also unwilling to relinquish responsibility. I have three babies at home, yet we schedule family steering committee meetings around her piano lessons and Bible meetings. We remain cordial for the sake of appearances, but the tension is impossible to dismiss. Inside I am dying to scream at her, "Shit or get off the pot, woman! Are you in or out?"

Much of what determines army wife protocol is nothing more than the practice of the Golden Rule and simple good manners; Audrey-Jill excels in these areas. She never misses an RSVP, a birthday, or a thank you note. The younger wives revere Audrey-Jill because she is so relatable and quick to laugh at herself. Though she misfires and needs an awful lot of encouragement and guidance. She is unjaded and full of the bright-eyed enthusiasm that so many of us have lost along the way. A breath of fresh Louisiana air in the frozen tundra of war. Audrey-Jill has no enemies, a feat that is a nearly impossible achievement in our competitive world. Since she lives off post as her husband insisted, I find myself worrying that she suffers without the nearness of army sisters.

the race for a brand-new home

Spring 2007. With almost no control over our lives,
when something pops up that we can control, even minutely,
we grab the opportunity and ride that monkey hard. Relentlessly.

◆

With their nine-inch nails
And little fascist panties
Tucked inside the heart
Of every nice girl.

—TORI AMOS

NOW WHEN I look back at the last twelve years of war, somehow the turds stand out the most in my memory. The people who act like total assholes. The goodness fades into the background, and I have to think a little harder to remember the goodness. I wonder what that says about me. Maybe it reminds me of myself, the greedy parts of me I want to pretend don't exist. It's easy to take the goodness for granted and cling to the bad parts.

Nothing brings out the monster in all of us like political greed. Oh, and the offer of new homes. People like Janet Findlay, who is headed out of Fort Drum that summer, and not eligible to move. She puts off visiting our new house for months, because it sours her stomach just that much. She has to gear herself up to visit our new, cheap hardwood floors and look at our gas fireplace and then skulk back to her lino-leum-floored duplex, the one we were able to leave behind.

After six years in the linoleum-floored ranch duplex, we move into a brand-new home. With the increased defense spending on the war, there is an emphasis on improving the quality of life for families. Maybe a new house will give the perfumed turds something shiny to hold our attention a little while.

Team Hawkins scores and moves into the new house before the Sweeneys, and Regina/Eeyore comes over with her precocious teenage daughter to take a look and to salivate and seethe, but says the visit is to plan her furniture placement. Unlike the familiar downtrodden Eeyore stereotype, this Eeyore has an agenda. Always an agenda.

The new houses are all cookie-cutter with the same floor plans and different facades. Sort of a metaphor for our lives.

Shortly after we move in, I see our new neighbors. She is a Korean-born woman with an ominous-looking, bald husband, a somewhat new major who does not have a history in the 10th Mountain like so many of the rest of us. Newbies in the division are rare. He drives a jacked-up Jeep and listens to death metal. Other battalion command-ers' wives are pissed that this junior major has jumped to the top of the housing list and has been assigned a brand-new house instead of pay-ing dues in the old, ugly duplexes. When I first see them as they move in, I assume that Mira Harwood is like so many of the other Korean wives, ever-amiable and soft-spoken. That her husband is a macho jerk. I could not have been more wrong about either of them.

Mira is my next-door neighbor and often my voice of reason and calm in the storm. Little riles Mira; but when it does, take cover. Mira is the daughter of Korean immigrants, but other than her heritage, she has almost nothing in common with the vast majority of Korean women married to American soldiers. She never seeks the camaraderie of her Korean sisters, and there is a plethora of them in our community. When Korean-speaking army wives speak to her in Korean, Mira tells them that she is Vietnamese, because she doesn't want to be invited to what she perceives as suffocating churches and because she doesn't want to be a part of the tight-knit military community of Korean women. She was raised in Virginia, and aside from a few characteristics of many Korean women (great cook, immaculate housekeeper, and a taste for designer things, especially Louis Vuitton) she is all-American.

Mira is private about her personal life, more so than most of us. It takes longer to get a pulse on her because of this, but when she lets her guard down, there is no one more real and trustworthy. Her children are happy and well-behaved, something that is almost uncommon among the children of senior army officers' kids. I see the behavior of perfumed turds' kids as clear indicators of what possible familial perfection they might fake. Mira makes her children her priority, and it shows in their behavior. She does what her husband expects of her with his unit, but she maintains the balance between her own life and the unit, a balance that so many of us cannot find. Mira is generous, introspective, adventurous, and bright, but behind all this, there is a vague disconnect with her life as an army wife. Which is refreshing. Sometimes she gives an impression that she is just going through the army wife motions. Like so many army couples, she and her husband appear to be direct opposites; privately he is the class clown, the life of the party. A heckler, like me. The tough caricature of an infantry soldier, he is hard living. But a big softie behind the exterior.

I spend that spring meticulously transplanting bulbs and shrubs brought from the Bassett Street house into the new flower beds. Mira's six-year-old son walks over each time he sees me bending over my flower beds and asks, "Miss Angie? Can I help you with anything? I'm good at weeding. I can help you dig those holes." Before I even call the Harwoods friends, they've already earned my respect through the behavior of their son.

summer of hurry up and wait

Everything and everyone is ready. Can we ever truly be ready?
Let the countdown to deployment begin.
What to do with all this nervous energy . . .

◆

My dog won't bite if you sit real still.
I got the anti-Christ in the kitchen yellin' at me again.

—TORI AMOS

AGAIN WITH TORI. Tori has a magical way of speaking to deployment angst, even before it's begun.

In the long weeks of the summer of 2007 leading up to the fifteen-month deployment, battalion commanders, their wives, and other division-level leaders attend a three-day team-building seminar on the shores of Lake Placid. It's part of our "get-ready-to-giddy-up" pre-deployment preparations. A fresh binder overflows with the most current Kool-Aid, given to our reverent hands for us to serve to the wives under us. Really, it is an opportunity to drink (alcohol, not Kool-Aid) to excess and schmooze with other command teams. Size up the competition. Some of the women sneak out of the mandatory PowerPoint snooze-fests to shop and sniff each other out. There's a new crop of division leaders, and this is our introduction. Many of the leaders at 10th Mountain have a history with the division and are returning for another tour. One of the new wives is my old friend and mentor from Somalia days, Carrie Barnes. Carrie likes to remind me that no matter how much time has elapsed, she is still my wise, older sister and can snap me into deference with a disapproving look or roll of her eyes. She patiently held my hand through my first deployment to Somalia, even though she had two tiny and needy babies then and probably wanted to punch me for my incessant whimpering and random dry heaving. I feel relieved that she will be around again for another deployment, this one the mother of them all, even trumping Somalia. Three times the length of Somalia.

When we aren't engaged in practical reality of what's to come, we talk about the salacious and exaggerated details of an email found on someone else's husband's army BlackBerry, an email reminiscing about the time he "titty fucked" his neighbor's wife in the woods behind our houses. We have to whisper words like "titty," but acronyms like IED and KIA roll off our tongues comfortably.

General George Casey is the chief of staff of the army, and he flatly tells us to prepare for an eighteen-month deployment, even as we are still reeling from the extension to fifteen months. As with so many moments, there is nothing to do but pour a cocktail.

Our brigade buzzes with rumors (which are true) of the affair between the deputy commander of our brigade (second in command of nearly four thousand) and another married lieutenant colonel, a female officer who is a close friend of Jack's and whose husband is serving in Iraq. Of course this is a huge scandal. Elizabeth Bianci and I are shown the dirty and shocking emails between them at Bunco (or Drunko, which is a more accurate description of the mind-numbing and way-too-gung-ho game of dice rolling). The emails were found by the deputy commander's wife on his government BlackBerry and were passed around delightfully by her thinly veiled BFF. Our brigade commander, the bumbling and BO-emanating Vick Petty, sweeps it under the rug and turns his anger toward others within the brigade who've discussed the emails. I'm at the top of that list. Whoopsies. Petty leers at Jack; they are polar opposites. Petty tries to be everyone's buddy, but ends up looking like a buffoon. He is in over his head with the upcoming deployment, and I can see the freaking-out in his eyes. He's nothing more than an overgrown, insecure schoolyard bully, and I have zero respect for him. I would use the word *sinister* to describe him, but he's too slack-mouthed to be sinister.

Greta, my youngest at two years old, is a biter and sank her teeth into him once at a brigade picnic. Somehow he has managed to work that tiny detail into every single conversation I've ever muddled through with him, so passive-aggressive. If he is going to act that way over a toddler bite, how will he endure Al Qaeda?

Though Petty is despised and written off as a bully by most in the brigade, his wife, Barb, is revered and respected. She doesn't mess with me. I wonder how those two ended up together; I wonder that about most of us. Maybe the word *revered* is too strong. She's not especially wily or formidable. But she allows the battalion commanders' wives to do their thing. She meddles to an extent, but it could be worse. She always shows up with a bottle of wine, and who could not love that quality?

The last couple of weeks before a deployment are sacred. Not a time for an avalanche of social events. So those are crammed into June and July, and half of July spent on block leave. June is a blur of picnics and lunches and seminars and classes to equip and ready ourselves. We disguise team-building as socializing. We would be spending the next fifteen months intimately involved, so no reason to fart around. Might as well get the show on the road.

I've spent the whole spring getting our new house set up and making it into the cushy dream house I've always hoped for. I painstakingly choose the colors for each wall. Devote weeks painting splotches of color on each wall so I can live with it and see it in every light. Finally I decide on the colors, and wait for Jack to eventually offer his painting services. Though I pretend that painting will be my own personal mission, I have no intention of doing the painting myself and take advantage of the fact that living with asymmetrical, haphazard splotches of paint will drive Jack bananas. My plan works.

I want to entertain. I am impatient to use this house, the house I finally have space to move in. Space to show off my culinary skills and feign humility at how easily I've created such a warm and cozy live-in home so quickly. Truly it isn't difficult with this new house, a fireplace in the living room, and an excellent layout of rooms. Perfect for guests. A huge, sweeping porch. Right at the apex of the cul-de-sac, surrounded by pine trees. Our house was maybe the best house on post, definitely in the best position.

Yes, I need to show it off as soon as possible. Especially rub it in just a little to old Eeyore, who still waits for her house with a peevish restlessness. I relish an opportunity to be pleasingly condescending. So Jack and I plan three sets of party/picnics. One for the battalion staff officers, another for the troop commanders and first sergeants, and a third for the other battalion commanders in our brigade and, eek, the Pettys. Tension already exists there, and we choose to ignore it. We chalk it up to growing pains. Jack has never had a boss he didn't get along with; somehow this is unfamiliar territory to us and ignoring it seems to be the best course of action.

The first two parties go off without a hitch, except that I've made each meal entirely from scratch, and Liesel shows up with a box of

Walmart-purchased brownies in a plastic container and plunks them directly in the middle of my table. The turd in the soup pot. A domestic, passive-aggressive act of warfare.

For the final party with the other battalion commanders and their wives and the Pettys, I brainstorm an excellent game to play. I come up with about twenty names of famous people from all eras and all sides of controversy. Kanye West, Madonna, Abraham Lincoln, Pol Pot, Matt Lauer, Saddam Hussein, Cinderella, Hillary Clinton, you get the idea. But one name is different. One I have a special idea for. Eeyore's husband, Fred, will get his own name. I print each name on a sticker and post it on the back of each guest as he or she arrives. Vick Petty gets Madonna, or maybe Britney Spears; I can't recall. But Fred Sweeney gets his own name. The guests can only ask yes or no questions about their identity to figure it out. For over an hour, Fred works the party: "Am I athletic?" "Is my wife hot?" "Am I successful at my career?" "Am I universally hated?" It is sublime. The best prank in history. Finally, well after an hour, he looks at me and pauses, lowering his bushy eyebrows. "I'm me. I'm me, aren't I? Very nice, Hawkins. Well played." I could see on his face he doesn't find it as funny as I do and will be gunning for me. Let him.

part three

deployment day
flavored kool-aid

*Finally, after months of preparation, changes in deployment
dates, and what seems like an endless trudge to the slaughterhouse,
the deployment arrives. The weeks and days leading up to this
feel like a loss of color—everything I see is in shades of gray.
We all operate on autopilot, disconnected from our emotions.*

WHEN THE SOLDIERS are finally gone, we start counting down
the days until their return. The color gradually returns as the
days pass. It's always the period leading up to deployment that's the
worst: the packing, the final weekend, the final meals, hearing Jack
choose songs for his "battle-ready" playlist on his iPod. All of that is
over when they finally go. It's a tremendous relief. The first few weeks
of the deployment, we all feel beaten up, and this is a period of recovery
and rebirth into our new normal. Our new battle rhythm on our own.

"Take this sinking boat and point it home, we've still got time, raise
your hopeful voice, you have a choice." The song "Falling Slowly"
takes on a whole new meaning. We are out of time, yet a new time is
just beginning.

I sit alone in Jack's Jeep and drop my head on the steering wheel.
For the first time in the months leading up to this moment, I cry. I've
just said good-bye to my husband in a most unceremonious, abrupt way.

No matter how many months we plan for this moment, it is always sudden. This is the seventh time I've sent him off on a long deployment, ranging from peacekeeping missions to battle, each one culminating in the slumped tears in the car. But this day feels different. This time he's responsible for over six hundred souls, not just himself. This time the risk of casualties is higher than ever before. This time it is for fifteen months, maybe eighteen. This time I am responsible for caring not just for my own three children and those other hundreds of families, but for my marriage, strained by this new burden and responsibility. My worry for his safety takes an odd backseat to the responsibility on both our shoulders.

Today is also the first day of a new school for two of our children. Joe is starting his first day of fourth grade, and Bridget is beginning second grade. Greta, our youngest, is in day care. Our new house falls into a crummy school district, so we have enrolled the kids in Catholic school, and aside from a brief tour over the summer, this is a plunge into uncharted territory. The kids don't even have the familiar, welcoming smells of their old school waiting for them at the other end of their bus trip. Somehow this lack of familiarity robs the kids of one more comfort, not just on the first day of school but also on the day they say farewell to their father.

We don't get to choose the day Jack deploys. It doesn't matter if it's a birthday, or Christmas, or today. If deployment day falls on the first day of school and he has to hug them good-bye for fifteen months, then that's how it goes. There will be no after-school cookies and excited stories about their new school for Dad. That will have to wait until the middle of the next school year. By then the excited stories about the first day will be nothing but a long-distant memory. Irrelevant in the mind of a child. But today *will* hang in their memories for a different reason. For the gut-wrenching good-bye.

All the other kids and mothers at the bus stop are exuberant and snapping pictures of the first day of school. A new beginning, a fresh start. For me it is both of those things; for the kids not so much. No one wants our stricken family huddled to the side in their first-day-of-school photos. My kids haven't looked forward to getting this dreadful day over with like I do. Fifteen months seems too overwhelming to fully grasp even for me; to them it's a lifetime. Nervous laughter and glee surround us at the bus stop, and my little family can't make eye contact with anyone. I can't bear the weight of my friends' sympathetic eyes this morning. They know that today is our day. Their own days of reckoning are coming or have already come. We each sympathize too well with what this moment means.

My tears have to wait. We huddled on the periphery, a desperate attempt to make light of the white-knuckled moment and focus on the first day of school. "Where is your bus pass? Make sure your sister finds her classroom. Try to sit together on the bus. We will order pizza for dinner, guys. I can't wait to hear about your new teachers." My attempt to pretend this is just a regular first day is feeble at best. I turn away and pretend to sip my now-cold coffee as we wait those last few moments for the bus. I have to be cold like my coffee to get through this part. Removed from myself. *Drink the tepid coffee, and remind yourself to hover above. This will pass.*

When the bus rumbles to a stop and it comes time for Joe and Bridget to climb the stairs, Jack quickly and lightly hugs (long hugs bring tears) both of our children and says, "Have a great day! I love you guys! Take care of Mom!" For a split second, it feels like a regular day, until I glimpse their faces as they take their seats on the bus. All the other kids wave except them. They look forward and away from us.

They aren't ready to start the countdown like I am.

Our moment of good-bye between Jack and the kids is a rip-off for both occasions. A gyp of the fun of the first day of school and a gyp of the open weeping of good-bye. We are forced to hover in the middle, and both moments are left unsatisfied. For the rest of the day brief glimpses pass through my imagination of the kids sitting at their new desks in their brand-new Catholic school uniforms, juggling the stress of adjusting to new classrooms, teachers, and students and wondering if they will hear their dad's plane fly over their school. Wondering exactly how long fifteen months will feel. They picture the paper chain that loops and cascades from our kitchen to the living room that moment. Our mark of the first day of deployment.

I made the paper chain a few days ago, one colorful link for each week Jack will be gone. The chain has sixty-four links of thick, printed cardstock. Some of us use white paper, but it will never hold up for fifteen months. Each Sunday, we will remove one link and write a memory or note from that week and put it into a shoebox. By week six, depending on what I've faced the previous week with the kids and the unit, I might be tearing the links off on Sunday night as I down a glass of wine, wadding them up and whipping them into the trash. Some Sundays will be sentimental, though, and we will put those links in the box. I hope Jack never stops to count the links when he gets home.

The kids aren't ready to start the countdown like I am.

The last week leading up to deployment is the hardest, and the longest. The dates of departure always fluctuate left and right, even up until the last day. He walks around the house humming "Leaving on a Jet Plane" and smiling in his childlike way. By the last few days, I am white-knuckling every agonizing moment. The weighty expectation of making the most of every remaining moment is smothering. Just last week, I abandoned a half-full cart of groceries at the commissary because I thought I was going to break down. I escaped to my car, but the tears never came. The last week. The last weekend. The last dinner. The last pancake breakfast. The last awkward sex romp, with no kissing. The last night, a night that brings no sleep for any of us. Last week we had the "talk." About possible funeral arrangements. He showed me where the keys to the lock box were. Each deployment, I want to confirm what his last wishes are in case he pays the "ultimate sacrifice." *I hate that term. As if getting killed is a choice, a preferred option in the multiple-choice test of war. Something about those words implies that making the ultimate sacrifice is the ultimate achievement.* Buried at Arlington National Cemetery or cremated and his ashes sprinkled? Where? I've heard him mention more than one preference, and I want to be sure. We finalized his Soldier Readiness Contract, a task I dreaded.

"Is there a section on there for the people I want nowhere near me?" I asked. "Like Liesel Leonard and Regina Sweeney? I will make that notation." Somehow, the people who are there with me fall second to the ones I don't want there.

Family members of terminally ill patients always say that despite the months of emotional preparation, death is always a sudden stab. An hour before I sat sobbing in the Jeep, Jack and I had eaten Burger King in an empty battalion classroom. We'd made awkward small talk about details like sign-up dates for the kids' fall soccer and when the cars would be due for oil changes. All things he'd left in extensive notes at home, the reiteration of them just a way to fill the empty quiet while we ate. Both of us wanted this part to be over. His uniform already smelled like the desert. Which was funny because these uniforms are brand-new. My mind must be playing tricks.

Now I gladly leave Jack for a few minutes for him to take care of some last-minute business. I walk around the courtyard crowded with battle-ready soldiers waiting to be called to buses. The cement courtyard weighed down with soldiers dressed in body armor and heavy, clumsy-looking weapons. Each soldier wears his mask, his battle face. The handful of family members in attendance wear the same. Stoic, strained, as if they've all left their bodies to hover above, watching with me. Together we are a cluster of unsettled and frightened souls sharing a certain congruence. What I want, though, is to rip off this fucking Band-Aid and get this over with. I want a Bloody Mary with a good, ugly sob.

I introduce myself to mothers of soldiers who've traveled from different parts of the country to put their sons on this bus and send them into a tangible hell masquerading as Iraq. Only a few wives are present. Most of them are veterans of this sick dance, so they've said their good-byes in the car and driven away to wait at home for the roaring sound of the C-17 flying over their houses. Then each wife will have confirmation that he is gone, and she will safely start marking the days until it ends. I can't take that route for this deployment. I am the commander's wife. So there I stand, trying to look reassuring and composed, listening to myself spout rhetoric about how we would not just survive the deployment, but thrive during it. *Ladies, we will not just survive this deployment, we will thrive!* A scripted line straight out of a binder full of the atta-girl stuff we are supposed to say. *Jesus, did I just hear myself say that crap?* The intricate, painful training I endure full of scripts for this day robs me of the ability to put a sentence together that does not sound scripted. I almost laugh at the absurdity. But another part of me hopes the line isn't a Dixie cup full of Kool-Aid, that it's the truth.

A dozen or so mothers are here. Fewer fathers. As I introduce myself I tell them that my husband's main goal is to complete the mission and bring everyone home safely. Even saying the words feels too intimate, acknowledging that in all likelihood, some will not be coming home at all. But unlike many of the things I'm supposed to say in these moments, this part isn't lip service. I also give the mothers, the ones who want it, my home phone number in case they need anything. In the moment, it makes me feel helpful, with a purpose other than looking like I want to get the hell out of here. I'm as helpless as the mothers, who at least have the privilege of not knowing the specific details of the uphill battle their sons will wage once over there.

Captain Ben Black, my personally chosen and still slightly disgruntled but committed rear detachment commander, comes to me a few times and squeezes my arm, the only person who acknowledges the mask of courage on my face. Sees the facade of strength. Everyone else is too focused on keeping his or her own shit together to notice.

"It's all going smoothly," he says quietly. "You hanging in there?" Then he rattles off irritation at some detail about a change in the manifest roster, a detail that goes right over my head. His attempt to distract me from the weight of the moment.

"Here it is. Finally. I had no idea so many parents would be here." As I say those words, I avert my eyes from him, feeling my autopilot mask shift and fearing I might cry. Ben isn't stiff and blank like so many of the other soldiers; he has an excellent way of making eye contact and connecting with people, a true empathetic nature. Ben shows his irritation at certain situations, but that's fine with me. He will always tell me what I need to hear, not what I want to hear. Today that empathy, the reason I initially chose him as rear detachment commander, makes me need to avoid him altogether. Saving the tears and emotion for later.

As the rear detachment commander, Ben says good-bye to comrades, which is meaningful, but not as wretched as bidding farewell to a husband or son. I can see it in his eyes, that what he most wants in that moment is to be wearing a rucksack instead of clutching a clipboard. Ben would rather be heading to Iraq than be left in the rear to take care of the families, wounded soldiers, and equipment left behind. *Left behind* is something we are coached not to say, though. It sounds insulting. Instead we use the term *rear detachment cadre*. A better ring, yet the same meaning. Ben commanded a company of a hundred or so soldiers in combat in Iraq a year before, so he has a firsthand awareness of where these men are headed. Some of the men he commanded in his past deployment are here today, now headed back. As I look at Ben, I feel a little guilty that I robbed him of another opportunity to go to The Fight, but there will be other opportunities. Jack and I are certain Ben is the right choice for us.

Nowadays, the best are hand-selected for rear detachment to help handle unavoidable family debacles. To help untangle the mess of catastrophic and inflated dramas between wives. Ben is good at his job, the best in the battalion in fact. So maybe in his mind, his reward is being our babysitter for the next fifteen to eighteen months. Well done. I'm lucky he doesn't hate me.

It is a perfect September day in 2007, sunny with clear blue skies. Our battalion will be the tail end of the surge, the brainchild of Petraeus, orchestrated to tighten the slippery hold on the stability of that country. I am aware that this is our generation of soldiers and their family's place in history. I am proud of my husband, knowing that despite the pressure and pain, these are his glory days. Beyond measure, I am proud of myself and proud of the families in the battalion.

There's one particular thing about the moment I want to freeze and remember. The faces. Each of these soldiers is someone's baby, someone's son. I feel guilty for not having an opportunity to know each of them by name. Because if they are killed, when the time comes for me to offer condolences to their mothers, I want to say with certainty and personal knowledge that he was a tremendous hero. I want to mean it, to know it. I have a moment of frantic regret as the battalion prepares to leave, and I realize that not even my husband personally knows every one of them by name. There is no way, and really it makes no difference whether we know them or not. Nothing, at that point, will ease anyone's pain.

I wait and sit on the concrete pavement of the courtyard with Jack in the last few minutes, and he reassures me with his usual crappy propaganda, things like, "We've done this before, it's no big deal." "Fifteen months is going to fly by, girl!" "You'll be so busy with the kids and the Family Readiness Group that you won't ever be lonely." "Please make sure the kids take their vitamins." Sometimes these silly comments are charming; sometimes they make me want to kick his ass. Today's a little bit of both, and like my desperate desire to have familiarity with each of the soldiers, I become aware that his words are meant to reassure himself more than me, even if he doesn't think so. So I smile and nod. I don't speak, because of course speaking will lead to tears, and that part I want and need to save.

Ben approaches Jack and me. "Sir, the buses have arrived. Five minutes until S.P." Army lingo for "Get your ass on the bus."

"Roger. Ruck up." We stand and he gathers his gear. The amount of shit each soldier has to wear is punishment enough. Flak vests, that heavy helmet, the weapons, night-vision goggles, and the sixty-pound rucksack. The idea of being a soldier, the details of it, are beyond my comprehension. It would be just my luck that I would get all suited up and realize that I need to pee. Once, to make me laugh, Jack told me about a soldier of his who, on more than one occasion, pooped his pants in the helicopter en route to a mission. After the soldiers were perfectly packed into place in the helicopters, no one was moving, no how, not even to poop. I would make a miserable soldier.

Together we make our way around to the front of the building, and I'm shocked to see the buses lined up right there in the immediate parking loop instead of on the road fifty yards away. I expected at least a two-minute walk. This is too sudden. I turn to him and whisper, "I'm not ready," and I feel the tears coming, but force them back. I see his tears and he hugs me, hard and fast. In that final hug, instead of being in that moment, all I can think about is how awkward and impossible it is to hug a soldier suited up for battle.

And that's it. Not our first rodeo.

I watch him climb the steps and turn onto the bus. There's no way I can or will stand there until the buses slowly drive away. I've done my job.

So here I sit in his Jeep that smells of army gear. Smells of him. It's only just after lunch, and I have time before the kids return. With shaky hands and a body that feels drained of blood, I drive three miles, the ugly sob guiding me home. I walk into the side door and see his jacket hanging in its place, and his cup from this morning, rinsed and in the drying rack. Fuck. It's time. I glance around the room at his magazines stacked next to his chair—that ugly, cheap leather recliner, an eyesore. So very little in this home is a direct reflection of him, except that chair. Everything else I've chosen and placed. He is little more than a guest in his own home.

I walk into the bathroom and stare at his sink with his few personal hygiene things neatly lined up. I feel limp. Everything is gray. I decide to lie down before I start my ritual. The bed smells like him, but it does not comfort me. I want that smell gone. It's going to be fifteen months, and I won't be one of those women sleeping with some old T-shirt, clinging to his long-faded scent. No. I'm a fresh-start girl. Today is day 1. Today we start counting down the days, 455 to go. So I get up and turn on my iPod. Loud. "Under Pressure." A poignant and perfect choice. I rip the sheets from the bed and throw them into the laundry basket, pausing to stare at the empty mattress—a prophetic blank slate. I'm on my own now.

Part of my deployment ritual is to remove all his daily things. It's easier for me. I compartmentalize his crap, and I compartmentalize my emotions. It's my coping style, and we each have our own. If I had to look at that tube of deodorant for fifteen months, pick it up to dust under it, wipe it down for fifteen months, I would surely lose my mind. No. My way is better. Fresh.

That ugly chair. I want all of this done before the kids return, so I drag it out to the garage. It does not come willingly; it fights me the whole way. It slams one of my toes, bringing a new round of tears and fury to my face. The chair does not want to go, but I won't let it stop me. Eventually it ends in the garage, pissed at me and defeated, but satisfied at having the last word by leaving a huge gouge in the new hardwood floors. That will be my one constant reminder of this day for the next fifteen months.

Reason number 67 that deployments don't suck: I won't have to endure the torture of effing *American Idol* or *Fox News* or any kind of f-ing loud sports show, like the UFC, which he loves to watch at deafening volumes.

Jack is a list man. I am too, to an extent. But he takes it to an extreme and makes matrices of what belongs in pantries, daily chores for the kids, packing lists, shopping lists, SOPs for everything under the sun. It exhausts me. The lists and spreadsheets neatly taped inside all of the cabinet doors and on the wall make me feel claustrophobic. I whisk from room to room and tear them down. They rip, they leave tape behind, it's messy. I don't give a shit for now. I will go back and remove the remaining edges of paper and tape later. This is my ritual, and I catch myself cackling as I wad the lists and shove them into the trash. I don't think too hard about the cackling; it's way too early in the ball game for the cheese to slide off my cracker. This part feels good. A rebirth. Euphoric sense of getting the fuck on with it, at last.

I miss my girlfriends and neighbors. In the week or so leading up to a deployment, we disappear from our seat at the playground, an unspoken rule of army wives. Allowing us to cocoon in our families and trudge through those last days alone with our husband and children. I heard them outside a couple nights ago, gathered around a fire pit in Mira's driveway next door. I heard Gwen Bautista's and Mira's raucous laughs and wished I could run over for just a quick glass of wine and the familiarity of my friends. As I lay in bed listening to the hushed voices and laughter, I wondered what I was missing.

No one will call today, though, and if they do I won't answer. Gwen waved to me from her driveway as I pulled into the neighborhood sobbing. I need this time to breathe and get my game face on. Right now I feel covered in bruises. But this is it. Day 1. Tomorrow I will see colors again. What hung before us for the entire past year, heckling us, is here at last.

I splash some water on my face and go to pick Greta up from her preschool class. It's early, but I miss her. This morning, Jack wasn't able to take her into her classroom as we had planned. We parked the car, and he got out to unbuckle her from her car seat, stopped, then looked at me with eyes full of tears and his lip quivering and shook his head. On autopilot, I took her from him and carried her away, checked her in, hung her little backpack filled with diapers and a change of clothes. Greta seemed to take it in stride, but for weeks after he leaves, she will cry and throw a tantrum, refusing to go beyond the parking lot at preschool drop-off. I want to go get her now; maybe we can snuggle and watch *Caillou* before the bus brings the big kids home. And I need a stiff drink. I can have that after I pick her up. Life in the army fishbowl, similar to life in the real world, makes us hyperaware of certain faux pas, and smelling of booze at a 3:00 preschool pickup clearly makes that list. Getting behind the wheel of a car after even one drink is unfathomable in our world. Schlepping to the commissary in pink pajama pants would practically make the news. Even on the day of deployment. In our fishbowl, we maintain at least an outward appearance of strength, control, and resilience; the ugly, snotty breakdowns are for behind closed doors.

Tomorrow I will place a huge catalog order with Hanna Andersson for the kids and a few tasty things for myself from J. Crew. Ease into our first days. Then before bed tonight we will at last hear the huge plane full of battle-ready soldiers fly over. Ben will call to confirm "wheels up," and that will be it. The finality that he is gone will be undeniable.

Tomorrow is day 454. Then I will stop counting. Tomorrow brings meetings and our new normal, establishing a battle rhythm. Tomorrow I can't hide and lick my wounds. But tonight I can.

non-combat-related casualty

Late September 2007. Reminders flow from my lips and my keyboard:
"Take time to adjust to our new battle rhythm. Fifteen months
is a long time. I can't hold my breath for fifteen months. Two
back-to-schools, two Halloweens, two changes of autumn colors."

◆

So let us not talk falsely now,
The hour's getting late.

—BOB DYLAN

THERE IS NOTHING more tedious than being held hostage during a presentation where the presenter reads slides to the audience, verbatim. If I doodle at just the right time on the PowerPoint printouts as they're read to me from the Proxima screen that takes up the entire rear altar of the chapel, it might look like I am intently taking notes. Instead I work intently to perfect a curlicue, or maybe it's a pumpkin. Halloween is right around the corner, and my pumpkins need practice. They look an awful lot like apples.

I find the timing of this half-day presentation on the organization called TAPS (Tragedy Assistance Program for Survivors) to be poignant and almost laughable in a sick way. The first month of the fifteen-month deployment isn't even under our belts, and every time I turn around, I'm being reminded to prepare for casualties. Not even my own husband's death, but any of the men under him, or any of the thirty-five hundred in our brigade. Somehow Jack's safety is barely on my radar anymore, eclipsed by the well-being of the men under him. As I doodle on my handouts, I can't help but look around at my five sister battalion commanders' wives and wonder who will be first. In a way the first KIA will be a sick trophy. *Trophy* is the wrong word. It becomes just another form of one-upping, comparing our tragic burdens against each other. We spent so much time preparing for this inevitability that it begins to feel like some sort of twisted contest. *Who will be first to pull out the casualty SOP manual and put into practice what we've spent a year preparing for?*

A heart-tugging video begins on the portable movie screen, and I stop doodling. Snapshots of folded flags, grief-stricken widows dressed in black, and children pulled close to their mothers passed on the screen. I will never be prepared for this, and I wish there was a way I could quietly escape. I don't need this reminder so early in the game. Thus we've officially arrived at one of many moments when I zone out and start imagining the most wildly inappropriate things that could happen. Maybe the chaplain could lift his leg and fart with a loud grunt. Maybe Regina Sweeney could spontaneously scream the word *fellatio!* at the top of her lungs. Anything to not see the women around me quietly passing the box of tissues.

Then I hear it, a name I recognize. Major General Mark Graham and his wife, Carol? No, it can't be the same family I remember from twenty-five years ago. A clear picture of the young couple from my childhood comes to mind. They lived downstairs in our building in Germany in the early 1980s, when my dad was stationed in Baumholder. I was twelve when Carol let me cut her bangs. She looked like an escapee from a concentration camp for weeks, but she didn't care. Their son was a toddler and I loved babysitting for him, though I didn't particularly enjoy babysitting at all. But I loved little Jeffrey. He had skinny, quick little legs and a belly that pooched over the top of his diaper. He was never not smiling or laughing. I played his parents' Linda Ronstadt record album, and we danced and danced around their apartment. The only time he sat still was when I read to him. Then he sat on my lap, leaned into me as I read, and didn't move a muscle. I was shocked at how vivid and sharp my memory was of Jeffrey, when neither he nor his family had crossed my mind for years.

I start paying attention and my stomach tightens and churns. Jeffrey had grown into a lieutenant, and as they flash pictures of him on the screen, I still recognize his wide, radiant smile. It covers his whole face, just like when he was a toddler. I feel sick, anticipating the direction this video is beginning to take.

Jeffrey had a younger brother who was a premed ROTC cadet, and the Grahams also had an even younger daughter, Melanie. As I watch the video, I learn that Jeffrey's brother, who wasn't yet born when I knew them, committed suicide as a cadet, still a college student. He'd stopped taking an antidepressant because Kevin worried the army system would perceive him as weak and pull his scholarship if they learned of it, and he was correct in his belief. Kevin convinced himself privately that he could "suck it up" and cope without the antidepressant. And then he was gone. Half a year later, Jeffrey was killed by an IED in Iraq. Within seven months, the Grahams were again down to an only child.

For the most part, tuning out the seminars and classes about coping skills comes easily to me. So much of it sounds like the same discourse after sitting through hours and weeks and months of lectures and training.

This moment is singularly different.

I glance down at the pumpkins I've doodled just minutes earlier and gather my things to leave the chapel in the middle of the presentation. I'm not sure where I'm going to go, but I feel hit right in the gut. I drive straight home without the stereo blaring my daily soundtrack of death metal. I'm halfway home before I notice I haven't turned music on.

General Graham is the commander of a division at Fort Carson in Colorado Springs, and without thinking it through, I look up his office number online and dial his secretary. I'm not sure what to say. This is not a well-thought-out plan. I'm only sure that I need to reach out to them. I wonder if they will even remember me after so many years. I can't get the picture of Jeffrey's wide smile and his little pooch out of my memory. We didn't even call him Jeffrey then, only used his nickname: Weed. Because he grew like a little weed.

"Umm, hi, this is going to sound unusual, but I am an old friend of the Grahams'. I just heard them mentioned in a TAPS presentation. My name is Angie Hawkins. My husband is an infantry battalion commander in Iraq now at 10th Mountain. But I used to babysit for Jeffrey when he was just learning to walk. My maiden name is McCormick."

"Please hold, ma'am. I will try to put you through."

I don't wait longer than two minutes when General Graham picks up. He remembers me immediately, and I fight the urge to cry at the memory of Jeffrey and the sheer coincidence of finding their family after all these years. I imagine Mark Graham sitting at his big desk and probably looking at photos of his boys on his desk. Gone. Both taken by the war, in their own way. One by combat, and the other in a non-combat-related casualty. The word *suicide* has a terrible stigma, especially in our warrior culture, and when a death isn't explained to us, we know. We just know. If anyone could break down the stigma of suicide, it is definitely Carol Graham.

Mark Graham gives me his home number and asks me to call his wife, Carol, says she'll be thrilled to hear from me. In the moment before I dial her number, I'm struck by what a lasting and shaping impression she left on me without even realizing it until this moment. When Carol answers, we both lapse into tears two sentences into the conversation. I'm not an easy crier, but I remember Carol so fondly and with incredible clarity. Carol was passionate and soulful, a free and kindred spirit who infinitely enthralled me with her brilliance and bravery to color outside the lines in a sea of young officers' wives who colored only inside them. She was what I wanted to be when I grew up. Back then, she talked to me for hours about thirteen-year-old girl stuff, like the big sister I never had. She didn't follow all the rules, but she followed the important ones and was smart enough to know the difference, and that taught me not to be afraid to march to the beat of my own drum. Within five minutes of our conversation, I realize she is just as amiable, generous, uninhibited, and emotionally raw as I remember her. We talk for hours that afternoon.

Suicide, KIAs, mental wellness, stress of deployment. My mind reels. I have an SOP manual for all of those things except suicide.

After I hang up, I walk around my house thinking about suicide and how it happens, the circumstances that drive someone to that point. Do warning signals pop up like in an after-school special? Is it a buildup of the downward spiral, or is it sometimes just one moment of desperation? Perhaps it's closer to each of us than we are willing to acknowledge. Maybe everyone is just one horrible, hopeless day away from being there. Maybe it's a perfect storm, the combination of that feeling with readily available means. A full prescription of lethal pills or a loaded gun in a drawer. I close my eyes and try to imagine how it happens, the decision to end your own life. Sometimes suicide isn't a long-thought-out event, but is just a really shitty day with an escape route. Maybe that's why I never want to lean over the edge of bridges. I am unconsciously worried the inner awful of my day might push me to the edge.

A week later, I will be forced again to contemplate what drives someone to end their own life.

Ben calls me with a "red message" on September 21, 2007. We're still in our first of fifteen months. I remember the call. He reports in his deeper-than-usual business-like voice, "Hey, red message. Non-combat-related casualty. Brigade surgeon. All notifications are made; family has requested no contact from anyone in the unit."

"The brigade surgeon? The new one, the new female you and Jack talked about? What happened?" I ask the question as I replay memories of Jack coming home last month and telling me how Petty had belittled her in front of the whole command group.

"She shot herself." Ben pauses before continuing. "Yes, her. The one Petty treated like shit since she was assigned to the unit in July. She was spinning before she left. Message says non-combat-related casualty, so keep the suicide part close hold. I'm sure there's an investigation." Our brigade surgeon, a vivacious female captain and Smith College–educated doctor, loses her beautiful future and her life to what the army calls a *non-combat-related casualty* within a month of her deployment to Iraq. Captain Roselle Hoffmaster was one of Colonel Petty's preferred targets of bullying, which the entire unit was well aware of, but helpless to change.

Roselle was a newlywed, had just bought her first house. She contracted into the army as a means of paying her way through medical school. I doubt she ever saw herself presiding for fifteen months as the lead surgeon over a hard-core infantry brigade at the tail end of the Iraq surge. The worst of the worst. I remember Jack telling me that she was struggling with little details like rank structure, and Petty rode her hard. His way of inspiring was to bully and berate. Jack told me he thought she would be okay, that she seemed to be toughening up. That he thought she would rise to the challenge and learn not to let Petty get to her.

In June of that year, our previous brigade surgeon, who was married with two children, approached Petty and professed that he was bisexual and thus nondeployable. "Don't Ask, Don't Tell" had yet to be repealed, and homosexuality was still a one-way ticket out of a deployment. At the commander's discretion. Roselle was his eleventh-hour replacement; she'd been in the army a handful of months.

And so Roselle entered a perfect storm with her assignment to our brigade. She was lost and overwhelmed, but new and learning. But by all accounts, she seemed positive and motivated, adjusting to the challenge. Committed to the mission and working on her "war face." The last thing she probably expected was that her biggest adversary would be her boss, not the typical enemies of war.

Jack told me later about Roselle's last day. He'd sat in a meeting with her in Iraq. Like many times before, Colonel Petty yelled at her and humiliated her personally. She left the meeting embarrassed and in tears. Within two hours of the meeting, Roselle went into her bunk area and shot herself with a military-issued sidearm. A pistol. She didn't leave a note. To this day, her parents are still unable to face the idea that their daughter took her own life. They've told themselves she was fumbling with her gun and it went off.

Everyone who was there knows it was self-inflicted.

Jack boarded a helicopter immediately after the meeting and flew back to his Forward Operating Base. When his helicopter landed a few hours later, he was met with a communication blackout order. He knew this meant there had been a casualty. His first reaction was that one of his own men had been killed in action. He made his way into his command center and was immediately briefed: "Captain Roselle Hoffmaster, NKIA. No further details." Noncombat killed in action.

In the many times I've thought of Roselle since, I can't help but close my eyes and put myself in her shoes on that last day. She had more than fourteen months ahead. Not to mention the austere chaos of a war zone, the blistering heat and smell of grit and desert, with the constant sounds created by helicopters and distant explosions. No solace in war. She wasn't trained yet to tune those things out. That was her backdrop for the remaining fourteen months. And like us on the other side of the ocean, she was braced for the casualties that we knew were coming any day. While we on this side were braced to deal with the emotional carnage of war, she would be the one faced day after day with blown-up bodies. The direct carnage. It wasn't if, but when. The devastating irony was that Roselle would be the first of those casualties.

Beyond those things, she had to endure this man every day, Petty, her boss. Instead of taking time to mentor her, he took each opportunity to publicly humiliate her in rooms full of our nation's toughest leaders and warriors. And all she ever wanted to do was be a family practitioner. I'm sure she wondered, *How in the hell did I end up here? What am I doing, and how will I make it through?* No immediately available support system, no one to turn to. She didn't have the girlfriends waiting outside with a glass of wine.

Though she'd confided many times to her husband and family about Petty's bullying, Roselle didn't want to burden her husband or family with her deepening distress. She probably faced each day thinking to herself, *One day at a time.* The night before she died, she left her husband an unremarkable, positive-sounding voicemail. She said that things were going fine and asked him to send routing numbers so she could set up an ATM account at the FOB (Forward Operating Base). She told her husband she would talk to him soon.

Sometimes there are escalating warning signals of a possible suicide. Roselle was not one of those cases. Roselle reached the end of a horrible day in a war zone, with over a year of the same, possibly worse days ahead. She lay in her bunk, felt a moment of hopelessness that coincided with a means. Her means was the pistol at her side. And in an instant, she was gone. No note, no good-byes.

Captain Hoffmaster's death was very hush-hush in our brigade, but we knew what happened. Roselle's widower stayed, or was kept, far from the wives. Instead of being relieved of command, Petty continued his toxic form of leadership for another fourteen months in Iraq. Jack had been Petty's second-favorite target, and with Roselle's death, Jack was promoted to the top spot.

The investigation into Roselle's death was completed in 2009, and Petty was indirectly implicated in contributing to her suicide, yet continued to serve. According to the whispers in our community, Petty was eventually asked to retire quietly in 2011. I wonder if he thinks about Roselle; I wonder if he imagines phoning her family. Making some kind of peace. He sent her parents a form letter after her death. No one else from the unit reached out to her family in the years since Roselle's death.

I also think of Roselle's mother. She'd raised a doctor, what a proud accomplishment for a mother. Her daughter was swept away by the army and not killed in combat, but killed by a toxic system.

If the mother hates the army, I can't say that I blame her. Even if she tells herself that it was an accident, somewhere deep down she must understand to some extent. And she probably can't bear to face how lost and terrified her daughter must have felt. In her shoes with one of my own children, I might have an identical reaction.

None of these details beyond Ben's brief red-message email are available to me until much later. In the following weeks, my intuition tells me that something is wrong by the tone of Jack's emails and the tense sound of his voice in our infrequent and short phone calls. Never do I think his tension is caused by his chain of command. We don't have a scenario in a binder for how to handle that. We are prepared for mission and casualty stress, not toxic-leadership stress.

I'm busy trying to establish the new normal with the other wives and with my children. It's easy for me to ignore the tone of Jack's voice. My calendar is full of meetings, coffees, trainings, welcomes, farewells, mixers. Constant events designed to keep us wives busy and engaged. Plenty to keep us distracted. There isn't a moment to sit idle and ponder what lies ahead.

The fall leaves turn, and I can't absorb a painful truth. Even as next year's leaves turn orange, yellow, and red again, Jack will not yet be home. And Roselle Hoffmaster will never come home.

my definition of loyalty

October 2007. Let's see if you've really got my six, if I can finally let my guard down. Let's see if you can be trusted.

DONNA HOOKER'S FAMILY is moving to Australia next week! Shit! The JEANNIE ball is buried in my closet. When we moved to the new house, I had to be sneaky to move it without Jack seeing and questioning. The Hooker family lives off post in Sackets Harbor, thirty minutes from me.

Ben, my battle buddy with the empathetic brown eyes, and I are getting along and figuring out our dance. For my kids, adjusting to deployment is a seamless and familiar transition. The real breaking-in period is for the new rear command team of Captain Ben Black and me. Still learning each other's facial expressions and voice intonations. Trying to establish where we fall with each other and who is in charge. A delicate dynamic; Jack is his boss, but what is Ben to me? I assign the REM song "The End of the World as We Know It" as his ringtone. Ben teases me and says that he can hear the theme song of *Desperate Housewives* play in his head as he rounds the cul-de-sac to my house, and he revels in using my term *perfumed turds*. I appreciate that he drops the formalities. There's nothing worse than being ma'am'd in the middle of a crisis. He confides to me that the wives are afraid of me, the first time anyone has been so honest with me. Maybe Jack has said something similar over the years, but statements from spouses are somehow easily dismissed.

Ben can do a spot-on impression of Jack, and I admire his gutsiness for having a feel for me so early on—a sense that I will appreciate his impression without even being remotely offended. The other members of the rear detachment crew, men who look at me out of the corner of their eyes—and I see this as a test of my solidarity with them—encourage and even goad Ben into doing it for me. They gather around in anticipation of the shenanigans, and I can tell by their expressions that this impression has been done often, and highly perfected. Ben leaves the room, throws open the door, and strides past us with speed and impatience, never looking up from his BlackBerry. "*What up!*" I hear as he passes me. I almost pee my pants. Someone else who gets my husband the way I do. Yes, I made the right choice in this guy.

A test of solidarity presents itself in that bowling ball. He lives within spitting distance of the Hookers.

I take the ball to Ben and lay out his mission. The ball needs to be waiting for Donna in the morning when she opens the door. He gets it. Ben delivers the ball.

From that day forward, I never question his loyalty. He is stuck with me; he can't divorce me or run from me. I and the other wives *are* his mission. A year from that fall, he will again stand next to me, squeeze my arm, and say the words, "I've got your back. My loyalty is with you."

porch pukers and the arrival
of the inevitable

November 2007. All the preparedness goes right out the window,
and no PowerPoint slide can prepare me for this part.

A WEEK BEFORE THANKSGIVING, we have three months under
our belts. Just a year to go. I am driving home from picking up
Greta from preschool when my phone rings. It's a Tuesday afternoon;
pizza night was a couple hours away. We live for pizza night at the
Commons. It is still our measure of time.

I hear the ringtone. Ben.

"Hey." His voice is serious. I can tell this is not a usual call to report
something humorous or absurd, or to vent. Ben is learning an awful lot
about women, and reminds me as often as possible that he will likely
stay single forever, and he has me to thank for that. But this is not one
of those calls. "Are you driving? I need you to pull over if you are."

My blood runs cold. If it was Jack, surely he wouldn't tell me on
the *phone.*

"I'm pulled over." Which is a lie.

"We had two KIAs today. Two enlisted guys in my old company,
Charlie Troop. Their vehicle hit an IED. Both killed outright."

"Oh Jesus. Were they married? Did they have children? Who
was it?"

191

"Only one was married, but his wife is in Texas. From what I can tell, they got married right before the deployment." I breathe a small sigh; there will be no grieving widow here, no schedule of weeks full of delivered meals.

There's a message from Jack on my answering machine. I'm relieved to have dodged that call. Waiting for me later will be a long email holding the details that I don't want to read. Our phone conversations end one of two ways: Either the ten-minute allotted morale call runs out and we lose our phone connection abruptly midsentence, or else we have so much to say that there's nothing at all to say. In those cases, after we endure an uncomfortable silence, Jack asks, "Anything else?" Which is army speak for, *This conversation has ended.*

When there's a casualty in our battalion, we hold a private meeting for other wives in the unit after next-of-kin notification is complete. We schedule meal deliveries for the family of the fallen soldier; we rally our troops. Always at the end of the official part of the meeting, as the commander's wife, I say a few words to the stricken wives. This is my first of those speeches, and somehow I don't feel prepared, though I have played out this moment dozens of times in my mind. I gather the women close to me in the corner of the chapel and remind them that our husbands are making history, that we are part of history. Our job is to take care of one another, and in helping each other, we help ourselves. I remind them that our legacy is the grace and strength we show on days like today. I remind them that we have an appreciation for freedom and life that will follow us forever, that never, ever before has there been a generation who has endured as much combat over such a long period. These words I sometimes force myself to say, picturing myself pouring overflowing glasses of Kool-Aid, but each time the speech rolls out of my mouth, I find myself believing it. Even if the dazed wives are lost in thought and not even listening, it resonates *with me*. I forget the petty competitions and my urges to smear dog shit on neighbors' blankets. I forget the one-upping. I feel our buoyancy and our bonds with one another. Our sisterhood and shared experience that no one outside of our world truly understands.

I avoid patriotic sound bites as much as I can—none of that "We are spreading freedom and keeping America safe" crap. I'm not good at insincerity, and I stick to what I can look the other women in the eyes and say truthfully. This is our legacy, like our mothers during Vietnam and our grandmothers during World War II. And I always end the speeches the same way: "Let's put our big-girl panties on and drive on with another day tomorrow."

Am I just slinging more of the army rhetoric with those pep talks? No. I mean and feel every word. Many other commanders' wives don't say a word at those meetings, but my responsibility is to rally my troops, and I'm good in those moments. I'm not insincere; I don't read from a scripted speech. Those are the moments I see colors the most vividly. Other times, colors mix together into shades of gray, but not now. Even through the harrowing swell of loss, I'm grateful to be in my shoes. There's a tangible beauty in that period—a beauty that will never leave me. In those moments, I wonder how or if, we, the wives, would be written into the history of this war. If anyone cared about the vivid colors I once saw.

a rewritten memory
and saving of face

My perception of the war is secondhand. I glimpse snippets,
and what lies between the snippets I fill in with
my own imagination. Like a movie.

THERE ARE LOTS of words in our army culture that we whisper or don't say at all. *Suicide* is next to impossible for us to say without flinching. A less impactful but still cringe-worthy term is *accidental discharge*, which means the accidental firing of a weapon. Usually when cleaning the weapon or loading or unloading it. Accidental discharges often result in punishment and always complete embarrassment. And to be the wife of the perpetrator of the accidental discharge adds an extra depth beyond regular humiliation. It means that your husband isn't adept at how to handle his weapon. And anyone who has ever seen *Full Metal Jacket* knows the fundamental intimacy between an infantryman and his weapon.

Ironically, our very first accidental discharge is one of our battalion's most senior leaders, the husband and chummy counterpart to witchy Liesel Leonard, whom I am still harboring resentment at for being a no-show at the wrenching chapel KIA briefing. As he nears the end of his career, this is his first deployment. Somehow that's possible in our world. Inconceivable, but possible.

The second accidental discharge isn't quite so straightforward. When the wife is beloved and valued, nothing negative or humiliating that falls on her soldier's lap is simple.

One of our platoon sergeants, Nate Shaw, is a kinetic ball of energy. His vibe screamed PTSD to me before the deployment, but Shaw is revered by his men. Jack and I are keen on the art of maximizing our team members' strengths and minimizing weaknesses. Clearly Jack is more astute at this talent than me, but I still try. Nate's wife, Anna, is humble, unflappable, and hardworking, never a wince of hesitation. She is Canadian, which kind of says everything you need to gain a good picture of her and what a solid person she is. Anna is her husband's greatest asset, which was not an atypical occurrence with army couples. It's shocking how often the wife is the stronger of the two. Scary, really.

A week after the two IED casualties, Sergent First Class Shaw shoots himself through the calf and returns to Fort Drum to recover. Humiliated and disgraced. Within a week, he winds up in the psych ward, claiming to be traumatized and haunted by seeing Colonel Hawkins "kill a haji with his bare hands." Ben retells Nate's horrific story to me, minus the gory details that I later fill in with my own imagination, and I am left feeling both mortified and also a little in awe. This is the piece of the puzzle that I still can't quite comprehend. Is reality as graphic and bloody and barbaric and intimate as I imagine it? Or is what happens over there more removed and calculated? I don't know, and I've rarely asked. I don't want a true picture, but I do. The imagined brutality is somehow the sexier scenario, and I realize how twisted that sounds. I almost need the brutality to justify my own grisly emotions and desperate sacrifice.

Beyond that, it occurs to me how little I really know of Jack's daily life over there. Does he hang out of low-flying helicopters doing badass tricks in the middle of the night, like in movies? Or does he spend most of his days sweating in his heavy gear through long, tedious operational meetings? I suppose I need to ask this at some point, but I don't know which of those two possibilities I would like for an answer. Somehow I think it's a little bit of both, with not much in between.

The day after Thanksgiving, before Nate shot himself through his calf and ended up in a psych ward, Jack emailed me a few photographs that I in turn disseminated to the wives. The pictures seemed cool, but innocuous enough. One photo was Jack and a few of his men, Nate included, all geared up with weapons in hand. The caption Jack sent was, "On an objective."

I thought it might rouse a bit of Thanksgiving pride in our families, so I forwarded the pictures to our troop-level leaders and asked them to blast them out to the families. Done and forgotten.

Now, just a couple weeks later, I listen to Ben retell Nate's interpretation.

"Nate is disgusted that you forwarded those pictures. I really wish you would have asked me before you blasted those out. So now he can't touch his daughters because he thinks he sees blood on his hands. He was fucked up before he ever went back. Your husband knew it. We all knew it."

Jack reveals nothing of Nate's too-vivid story, and I don't bring it up. But it keeps me awake at night and I wonder. Who am I married to? Do I love this possibility or loathe it? Or do I hover somewhere between the two extremes?

tip of the spear

The families in our battalion understand the dangers of IEDs. We grasp the concept of the stress of our husbands conducting combat patrols with the vivid possibility of disappearing in the flash of a second. We understand defensive stress, not offensive. A new ball game for everyone. And a year to go.

JUST BEFORE CHRISTMAS, our battalion is hand-selected for a new mission. Our soldiers move from routine combat patrols in a specific area in Iraq with a high likelihood of striking IEDs to a solely lethal "kill-capture" mission under the umbrella of special operations.

Suddenly, our conventional reconnaissance battalion has become an elite 750-soldier air assault special operations task force conducting missions blanketing the northern half of Iraq. We do not see this coming, and I didn't know it was even possible. But I am certain if anyone can lead such an intense mission, it's Jack. His laser focus, relentless disposition, and inability to ever acquiesce to the horribleness in any situation are qualities that have built him precisely for this moment. But am I built for it?

Special operations forces consist of all volunteers who sign up for additional intense training and a selection process, all hard-charging thrill seekers. None of whom are "stop-lossed" soldiers, soldiers who would choose to leave the army, but are forced to continue because of the war. Conventional reconnaissance and infantry soldiers go through basic and advanced training, but not all have completed ranger or special forces training.

The wives are usually not much different from their husbands. They mirror, in most cases, the attitudes and experience of their husbands.

Within three months of arrival in Iraq, Jack's battalion is suddenly selected for this humbling and daunting elite special operations mission under the command and control of Stanley McChrystal. The new assignment completely isolates and separates the battalion, now renamed Task Force GHOST, from its parent brigade, something for which both my husband's soldiers and our families are unfamiliar. This new mission brings about a total paradigm shift; we no longer have access to information about where our husbands are or what they do. No more little articles in the local paper that show our guys conducting combat patrols or handing out school supplies to poor Iraqi kids.

Because this mission falls under special operations, it will be completely covert. The media will not cover it in any way. My husband and his men love every minute of it; this is his gritty and dirty dream come true. Jack is at the tip of the spear, and that's enough for me. I don't need a silly picture of him shaking the hands of village leaders in the newspaper. But our wives do. They don't understand. Over the years, our families have grown accustomed to seeing their soldiers on the news and in print. Having tangible evidence that they are appreciated and respected makes the bitter pill of sacrifice somehow a little less bitter. With this new mission, we give up the ability to cut out newspaper articles for a scrapbook. But we gain something that is hard for me to put into words for many of our confused wives.

Ben has become my closest ally and the safe place for me to dump my pent-up frustrations at the other wives and my husband. For lack of a solid battle buddy in Liesel or Audrey-Jill, Ben becomes my battle buddy. Almost like the bratty little brother I never had. To this day, Ben and I remain very close. The bond between battle buddies can never be underestimated or forgotten, no matter how much time elapses. There is an unavoidable intimacy in the challenges we faced together. Ben and his cadre have two other roles as rear detachment: They train newly deploying soldiers and babysit the "naughty boys," the soldiers who are too ill-disciplined or too broken to head back to combat. Along with his handful of other very capable, experienced soldiers, Ben is in charge of corralling the dozens of AWOL soldiers left behind. His itchiness is palpable and my sense that he would prefer to be in The Fight is inescapable. He reminds me at every opportunity that combat has nothing on us bitches back here. I suspect that Jack had a very different repertoire with Kate O'Malley when he was rear detachment commander. The same kinship, but a different way of relating. Ben and I relate through mutual whining and consoling.

I learn of the new mission from Ben. When I stop by the office to make copies of a roster, he asks to speak to me privately. After he reads and explains the official email detailing the new mission to me, he leans back in his chair and pauses for a second. Then he says with a scowl and flaring nostrils, "This is hard to admit because I can't change where I am, but this is the coolest goddamn mission ever. It's so badass. And I'm here." Ben flares his nostrils when he is stressed or angry, and Jack clenches his jaw. It hasn't taken me long to learn to read Ben's little signals, although there is nothing vague about his words today. For a second, I remember that he's here because I asked for him, and I feel guilty again. I want to tell him that he's holding me together and that I need him more than Iraq, but that would sound ridiculous.

Ben can't run from me, no matter how much shit I dump in his lap. Even though he has a long-term girlfriend, Ben is still single and I forget that he might be completely overwhelmed by the constant lady drama. This is a fresh hell for him. Yes, combat might come more naturally and even easier.

Battalion commanders' wives are considered senior spouses, but sit at the bottom of the pecking order of senior spouses. Above me are brigade commanders' wives (like Barb Petty), senior staff's wives, and generals' wives (Linda Stewart). As a battalion commander's wife, I'm still in the trenches with the families under Jack's command of over 750 men. After his battalion command and in future senior leader positions, my role will become that of an advisor (mega perfumed turd), no longer directly mentoring younger wives at the battalion level. This is the last chance for both Jack and me to be in the trenches, and ultimately it's where we thrive. Even if I feel exhausted before it's even started.

My job is to equip the confused families for yet another new normal that comes with the new mission. As I've said, I'm not good at following scripts, and this mission has some seriously rigid scripts for the families to learn and live. We wives can no longer communicate daily with email and phone calls, and we are never allowed a clue about specific details of Task Force GHOST's missions. We are no longer a part of our brigade and division effort, our chain of information stopped.

I, too, am tired before it's even started. My kids' diets consist of stuff I buy from the Schwan man and McDonald's. They surely feel my restlessness. We all fall asleep in our own beds, but each of them gravitates to my bed by morning. We huddle together. None of them are aware of the sleepy march that brought them to my bed. Sometimes, but not often enough, I wonder about the long-term scars and other effects this will leave on them. This is what my kids will remember of their childhoods: a father back and forth to war and a mother too exhausted from supporting others to hold up her own babies.

The transition to the new mission is supposed to be a secret, but I'm not stupid. Nothing is a secret.

Jack immediately favors and feels confident with his new bosses, Lieutenant General McChrystal and another colonel who is a lifer in the world of special operations, both of whom have a cult-like allegiance from their men. Yet Jack continues to fall under the rating scheme and performance reviews of Colonel Petty, who continues to target Jack and his men with bullying behavior. Something that seems like such an innocuous detail paints an entirely different vibe of stress. Jack still has Petty to battle, a situation that takes a toll far worse on him than the enemy ever could.

The new mission is a tremendous readjustment for all of us, yet we are humbled and proud beyond measure to be at the tip of the spear. We are no longer waiting for action; our soldiers go looking for The Fight. The weight of it shrouds the faces of our wives and my own reflection in the mirror.

Something that comes along with the new mission is the addition of a company of around 150 soldiers from Eeyore's husband's battalion, which is now part of our task force. Eeyore is not pleased to lose their Alpha Company and pouts at a Christmas social. I make sure to express my humble pride loud enough for her to hear. The placement of a perfect perfumed-turd passive-aggressive zinger is equal to the flush of an orgasm. It is sublime.

We follow strict guidelines about the dissemination of information, and protocol about which units "belong" to us. Referring to our manuals of protocol is supposed to remove the element of personal judgment and feelings. *Hey, I'm only following the guidelines; it's not personal.* Further complicating this is the wife of the Alpha Company commander, Nicole Messer. This sneaky young wife of a captain plays Eeyore and me against each other, and it doesn't take long for Eeyore and me to figure this out. Luckily this aspect of Nicole's personality gives Eeyore and me common ground. We are united against Nicole. Nicole proves to be a bratty beast who challenges me at every opportunity. Ben calls Nicole the Rhino, because she pushes her complaints and games at us like a rhinoceros.

So at this Christmas dinner, Eeyore refuses to acknowledge the mission change. Instead of talking about it or anything else vitally important, she corners me away from my table—and from where I even could grab a cocktail—and delivers an emphatic yet boring-as-hell story where she was again the victim of some perceived injustice. The tale is loaded with irritating, irrelevant, and dull details. Most of all I am pissed to be trapped without my cocktail. I'm not listening, and she doesn't even care enough to notice that her audience has left the building, is there in body only. I do have a new piece of Juicy Fruit in my mouth, and it is stale by the time Regina takes a breath.

Between making sure that about-to-pop-with-pregnancy Audrey-Jill doesn't throw herself in front of a snowplow and monitoring philandering wives' antics online, I just don't have time for Eeyore's bullshit. I don't have time for anyone's bullshit. I think of those easy conversations with wicked smart Elizabeth, when I had it all figured out and thought this would be easy. The Gods of Flippant Women were surely watching over me and preparing my delightful reality check.

Ben and I talk over the misadventures and plights of our families on the phone nearly every night, and I am grateful that his presence anchors me. Beyond helping me work through complexities with the wives, he reassures me that no, he hasn't noticed the fifteen pounds I've gained. *The stress is not making my ass look big.* The merciless job of being my anchor takes a yet-unseen toll. Ben's job is more than just the Sid to my Nancy, though I often forget.

treadmills, snow, and escape

With no end in sight, I can't do this for another year.
Something has to change. I can't control any of my chaos,
but I can control the size of my ass.

◆

Years go by and I'm here still waiting,
Withering where some snowman was.

—TORI AMOS

JANUARY HAS ALWAYS been my favorite month. No one expects much of January, and there's an excuse to hibernate and retreat. I love the isolation and retreat that are easily offered excuses from routine activities. In particular, January 2008 is an extremely cold and snowy month. Which says a lot considering January in the North Country is nothing short of arctic in a typical year.

I lose track of the other days of the week in that month, but I remember with accuracy that the kids do not have a single Wednesday of school in January and into the first weeks of February too. Either we're snowed in, or the temperatures don't rise above negative twenty and the school buses are deemed inoperable.

Wednesdays are meeting days. Steering committees, community leader pontificating sessions, family issues tracker meetings, blah-blah. I relish the legitimate excuse to hole up in our house and immerse myself in watching *Caillou* and *Napoleon Dynamite* with the kids. Our full schedules weigh on us; both the battalion families and my family are overscheduled. We need respite from the carnival of activities we've created to keep everyone moving forward and not allow them to dwell and stew and perseverate about the fact that we still have three seasons to go. Spring is months off. Then summer and another fall and possibly another snowfall before the men return. We don't want anyone thinking too hard about that. Busy is better. I crave the tiny reprieve from my hamster wheel, though.

Deep into winter, my neighbor and partner in crime, Mira, asks me if I want to train to run the Army Ten-Miler race in Washington, D.C., in October. She assumes I'll immediately say "no way," as I'm not a runner. Unless it's to be first in line for dessert or a cocktail. This is January 2008, and I am the heaviest and most out of shape I have ever been. Nothing fits. Stress makes some people gaunt; it makes me fat. I accept Mira's offer, and it catches her off guard. No more pints of Ben & Jerry's go to bed with me each night—pints that I force myself to finish because I don't feel like trudging downstairs to put them away. Gradually learning to run gives me a focus beyond my marriage, which has been ignored by the weight of both of our roles. Running is loathsome, but I won't let it beat me, in the way that so many other things in life are beating me. No one runs outside with the snow, and the gym is just another venue for perfumed turds to pontificate. But in the gym, I keep my eyes down and focus. The treadmill is my salvation from chaos. No small talk. No minutia. I need one turd-free zone, even if I have to be rudely antisocial.

It's easy to throw in my headphones and lose myself in the maximum volume allowed by my iPod.

Anyone perfect must be lying, anything easy has its cost.
Anyone plain can be lovely, anyone loved can be lost.

NOW EVEN THE men from Bare Naked Ladies seem to be singing to
me. Something about this point in my life feels strangely as if so many
of my favorite songs are directed right at me. Speaking to me. Telling
me to do something, but what? Run. That must be it. Because it's all I
can control right now and for the foreseeable future.

Running on the treadmill floods my mind with memories. The
memories that are like the guest room in our house. *The room we do
not speak of*, is what I call it. It is full of piles of shit that don't fit neatly
elsewhere in the house. I stuff it into the guest room and keep the door
closed. Out of sight, out of mind. Heaven forbid I have a visitor and
have to deal with that room.

The dead of winter offers a fabulous excuse for why I won't run
outdoors. I can't pace myself on the road; I sprint and get winded. On
the treadmill, I can set the pace and stop thinking about what's around
the corner and let my guard down.

I lose almost thirty pounds by the time the race arrives ten months
later. Although I eat far less, I still pop the cork on many wine bottles, sometimes alone and sometimes with the perfumed turds. It feels
good to not be alone in this, although, in private, we each fight our
own demons.

Running for the first time in years, I can't help but think about
Sackets Harbor and the winter and spring Jack spent in Somalia in
1993. Feeling myself pant for breath took me back there, back to
teaching those cheesy aerobics classes in the old barracks gym right
on the old Madison Barracks. When I look out the window from my

treadmill, my eyes fall on a heavy blanket of thick snow, just like in Sackets. Only these buildings on post are new, nothing like Sackets with its towering barracks from over a hundred years ago. The buildings that saw everything and refused to give up to time and storms. The snow only made the buildings look that much stronger and sturdier. As if they were rundown and weary, yet deeply unaffected by the winter's fist. Stubborn and determined. I wonder if some of that rubbed off on me over the years.

The winter Jack was gone to Somalia, the snow was so deep and the temperatures so low that I only left the house for a few reasons. To walk to the mailbox hoping for letters from Jack, which would come about every two weeks and would arrive in a rubber band of ten to fifteen letters at a time. Just like in some old Lifetime movie. A stack of letters covered with grime and smears from his life in Somalia, carried through the perfect white snow on the other side of the globe to our frigid little apartment. The letters held together with a simple rubber band. I always saved the rubber bands, even though I knew the mailroom dude on this end put them on and it wasn't like they had real sentimental value. Just sentimental by association. But I kept them just the same. Maybe I went a little bonkers with all the solitude of that winter.

Every day, I bundled up to walk our dog Justice, a Bouvier des Flandres, around the polo field and to dump my little bag of daily trash in the dumpster by the tennis courts. These were the pre-UGG days in the North Country, so what boots did I wear? I can't even remember. Justice loved the snow, the deeper the better. Some days we were brave enough to trust the ice-covered bay and skid around the edges, right behind the abandoned buildings. I worked a few days a week teaching aerobics in one of the rundown buildings that had been converted into a gritty and very barren gym. I always walked to work; the gym was just across the polo field, on the water.

The little family-run grocery store was right next to the mailroom, so I rarely had reason to dig out my peppy black sports car from under the pile of snow left by the morning plow. Sackets Harbor has a booming downtown scene now; back then, I think one restaurant stayed open all winter, the Harbor Master. A couple fledgling boutiques, but that was it. I rarely went downtown anyway. Everything I needed was right there in the old barracks. A sleepy and introspective period in my life, but I loved walking around the barracks and getting lost in my imagination of what it must have looked like just two or six generations earlier. Those buildings had eyes, personalities. I was barely twenty-two years old and felt like I'd been dumped in *The Shining* on some days, but it was our first home as a couple and full of defining memories. I couldn't wait to start my life with Jack; in those days, I didn't go ahead and start without him like I do now. In those days, deployment lengths weren't predetermined (though they were shorter), so wives and families were held in perpetual limbo. The soldiers could be home next week, or next summer. We just had to wait it out, surrender control. Whenever I look at pictures of the old barracks, I can't help but go right back to that time in my mind, and how something as simple as a place stayed with me and sustained me for so long—long after we left Sackets in our rearview mirror.

a cathartic levy break

*"Do you have any concept of how many women have
threatened to kill me just in six months? Three. One said
she would bash my head in with a snow shovel. These bitches
have nothing on Al Qaeda. I don't want this job anymore."*

—CAPTAIN BEN BLACK

AUDREY-JILL'S BABY IS on the way, and I spend an entire day at
her hospital bedside. In the twelve hours I sit by her bed, Audrey-
Jill's face of pleasant composure only slips when she asks me why I
think Stan hasn't called yet. Are they on a mission? I don't believe they
are, but I tell her that they're probably out of the net. He would call if
he could. My mind is distracted; today is the worst day for me to spend
here, but Audrey-Jill would do it for me or any of the other women
in the unit. The idea of her lying alone is out of the question. The
memorial service for the two soldiers we lost is tomorrow. We just lost
seven additional soldiers last week, and someone has to drive through
a blizzard to pick up Audrey-Jill's parents, who are as Southern and
unaccustomed to our unforgiving winter as their daughter.

I ask Ben to pick up Audrey-Jill's parents from the airport a hundred miles away. Ben argues that this is an abuse of power; I tell him
to make it happen. I'm sure he must be just venting. Then he bellows
a chain of four-letter words into the phone, and I hold it out from my

ear to stare at it. Surely he's not talking to me like that. Surely someone walked into his office and a sad little private is the receiver of the
furious rant.

"Are you talking to me? Ben?"

Click. The line goes dead.

I will have to sort that nonsense out later. My job now is to get
ahold of Jack through emergency channels, a Red Cross message, and
beg him to force Audrey-Jill's distracted husband to call. And, from
the hospital halls, to orchestrate the last-minute details of the memorial service. And to plan a mini spa day for the wives this weekend.
Oh, and I think it's one of my children's birthdays. That's somehow
the least of my concerns. Thank God for the neighbors who took her
bowling. Maybe she doesn't notice that Mommy isn't there. *It's just
her third birthday; she won't remember and torture me with guilt for
years to come. I hope.*

Ben cleans out his desk, prepares for the phone to ring from Iraq,
relieving him of his agonizing duty of guarding the flock. He confesses
to screaming at me and offers his resignation. The last thing he expects
is an apology from me. I do apologize, though, because he doesn't
deserve to be treated like my whipping boy; that job is already taken
by my absent husband. Ben has taken a gross amount of my shit in the
past few months and I probably deserve what he dished out. I'm sure it
felt incredible to yell at me. In many ways, Ben can't quit me, though.
He can't run, which is something I've taken advantage of. So I'm safe
with him, free to be myself. This is a luxury that none of us feel with
our own husbands. Our guard is held up with vigilance. Keeping our
distance is our survival. Ben is stuck with me. In all his mighty, zesty
infantry-ness, he is for this time stuck here with me and our posse of
wives. Ben, Jack, and I have formed a bizarre triangle of teams and

information dissemination. Jack shares certain tidbits of data with me in phone calls and emails, but sometimes says, "This is just between us. Close hold." Does that mean close hold from Ben, too? Isn't he in the inner circle? And other times Ben says, "Let's not burden your husband with this; we've got it covered. I don't want him to think we can't handle the piddly shit." I suck at secrets, and I lose track of who doesn't want what to be told to whom. And yeah, it has all come to a head today. That tirade was well earned by Captain Ben Black.

index cards

"The media gives Americans a number to count casualties.
Not a name or a face, but a number. To us, the loss is deeply personal."

—EULOGY FOR OUR 10TH MOUNTAIN SOLDIER

EMPTY DESERT COMBAT boots and poster-sized pictures line the front of the chapel. None of the faces are familiar to me, but they were Jack's soldiers. I listen to a general give eulogies; he didn't know them either. But he strikes a beautiful chord with his words. "So few of our men serve these days. To the rest of the nation, it's hard for them to feel the war personally. Their lives go on untouched by its constant presence. But for us it's different. For us it's deeply personal."

The mothers and widows of the soldiers are here. One of the widows is showing an obscene amount of cleavage, which I hope is accidental, and at a reception earlier in the day, I overhear her lament that her soldier escort hasn't hit on her yet, and doesn't he know how hot she is—is he blind? It's like a topic for *The Jerry Springer Show*: "New widows offended when not hit on at their husband's funeral." But instead of judging her, I try to tell myself that she's out of her mind with grief.

One of the mothers grabs my hand during the ceremony. I made index cards this morning with each soldier's name and his parents' names, hoping they might believe that I knew their son, or at least not

ask directly if I did. They don't quite understand who I am or how I fit
into the picture, what my role is. "No," I explain, "I'm not the chaplain's wife. I'm the commander's wife."

"But I thought that was the other lady, her over there."

"Well, she is, too. Her husband is the brigade commander. It's just
a different level." Why am I trying to explain this, here and now? And
whose mother is she? I'd really like to pull those cards out of my purse
and refresh my memory, but I can't do it with her clutching my hand
and whispering to me. I made sure that Ben had someone put dozens
of boxes of tissues in all of the pews. Controlling the things I can control. One of the younger wives in the battalion, the Rhino (who is one
of the wives attached to us from the other battalion, of course, so I
tolerate it even less for this reason), tries to boss Ben around in front
of other soldiers, and he whispers to me to put her in her place or he
will do so. His recent meltdown broke the barrier, and Ben is embold-
ened; he earned his bragging rights by chewing my ass. He's afraid he
will go off on the Rhino if he even has to open his mouth to talk to
her at all, so I do his nasty bidding. She leaves in tears. Angry that the
Kleenex boxes weren't positioned to her liking and that she didn't get
a personal introduction to the grieving mothers. She arrived late and
couldn't jockey for prime seating in the chapel. We are a hotbed of
displaced anger and neurosis. Every one of us.

After the grueling remembrance ceremony, I break down in the
restroom when the enormity of responsibility on Jack's shoulders hits
me. I feel like shit for being so angry at him. This is when I finally face
something I've carried but ignored in the back of my mind: We are
fighting a futile war. How many of us feel responsible for each death?
Does this mother even know that I never heard her son's name until
after he was killed? Was he there that day I said good-bye to Jack?

Carrie Barnes is there; my kids call her Aunt Fannie, the woman who has been like my big sister. She held my hand when I fell apart during Somalia. With two young children of her own at home, Carrie nurtured me. Now I hear her knock on the bathroom door. "Ang? Are you okay?"

Where is my Xanax? I left it at home. Last week the doctor graciously gave me exactly ten when I begged at a routine physical, explaining to him the extra heavy upcoming week. Two are gone already. I need its numbness now, but I've left it at home in the medicine chest. Didn't want it in my purse, mocking me and making me feel like a sad character from *Valley of the Dolls*. I wipe my tears with toilet paper and tell Carrie I'm okay, I'll be out in a sec, the eulogy just caught me off guard, gimme a sec, Aunt Fannie.

How has the impact of this on Jack slipped past me? He seems so impervious to the pain and loss, focused on the mission and able to compartmentalize it. I thought I was good at that, too. The moment of giving in to the tugging and ever-present emotions takes me over, there in the restroom. I can't bear the thought of Jack feeling what I feel now—but so far away and in a world I can't even fathom.

Looking back, my shift was in that exact moment there in the bathroom stall. The one that turned my gradually darkening soul pitch black. With Mira and our friends, we later give this phenomenon an official name. The black soul. We've learned from our years as army wives that giving something a name somehow makes it more palpable.

THERE'S A NEW program in the division that's intended to be helpful, but is in reality just creepy. Civilian counselors and therapists, most with zero experience and knowledge about our lives, now lurk in the corners waiting for one of us to flip out. Of course one counselor is present in the next stall when I break down and sob at a volume that frightens even me. *No, don't you dare hug me, lady. For reasons beyond the fact that you didn't wash your hands. My soul just turned black two minutes ago, but how could I tell you that?*

Over cocktails later that night, Mira and I theorize that the counselors are secretly keeping statistics so that long after the war, they can tell the rest of the world how fucked up and disturbed we were. A covert social experiment sponsored by the government? It sure feels that way. Maybe I should have tried to explain our black-soul phenomenon to that loitering counselor.

before i became steeled

Obsessing over every single day, smelling his shirts, not leaving the house for fear of missing the one phone call that comes every six weeks. Ain't nobody got time for that shit anymore.

SOMALIA ROLLED AROUND on a regular Monday afternoon in December 1992. In my journal that night, I spelled it "Simalia." That's how unfamiliar I was with it. Jack barely missed the first Gulf War, and anyway, I didn't know him then.

After a briefing on Tuesday night for the families, complete with maps and tentative details of where they would be and what they would be doing, I puked in a trash can right in the entryway of the battalion. Less than a mile from where I would watch another woman retch fourteen years later as we waited to hear who was aboard that Chinook that we knew belonged to us. I puked because I didn't want Jack to die, because we had no idea of the duration of the deployment, and because I was so in love with him. I watched the clock every afternoon back then, waiting for his boots to clomp through the door of the little apartment we'd shared for just a few weeks. I barely even knew him, but I knew it was right. The things I loved about him were the things that were so very different from me.

It often struck me as funny in an ironic way as the years wore on and the leathery bitter dug into the fabric of who I was. With each deployment, I became more stoic, more removed. Less concerned with his safety and more concerned with carrying on with the details and caring for the growing number of families under his command. I quit holding my breath through each deployment and just picked up and carried on. But each one took a piece of me. Each one made me a little harder. I stopped crying in movies and started weeping out of the blue in the shower or the commissary parking lot.

Before I'd heard the word "Somalia" fall from his mouth, our wedding was less than two weeks away. In two weeks and one day, we were supposed to be in the Bahamas. Instead he would be in a balmy climate of a different kind; I would be in our empty apartment in Sackets Harbor, slugging NyQuil and hanging on Christiane Amanpour's every word reporting live from Moga-dee-shooo. Back then I left his things out—his shaving cream sat in the prime spot on our already-tiny bathroom sink for over six months. I went through the first few deployments like that, pining.

Back then I felt my worry. I wore it on my face. I lay in snow banks and sobbed without giving a rat's ass who was looking. I didn't know then that I would eventually develop a callus from the dizzying merry-go-round of deployments. The cliché is pathetic but valid: A heart can only break so many times before it becomes unbreakable. It took mine awhile, though. It was maybe the summer of 2006 when I checked out. No more sobbing over what lay beyond my scope of control. Just wasted tears. Eventually I would figure that out. But it would take a handful of deployments to steel me.

My wedding was planned and replanned four times, my eternally optimistic self believing the promises that he would be home soon. Each time, I sent out invitations again, licked the stamps, and copied three hundred addresses to guests. Even though we got hitched quickly by his unit chaplain the night before he deployed, I still wanted the wedding. The fact that we were already married was a minor detail as far as my bride-obsessed brain was concerned. Eloping before a deployment for practical purposes is an unfortunate and unromantic reality for many army couples. But it doesn't stop an eventual fairy tale wedding. Somalia won't stop mine, either.

Each of those four times the wedding was rescheduled, I took one pound of hamburger meat out of my freezer to make Jack's favorite homecoming meal, one of three things I knew how to make at age twenty-two, and each of those four times, I refroze the meat when his boots didn't make it through our tiny front door. When I eventually made the grotesque casserole, the meat was rancid. I was too blinded by the glee of his impending arrival to notice. And he ate the entire pound without even stopping to take a drink of water. He had lost twenty pounds in Somalia. I wanted him to finish eating so I could jump his bones again. *There is no sex as good as post-deployment sex.* He spent the next three days in the bathroom, or sharting himself at work. He had to "take a knee" in a formation of soldiers, the kiss of humiliation for a hard-core infantryman.

It's still his favorite dish, though. War and rancid meat.

eighteen days of polite face

An admission of horror, a closely guarded secret,
and the last kind of vacation I would expect him to want.

IN EARLY JUNE 2008, Jack comes home for his eighteen-day R&R.
My anxiety leading up to this visit is overwhelming. Joe and Bridget
have little interest in going to the airport to pick him up, and both
insist they would rather stay with a babysitter than drive an hour and
a half to the airport, but I force them into the minivan anyway and we
head to the airport. Greta doesn't quite understand what I'm trying to
explain when I tell her we are going to pick Daddy up. Ten months is a
long time for a child. Jack has grown as intangible to us as a ghost who
pesters us in the night but who is forgotten during the bright light of
day. I've spent the last ten months playing mother to everyone but my
own children. I procrastinate dealing with them. Even on the rare occasion that I read a Junie B. Jones book at bedtime, my mind is anywhere
but in the moment. My mind is on the battalion. On the games I play
with the perfumed turds. On the little nugget of information I forgot to
pass along to Ben at our family update meeting today. My mind is also
on Jack and how to handle him when he gets home.

We wait for his plane to land, and I realize I am a shmuck for not
making big WELCOME HOME posters for us to hold. I am too worn out
to even consider making a poster. Finally we see him walk down the

long corridor from the plane, and my lip trembles as I hear that cadence of his boots on the hollow floors. He hugs me and whispers, "I love you so much, Ang." He smells like the mistress, but now he's home. Maybe eighteen days is enough time to mend things and find some calm.

Joe, who is now ten, is stoic and seems uneasy on the drive home, but gradually warms up. Bridget, barely eight years old, cries from the time she sees him until we get into the car; she is the most outwardly emotional and tenderhearted of the three. Greta, at the age of three, won't even make eye contact with him, which tells me she remembers him. She's angry that he's been gone. How that must feel for Jack. I've become so engrossed in surviving myself that it's moments like this that I am reminded of how lost and off-kilter he must feel to be treated like an interloper in the first moments back with his children.

We walk in the door to the house, and I see his eyes scan the living room for his missing recliner. But he doesn't say anything. He doesn't need to. Our marriage is still a mess of tension. We never fully recovered from the meltdown that started two years earlier after the second Afghanistan deployment, both of us not just haunted by the horrors of the past ten months apart, but too weary to share what we've each endured. We are guarded around each other, not so much because we want to be steady for the other, but because we don't trust the other with the hell we've been through.

He is frustrated that I haven't held the children to his standards of a daily physical workout and an hour of daily reading, and I resent him for having the nerve to judge me. If we are alive at the end of this, I consider it a success. Ben allows me to let it all hang out; Jack demands more.

When Jack's home, he's a more involved and physically present parent than me, but I'm a more emotionally aware and connected parent—except for this deployment. This one leaves the kids pretty much without either of us. Jack doesn't see the nuance separating the two parenting styles. So we spend those eighteen days walking on eggshells and pretending things between us are anything but shallow.

sleeping in the company of skunks

The last thing I would expect, he wants to camp on the river
for four of those sacred eighteen days. No shit. He camps in
the Iraq desert for over a year, has eighteen days to sleep
in an air-conditioned house, and suggests a camping trip.

B EFORE HE GETS home, Jack sends a spreadsheet with the details
of the camping trip and reassures me that I only have to show
up. He will do all the work. Camping, even glamping, is not my gig.
Camping is for homeless people. What I'd really like to do is send him
camping alone with the kids and take a break, but that's out of the
question. The rumor mill would explode with assumptions about my
marriage if we even think of spending one day of precious R&R apart.
In our circle, and even to each other, Jack and I pretend that we are
resilient. Still the perfect army command team. Our smiles hide the
screams. So off we go, on a lovely fucking camping trip. Hooray.

Reluctantly, I agree to the camping trip, and we arrive at the gorgeous campsite on a cliff overlooking the St. Lawrence on Wellesley
Island. He sets up the tent with the speed and finesse of someone who
has been at war for ten months. Each of us has one mildew-scented
sleeping bag, no pillows, one hand towel, and one tin cup. Water from
that rusty pump thing to drink. To eat, there is one loaf of Wonder
bread, a jar of something called Goober Grape (peanut butter already

mixed with jelly, both extraordinarily lazy and extraordinarily genius),
one package of hot dogs, and a bag of marshmallows (those were my
contribution). Oh, and two boxes of bland protein bars that my kids
wouldn't touch even if they were in a refugee camp. On the way over
the bridge to the island, there was a neon sign flickering the word
LIQUOR. I'm headed back that way to stock up, then all will be right
with the rest of this.

The kids fall asleep, bellies full of preservatives. Jack has built a
divine fire, and I drink wine straight from the bottle (the tin cup makes
it taste weird) and Jack sips his rusty water. For the first time in almost
a year, I am comfortable with his presence. His personal presence, his
phone presence, his email presence, even his invisible presence.

"Something bad happened," he says. "Things are bad with Petty.
It happened—something that was just an accident—and he's using
it to screw me. To mess with my mind, like he did Hoffmaster, Ang.
He's got it out for me, and I don't know why. The soldiers in our task
force are pissed because Petty doesn't recognize any of our accomplishments and I make excuses for him to my men instead of siding
with them against Petty, but what am I supposed to do? If I side with
my men—the soldiers who think Petty is a bastard—we will lose the
sense that we are still a part of the brigade team, even though our
special operations chain of command has been awesome to us and
supports us all the way. All Petty cares about is that my men don't
wear ball caps and 'pretend' to be special forces. Can you believe
how stupid that sounds? I have to do the right thing, though, and
be diplomatic."

Jack continues staring into the fire. "Petty went nuts when
Hoffmaster killed herself," he says. "His paranoia has made him unfit
to lead, and I thought my men and I would be safe away from him in

special operations. I can't believe he wasn't relieved of his command. How did the Hoffmaster tragedy just disappear? The way he treated her, I can't fathom how she must have felt. The special operations standards dictated that we request special clearance to include Petty and his command sergeant major in our missions, and that really pissed him off. He acts like I withhold shit on purpose. On top of that, Petty's commander tried to cancel our tasking to special operations entirely and clearly wants to see us fail. Neither of them even acknowledges us except negatively, let alone bother to visit us. I've been told by Special Operations Command to disregard this tension, but he's still technically my boss. I'm just a pawn in a shit sandwich. Petty is a psycho. And then that incident."

His foot is tapping faster than I can see. A signal that his anxiety level is piqued. *My noncussing husband used cusswords twice.* I have no idea what he's referring to with all this. He opens his mouth ready to elaborate on what he keeps alluding to, and then I feel something wispy brush my leg at the top of my calf.

"A wild beast just touched me! Jack! Motherfucker!"

"Ang, your mouth has gotten terrible since I've been gone," he hisses at me, forgetting he just used a rare curse word only seconds before.

A huge spotlight, ready at his side, beams at the perimeter of where we sit. Nothing. Okay, Jesus. Maybe I imagined it. *Back to your story. You cussed. It must be serious.*

Again, not only the pokey fur brushes me, but the bump of a body.

"It's here again! Jack, do something!"

"Relax, Ang," he whispers and shines the light again. I see the red asshole of the biggest skunk I've ever seen, the asshole leering at me. Tail raises, and shiny Pepé Le Pew fur glistens under the beam of the spotlight. I freeze a scream.

"*Move to the right! Move to the right! Move—mooove!*" Jack's booming but controlled, commanding voice jars me almost as much as the skunk's ass, which is mere inches away.

Which way is right? Jack shoves me into the dirt, off the uneven stump from where I'm perched, right on the edge of his confession and two-thirds through my bottle of gross merlot. Now I'm under siege, part of a weird Black Ops offensive on Wellesley Island. Not Al Qaeda, but a humongous skunk waddles into the distance. The creature is as scared by the flash-to-bang military outburst as I am. The skunk wants no part of the madness or the impending confession and scurries into the darkness, with Jack hot on its trail. Somehow the skunk deems us unworthy of its toxic spray and we are spared.

The next morning, the vibe of dark harmony is gone and the shrill voices of our kids who beg for a fishing expedition replace the silent anticipation where a confession nearly fell last night. Jack must have been moments from describing to me the incident that sent Nate Shaw to the psych ward. Six months later, and Shaw is still too broken to return to combat. Maybe I can work it into conversation, casually.

"I think Anna Shaw wants to resign as the Alpha Troop FRG leader. Which will suck because she is one of our greatest assets and her coleader was Mallory Bond, and anyway, we asked Mallory to step down after the Starbucks drama." I trail off for a second. Oh shit. Jack is still mad over the Starbucks drama, and this is not a good time to bring it up. So I quickly change the subject back to Anna. "Mallory's a hot mess, but Anna is the best of all the FRG leaders, and I need to keep her in place at least until the end of the deployment. She's the glue in that group. Jesus, Jack. Aren't you curious about Nate, about how he's coping?"

"Coping with what? That he had an accident and shot himself through the leg because he wasn't paying attention?"

Not his shot-up leg. His shot-up conscience. I can't believe Jack has the nerve to discuss this in such a cavalier way, as he slaps the PBJ paste between pieces of crumbly bread. As if he's checking off a block on one of his inane lists. I hear my voice raise as I remind him that Shaw is traumatized and half in the bag every day.

"Why?" he says. "He's just embarrassed that he looked bad in front of his men for shooting himself in the leg." He chuckles with a polite disinterest that would fit small talk about a missed homework assignment. *The kids will never eat those sandwiches with the crust not cut off, but he wouldn't know that.*

"Because he saw you break a haji's neck, or strangle him, or whatever! One of those bad guys you killed on Thanksgiving! Because you couldn't use a firearm! Because the room was too small and a firearm blast would have blown everyone's eardrums! Because the haji was going to kill another soldier! He told Ben every grisly detail! I get that it's your job and you had no choice, but *fuck*, Jack! How can you be so removed? Shaw is haunted! He says his hands are covered in blood and he can't touch his little girls because of the images of blood!"

After examining my face for a couple short seconds, Jack cracks into laughter.

"How in the hell can you be laughing?" I ask.

"Wow, I did that? First I've heard of that! Ang, listen, his soldiers lost respect for him, and I guess he needed to save face back in the rear. That wild story is made up to cover his humiliation. We killed those enemy with a hellfire missile. They were crawling in the brush attempting to ambush one of our checkpoints. We tracked them for hours with our intel. There was nothing left of them to strangle."

There was no intimacy in those deaths. It existed in others, but not that one.

Please, God, let there be cell service out here in the boondocks. I race to the foul public restroom and hit #2, speed dial for my BFF. Ben. His boss did not twist someone's head off or participate in whatever grotesque mental image, imagined or real, I was left with after my conversation with Ben months ago. I'm not so sure he believes me.

After I hang up with Ben, a thought occurs to me. That's not what Jack was trying to tell me last night.

"cover your panties
on the flagpole"

*Jack wasn't the only one holding a secret in those eighteen days.
I have my own secret.*

I AM SICK WITH worry that Jack will catch a whiff and overreact to
what I've already handled and put to bed. Will jump to the worst
conclusion instead of seeing the nuance of the situation and the bigger
picture of the Belinda Becks of our life. Belinda hides behind a helpful
facade and her binders full of a plan for any situation, from where to
store her seasonal wreaths to how to color-code a roster of volunteers.
Well beyond my antics of coveting bowling balls. Her attack was well
aimed and personal. Clawing, knife-twisting. And when confronted,
she met the challenger with mock confusion and complete denial.

I hold my breath during the month leading up to Jack's eighteen-
day R&R. Anticipating fallout from the rumor mill and relieved at
Barb Petty's support and her suggestion that neither Jack nor her husband (the psycho bully) needs even know what happened. But still.
Word travels fast. I've reveled in a juicy piece of gossip like this too
many times to count, but I've never been the topic.

The weekend of Mother's Day, a month before Jack's R&R, I join
two minivans loaded with other perfumed turds heading to dinner
and a comedy club in our small harbor town. It is the same place I

lived during the months that I waited for Jack to return from Somalia fifteen years ago. The other wives and I falsely tell ourselves that it is safe to get wild and crazy here, that no one knows who we are. Mira and I slug down too many appletinis, a disregard for pacing our drinks, each of us caught up in the excitement of being somewhere besides hidden in our homes with a cocktail in hand. Spring is here and it has been a long, hard winter. We get drunk quickly, each of us sharing war stories of our week, exaggeration fueled by booze. All of us are either just ending our husband's R&R or bracing ourselves for its nearing impact. Mira is dying to hear the details about how Ben and I fired uncouth and brazen Mallory Bond earlier that week. But Mallory had to go. Ben hated her, and I wasn't her biggest fan. The girl never learned her place in the food chain. She was guilty of blatant indiscretions, both with her genitalia and with her flapping lips. No pun intended. Rear detachment has devoted weeks to catching Mallory Bond in action. She was rumored to be engaging in not just an affair, but the bigger offense of violating the tight-lipped policy of operational security by yapping about our battalion's über-secret mission, at Starbucks. She did not go easily; it has been a long week of damage control for our team, and I need to vent and guzzle those sick, too-apple-y drinks.

"Angie, isn't your rear D single?" a perfumed turd from another brigade asks. "He's cute. You guys seem to get along really well. I hope my husband lets me have a rear D just like that when we deploy next year." It doesn't dawn on me that these women think my rear D is cute, and it feels like these older women are asking to take my younger brother on a date. Weird. I take a hot second to place in my mind where the woman asking the question lives. Yeah, between Eeyore Sweeney and Belinda Beck. Dreadful.

We cut the night short when Mira hurls in the bushes. During the drive home, we debate whether this qualifies her for the porch-pukers' club. The appletini overindulgence leaves me in a fog the next morning, but my responsibilities to the unit don't care about my night of escape or the hangover headache clenching my brain when my phone rings at seven o'clock on Mother's Day morning.

It's Ben's REM ringtone. News that one of our lieutenants lost his leg that morning and a sergeant will have a disfigured face for the rest of his life, if he survives.

Two days after the puked appletinis, Belinda "Kiss My Grits!" "Flo" Beck, who has a reputation for vicious gossip and playing superb politics, spreads a rumor that Fort Drum is "buzzing with talk about Angie Hawkins canoodling with Captain Ben Black." Within two hours on a Tuesday morning, two mutual friends who both live out of state call to tell me that Belinda is spreading the story like the plague. Of course, her story is told under the false pretense of worry that I've lost my judgment under the immense pressure of Jack's command, and *what can we do to help poor Angie?* All of this because we didn't invite her out for our night of shenanigans. Inviting her never even entered my mind. Can that woman even have fun?

For years I've had Belinda's number and I've known that her motives were never pure, but I also knew she offered a contribution to the team. Is it better to be a barely contributing slug like Regina Sweeney or Liesel Leonard, or be a hard-bitten, backhanded Belinda Beck type? Belinda works her ass off to be the best at everything. She is the first to volunteer to help a comrade, the first to shovel snow from a sick neighbor's driveway, but she does it all for the credit and brags about her good deeds at every available opportunity. She is what we call a *spotlight ranger wife*. Her sole goal in life is to claw her way to the top of the turds, fooling herself into thinking that no one sees through her facade of perfection. *Those who try the hardest generally have the most to hide and the most reasons for trying.* All of this I've overlooked in the years I've known her, mainly because I feel sorry that she tries so hard. Until now I've felt nothing but a sympathetic pity for Belinda. This bullshit is a game changer.

If Jack gets a whiff of the rumor, he will lose his mind. Since day one, he warned me against rumors and the importance of safeguarding our images, keeping a professional distance in my relationship with Ben. Or as Jack refers to him, *Captain Black.* "Your reputation is all you have."

Ben is more than my rear detachment commander; that much is true. He's become like a girlfriend, or maybe a little brother. Jack wouldn't understand that the nature of our relationship has nothing to do with canoodling or a romance. It's survival. Our closeness is a product of what we endure together. He makes me laugh, he makes me feel safe. He gets me and can put me in my place. Isn't that the goal? To work well together? How could we not be tight? It pisses me off that Jack would expect me to work so closely in support of his mission with someone, to navigate our ugly waters and not be close to the person he left back here to be my partner. Jack doesn't expose himself to anyone, not even me. He is autonomous, and my nature is diametrically different. I have a fundamental motivation to be understood—a motivation Jack lacks. I still am unclear about what his fundamental motivation is, exactly.

After I as nonchalantly as possible tell Ben of the rumor the day after Mother's Day, it takes me days to talk him off the ledge. He knows Jack and his reactions nearly as well as I do. He shouts into the phone, "This is my career! Don't you assholes have anything better to do than gossip about each other and make shit up? One of our soldiers lost his eyesight this weekend, and another his legs. And *this* is what she's talking about?"

Barb Petty calls Belinda and chews her a new asshole; I love Barb, despite the fact that her husband is a raging wacko. *Barb always has my six. I got your back.*

That night I call Belinda for the fifth time, and she finally answers.

"Hay-lloooo, Beck quarters. Beliinnda speaking." She drips with molasses, her words sound sugary, but trail off with a subtle bitterness. *Kiss my grits.*

"This is Angie. How are you?" We exchange a few back-and-forth pleasantries. I want her to sweat a little.

"Belinda, you've told people I'm canoodling, whatever that means, with my rear detachment commander"—*don't say his name, don't establish intimacy*—"Don't even deny it. Why would you do that?"— *I know why, duh*—"We have a history. Jack and I have known you and Larry for years. Belinda, you have a terrible reputation. But guess what? I always stick up for you, try to convince people that you are well-intentioned and that your heart is in the right place." My heart is racing and my blood is pounding in my head, the head that has barely recovered from yesterday's appletini hangover.

She's been stammering and interrupting since I started my speech. Now I let her speak. "Angie Hawkins! I have done no such thing! Where on earth did you ever hear that? I am too busy with my own battalion and planning a bridal shower to worry about you and your silly nights of shenanigans."

Is she really denying it? Okay. Let's go to the mats.

"I heard it from Paige Evans. And Gwen Bautista. And Lindsey Grundy."

A gasp. One that I will never forget. It screams of Flo from *Alice*. "Why would thaaaay tellll youuu thaaaaaat?" Feigned indignation. I almost laugh. That weird character flaw of mine again.

Now I'm screaming, not giving a shit that my windows are wide open. She is busted, and her gasp is the closest I will come to a full confession.

"Because they know you for who you are. And they know me for who I am. You are a back-stabbing, opportunistic, marinated-in-jealousy, white-trash, social-climbing bitch!" *Thank you. No, I didn't preplan that insult. It came naturally and it begged for a grand genuflect at the end. I stood in my dark kitchen with the phone in my hand and bowed deeply, so proud of my perfect put-down. My inner mean girl is off her leash.*

"I will not be verbally abused by youuuu, Angie Hawkins. This is not over! You better watch yerself, missy! The higher Jack climbs the flagpole, and Larry is gonna climb higher for sure"—never a missed opportunity to one-up—"you better know that more people can see your panties!"

And the phone slams down, maybe both of us at the same time, neither of us with the firm sureness of who hung up on whom first.

Am I overreacting a bit? Displacing outrage? Not this time. Despite our earlier small insults and eye rolls at each other's words, behavior, and postures, we have been sisters. I feel punched by Belinda. Punched by her blatant kick when I am down and vulnerable, weakened and stressed by the deployments and our casualties. That night, I learn two lessons: One, discerning between friends and frenemies is a critical skill, and recognizing the fluidity of everyone between those two extremes is even more critical. Two, Jack never needs to know a word of this. He will think Ben and I have given an air of unprofessionalism, and we probably have with our level of comfort and the familiar way we speak in public. We bicker. We finish each other's sentences by now. He is my brother. Of everyone in this equation, Ben is the least deserving of the potential fallout from such a rumor. Hasn't he taken enough shit already?

Belinda? Karma caught up to her. A year after our fallout, her husband had a full chickenshit meltdown in Afghanistan. Larry Beck locked himself buck naked in his hooch; those outside heard him alternate between singing dirty cadences and sobbing. Larry is a severe alcoholic and porn addict and had never made it through an entire deployment. Alcohol withdrawal always got the better of him. The rumor mill swirls with whispers that Naked Larry was lured out of his tent by MPs, and in front of his troops, the general in charge relieved Larry of command, the army's version of *you're fired!* He was handcuffed and carried off in a helicopter and eventually back to the States and finally a psychiatric evaluation in Walter Reed Army Medical Center.

Normally I would hesitate to believe rumors so seemingly far-fetched, but somehow I could picture the exact scenario the rumors painted.

For months after Larry got home, we worried that Larry or Belinda's mental state might lead to more drastic outcomes. To this day, Larry still serves on active duty as an army colonel. He's even a graduate of the elite war college, through some tiny glitch in the system that left his peer group, and me, baffled. Somehow he escaped the media attention that others weren't so lucky to avoid.

stuffed french toast and
what i can never forget

Fish and visitors get old in three days; it's time to giddy on up.

THE EIGHTEEN DAYS of leave creep by slowly. I hear other wives lament that leave goes too quickly, but I'm tired of holding my breath with his body in my house. Not ready to exhale until this deployment ends. Arguments brew that neither of us is willing to indulge in, things about the kids and where they park their bikes at night. I banned his recliner to the garage ten months ago, the day he left, and a dozen times a day, he hints at missing it.

R&R is only a tease. A dangling carrot that I won't reach for because it's going to be jerked away.

He's heading back to Iraq in two days. Five months to go, no time at all in the big picture. With ten months under our belts, this will pass in a blink. I get a babysitter, and Jack takes me to brunch at Tin Pan Galley, our favorite little family-owned restaurant in Sackets Harbor. Everything monumental seems to happen in Sackets.

At some point during the meal, I can tell Jack is trying to say something. He clears his throat and begins: "I started to tell you something while we were camping, and hey, it's not even that big a deal. But I want to tell you." I can't even quite recall his timing of this statement, before we ordered or after our food was in front of us. But I remember his right foot tapping again.

As he begins to retell what happened, I can imagine dimwitted and floundering-for-power Petty screaming at him over the radio, trying to posture himself over Jack even though Jack's operations don't fall under his command.

Does Jack hope the nonchalance of our brunch setting might ease the horror of the story he tells me? We've never spoken of it since that morning. I've never brought it up to my friends, the ones whose husbands in all likelihood have faced similar tragic situations.

Jack, a man who loves family and children as much as or more than most, is responsible for ordering the bombing of a building in a remote village in the middle of the night in the spring of 2008, killing a handful of civilians: two women and three young children. The insurgents who hid alongside the innocents were also killed in the bombing. The Iraqi civilians hid in a building, refusing to come out, and were eventually assumed by Jack and his men to be a large group of male insurgent targets. Over several hours, Jack followed strict protocol (rules of engagement protocol) and an escalation of force in an attempt to persuade the people to surrender, but they didn't.

I wonder how those mothers felt in those few hours, if they felt sick with terror and prayed for the foreign-speaking men with interpreters over loudspeakers, guns, hovering helicopters, smoke bombs, and blinding lights to eventually give up and leave if the Iraqis hid silently enough. What did they tell their children in those hours? Had this happened before to them, or was it just another day in the hell of Iraq?

Eventually Jack made the call to bomb the building. Within a few minutes, the building burned to rubble, and once the objective was cleared, Jack and his men discovered that among the insurgents were also women and children. The three children were close in ages to our own. For just a second after he finishes speaking, all of a sudden my soul doesn't feel black, my numbness is lifted. The horror, anger, sadness, grief, and disbelief punch me right in the gut. Who can I blame this on? Not Jack. Not the women and children. Then who?

How many other people who were connected to the chain of events that night are also haunted? How many commanders up and down the echelons approved the bombing of that building? Do they each bear a heavy feeling of responsibility like Jack?

The other senior wives and I suffer the possible bloodshed of our own husbands and their men, but also bear the weight from the *causing* of bloodshed. Civilian bloodshed. The guilt from being married to the man who leads a soldier to his death is as heavy on us as the senior leader himself. The leaders themselves, like Jack, aren't left with the task of dealing with angry and confused wives, the grieving and stunned mothers, and, worst of all, the crushed fathers who lean against walls because they've lost the ability to stand straight.

I feel horribly responsible not only each time my husband loses a soldier in combat, but also for the civilian casualties, the innocent women and children lost just by virtue of their living in a war-torn country. The civilian casualties are never mentioned in my circle, but surely are thought of in private. These are the thoughts we don't share with each other, the burdens and pain that are our own. The Iraqi and Afghan mothers whose front doors are kicked in by our husbands and the terror those women must have felt and still feel to this day.

And then an instant later, the black-soul phenomenon returns and rescues me from my warring emotions and rage and gives way to pure exhaustion and depletion. Too numb to feel anything except weariness.

the treadmill, still

"You know, this ten-mile race is outside. It's different from the treadmill. You really need to start training on the road."

—MIRA HARWOOD

THE REST OF that summer, I research online for a way to amp the volume on my iPod. I need to drown out the sound of Jack's brunch story with loud Rob Zombie and Breaking Benjamin. Logging miles on the treadmill and blasting loud music are my solace from the images and sounds that burn inside my imagination. Running on the road is still out of the question.

The world is full of two kinds of people. Runners and everyone else. I suppose the cliché can be applied to any group of people who hold themselves above the average joe. For some people, running comes so naturally. Not without effort, but running goes along the grain of how they are built. I am without doubt in the second group, but still I struggle to be in the first. Every step is a struggle, yet once in a blue moon, I hit a stride and can go for miles without noticing. And without wondering if the smoke killed those women and children or if it was fire. Those transcendent moments of losing myself and my thoughts come without warning and without a formula. They just happen, and the quest for another moment like that keeps me running. Keeps me pretending.

Our family is under constant, white-knuckled strain. But at least women who feel the same, even if we don't talk openly about it, surround me. My children are robbed of their father's physical presence and robbed of my mental presence. I am still anywhere but with them, lost in the images that overwhelm my ability to connect with them in the moments they need me most.

"chicken piccata: what an economical choice for an army wife"

A new wife arrives in the battalion, a brand-new bride of our new soft, pretentious major. Jack won't like him, I can tell. The major tries too hard to be intellectual, when Jack values hard work, standards, and grit far above intellect.

O NE OF MY favorite men, a major, in the unit is leaving the task force and heading to a job on brigade staff. He has been our suspiciously single major, which would have seemed more bizarre ten years ago, but now we have dozens of career officers who haven't had time to find a bride. This is not one of those. I think he prefers being single. This fellow is so unlike the others in our unit, snarky and lacking in typical bravado, not effeminate, but scholarly almost. Not like a typical soldier. Once before the army he was almost a priest, is a Yale grad, and is older than my husband. He quotes Thoreau. In the year that I've gotten to know him before the deployment, he fascinates me and I like him. And he doesn't like me, I can tell. I set up a Girl Scout table to sell cookies in the battalion one afternoon last year, and he came at me with an open wallet, asking, "How much will it cost me to get you to leave?"

His departure leaves a vacancy in our command group, and a new major is assigned in his place, this one just married. His new bride, Jodi Horatio, kept her own name—very rare in our world, a definite sign that she will not play ball with the rest of us. She has an axe to grind and numerous preconceptions about army wives. She has her "own" job and will not be defined by her husband. I suspect she will be lonely very soon if she keeps up this pretense. I invite Jodi and her husband over for dinner before he leaves to join the battalion in Iraq. He is soft and out of shape, just as Ben described.

I serve homemade chicken piccata. She makes a snotty comment that I've chosen an economically friendly meal and brags about being antiwar, and furthermore, why do we not have troops in Darfur if we are so concerned about human rights? Oh boy, does she have a lot to learn. I feel the eyes of the other guests on me, waiting for me to unleash on her. These are the things we don't say, and if we do, we don't do it in an open forum. We say them drunk and to our trusted confidantes. We earn the right to say those things. She needs to take a step back and learn from what happened to Mallory Bond. I hope the war stories of how we made an example of Mallory will make their way to her.

The brigade hosts a huge party for the families in celebration of marking a year of deployment. I feel like I've aged ten years. I attend FRG meetings and Sunday dinners, and it all becomes a blur. I am constantly revved up for more banality. We host a craft night to make elaborate care packages to send to Iraq. As I stand there contemplating evil thoughts of what I could put into that box, Mira tells me she might fill her husband's box with the piles and piles of shit from his beloved dog that she's been left to clean up after. We eye Audrey-Jill in the corner, looking bone-weary but still smiling. That baby of hers never stops crying.

part four

the home stretch and
the inevitable moment

I hope the knowledge that she isn't alone helps guilt-stricken
and sweet Mira feel better about her own meltdown.
But even so, Mira might carry the feeling of a mother's regret
with her forever. We each have our moment of breaking.

KOREANS ARE KNOWN for their exceptional mothering skills, a stereotype for sure. An off-the-books stereotype about subservient, U.S. citizenship–seeking Korean wives exists in the army. Many Korean wives speak in quiet, broken English and have macho, stern husbands. But their Korean American communities and churches are extremely close, and they stick together. Not Mira. When Mira and Mike Harwood moved in next door a year and a half ago, my mind went straight to the stereotype. The first time I saw Mira's husband, he spent the day in his garage working on his gritty, jacked-up Jeep and listening to Rob Zombie. Yeah, I had his number, or so I thought. After Mira and I became close friends, I admitted my first impression to her one night over booze. We laughed and grew closer for my admission.

Just days before we drive the nine hours to Washington, D.C., for the Army Ten-Miler race, Mira confides in me. I have often admired her calm patience with her children, her presence in the moment with them. Mira doesn't avoid mothering like I do. But we're fourteen months into single parenting and KIAs, and that takes a toll on every aspect of how we operate. We each have our own threshold, our own breaking point. Our own private moments of feeling the cheese slide from our crackers.

One late September morning, Mira reached hers. One of her kids threw a small tantrum before school over which shoes to wear. *Hello, breaking point.* Mira smacked him more than once with a shoe, screaming and swearing at him in Korean and English. Poor second-grade Matthew was stunned and stained with tears as she shoved him onto the school bus minutes later.

A matter of days before Mira's confession, I jerked my ten-year-old son Joe so hard that his glasses flew off. He and Bridget fight bitterly, and it makes me climb the walls. One afternoon I snapped. Joe is still barely speaking to me. Aside from being riddled with guilt, I'm furious for being in this position. Frustrated for having all of this on my shoulders alone. Maybe I'm wrong to deflect guilt in this way, but it feels bearable and plausible to place at least part of the blame on the war, and on Jack.

more than a race

The culmination of ten months of training arrives.
If I can finish this race, it means I can beat this deployment.

Octob"OCTOBER 2008. I signed up for this race ten months ago, when the end of the deployment seemed so far off, when it seemed I had forever to prepare. Now here I stand. Jack's been gone for fourteen months and will be home in three weeks. I want to be anywhere but standing here, but I have to do this thing. It won't be one more thing that gets the best of me. Oh, the ultimate humiliation of not making it ten miles. *Fear of social humiliation can be highly motivating.*

I've lain awake most of the night before the race and stared at the digital clock in the Crystal City high-rise hotel I am sharing with two snoring friends, Mira and Gwen Bautista. Trying to focus on the race instead of everything fucked up about my life. As I tie my shoes before dawn to board the train to the starting line, I feel both deflated and yet more determined than ever. Diametrically opposed emotions, pretty much the theme of my life. Intense highs and lows without a whole lot in between, but I crave tranquility and refuge. Today will not yield either of those elusive rewards, but I'm ready. *Smooth seas do not make skillful sailors.* The triple venti latte was unavoidable. A potty break every mile will be the price to pay.

This moment at the starting line represents more than just logging ten miles of pavement; it's the culmination of surviving our longest and most treacherous deployment. Frantic water treading and near drowning. Living in a perpetual state of fight or flight. To survive I have detached myself from my marriage and Jack, an obvious defense mechanism, though the obvious part eludes both of us then. I dread welcoming him into my home. Yes, my home. I wonder how many other wives wrestle with this dread. I am too exhausted to try to fix it. How could anyone maintain intimacy under these circumstances? And this is what insults me above all else. That marital intimacy is expected to endure such long separations. I've given everything of myself in support of these past fourteen months, not to mention the past sixteen years, and it isn't enough.

I am ready to run. Ready to beat this bitch once and for all. I haven't run a single step on the pavement in my months of training. Ten miles of pavement stretch ahead of me now, taunting me. Egging me to come and get it. I couldn't walk a mile ten months ago. Now I'm ready to run ten miles.

So here I crouch and wait for the starting gun at the base of the Pentagon with Mira and the other turds. Carb-loaded from the previous night and armed with runner's goo for energy. Instead of a supportive "Git it, girl" email from Jack, I got an email the night before asking why I needed to spend $200 on bras, and then another long email directly linking my lavish indulgence in bras to my disregard for our family. So I haven't slept well. *Aren't you fighting a war? Leave our online bank tattletale feature alone, won't you? Quit tallying up the amount of money I've spent at Starbucks in the month of September in an Excel spreadsheet, and try some sleep.* Yes, I've overspent on this deployment. I haven't saved a penny. I've bought the kids almost everything they've asked for; I've spent a fortune on the unit through entertaining and gifts. Just the expense of babysitters is breathtaking. Somehow Jack doesn't understand how expensive life without him is.

Each of the perfumed turds at the starting line is on her own journey, some of us getting ready to send husbands off, some of us (like me) feeling the butterflies of an impending reunion, some treading the muddy waters in the middle of home or gone. All of us in our own lurch, our own ever-changing battle rhythm. No one knows the extent to which my marriage is in shambles. More than fearing gossip, I just can't formulate the right words to capture how I feel. I can't share that weakness.

But this morning I have this race, and none of the noise in my head will play a part in today. Today I will run in front of the noise. Today I wish for a moment of clarity to take me away. An answer to solve everything. Maybe calmer seas lie ahead for us. But maybe chaotic seas are our home. Maybe that's where we thrive. What would we even do with peaceful waters?

This is one of those defining moments in life. I will remember this day and place other events in order according to "before the run" and "after the run." I've worked my ass and thirty pounds off to be standing here with the other thirty thousand runners. Every step of my training on a treadmill that stared out the window of the gym, at piles and piles of snow through the winter, then the thaw of spring, the heat of summer, and finally the first peek at fall before I am as ready as I will ever be. Before this early October day. Runners are prohibited from wearing iPods, and my angry death metal will be missed, but today I have more than enough fire in my belly to make up for its absence.

Fire and determination resonate from the other runners, the soldiers, the wives, those who run in memory of a fallen comrade.

Wounded warriors surround me, many of whom are amputees. We have our own reasons for inhabiting our positions at the start line, but we share a fire that fuels each of us.

Mira and I wait toward the back of the crowd for the sound of the gun. Mira is preoccupied with worry that we won't hit the designated halfway mark in the required time, resulting in the shameful pickup by the losers' bus and disqualification. I know we will make it.

"What do you know?" she says. "You've never even been off a goddamn treadmill!" Mira shoots this at me, only half laughing. Instead of feeling shackled by fear, all I feel is resolve.

little bombshells and
my nugget of strength

I can identify with the bravado Jack feels from staring at death.
I faced death too, but no one waited at home for me with a yellow
ribbon. Each of us has a silent source of strength. That thing that
defines us, the one thing that gives us muscle and buoyancy.

◆

And if you lost it all and you lost it,
Well we'll still be there when your war is over.

—STARS

THE FIRST COUPLE miles pass with ease, and I stop to pee, motioning for Mira to go ahead. I shout to her, "I will catch up, Koreana!" which is my nickname for her, but really I want to run this thing alone.

Why haven't I run outside with my friends in our months of training? My reason is fear. Fear of open road keeps my ass on the treadmill. Deep in my mind is a distant memory, the one thing I never told to anyone. The thing that tried to kill me is the very thing that gives me tenacity and courage. It's the one thing I never told another soul in my life, not even Jack. Me, the girl who is incapable of secrets. Except one.

During Jack's deployment to Somalia in 1992 to 1993, my attention to televised news was solely devoted to watching Christiane Amanpour report on the soldiers from Mogadishu for CNN. Local news held zero interest for me. If there was a psycho murdering rapist on the loose, I didn't know or care. *Stupid move, Hawkins. Never let your guard down.* In all the years since, I still find myself about twice a year looking online for records or reports of a similar attack. Each time I escape to Sackets I wonder, *Are you here? Do you remember me? The girl you wanted dead? The girl whose name you didn't know?* The idea that he wouldn't know me and I wouldn't know him overwhelms me, incomprehensible to experience my closest call with death with a person, evil or not, and not know who he was. Different, but similar to Jack's possible brushes with death in combat. All very random. Impersonal.

Well past midnight and a little past drunk after a night of playing cards with friends in Sackets, I set out to walk the half mile of open space between my friend's apartment and mine. I found a place on the curb free of snow to sit for just a minute to look at the brighter-than-usual moon and mull over whether or not to vomit. Just an open field on one side of me and buildings abandoned after World War II on the other. The sound of approaching footsteps barely registered in my mind. I didn't hear the low rumble of the diesel truck. I wasn't drunk to the point of being sloppy or incoherent, just introspective. Two and a half glasses of wine at most; I was a lightweight then. I sat and got lost in a moment of missing Jack. I raised my head from the cradle of my hands in time to feel someone shove me to the gravelly pavement and then fall on top of me. I didn't feel pain, just felt shock. It sobered me right the fuck up.

MILE 3: I look up from the pavement and see the mile-marker sign along the road. Runners pass me, and I pass only a few. I'm relieved to be on my own for the rest of the race. The absence of the treadmill forces me to remember that night fifteen years ago. The night that kept me from running outside for so many years.

The man who pushed me to the ground didn't rape or kill me like he planned. We were on gravel, and the cold was piercing and raw. I was facedown, I think. I think this because there were little pieces of gravel embedded in my left cheek afterward. And because I remember the sharp and larger-than-normal piece of gravel that dug into my chest. My right arm was pinned under me, and I remember gripping that rock, not hoping to use it as a weapon, but to keep it from digging into me. Some of the details are crystal clear twenty years later; others almost nonexistent. I never saw his face. I never saw him. I knew he was going to kill me. He had green army tape; I remember seeing the roll lying there after he tossed it presumably from his pocket. I recognized it and knew it was meant for me. His car or truck, whatever it was, was still running. I lay there recalling a self-defense expert on *Oprah* who said, "Never allow an attacker to take you to a second location." We could have been there five minutes; it could have been an hour. I remember that he smelled vile: BO, bad breath, cigarettes, even shit. To this day I tighten around stinky people. Maybe it was the shock, but I didn't feel pain. Just the overwhelming horror and surprise. I don't remember screaming, but the next day, I couldn't speak. A result of the choking or endless screaming, not sure which. Again, I knew he was going to kill me when he was ready. I was not ready.

MILE 4. I watch the other runners, wearing their Wounded Warrior hats, and shirts custom-made to let everyone know they are running in memory of a KIA soldier. I feel petty for my secret, and even worse for using it as a source of strength.

He was not much larger than me, a small man, judging by the feel of him on top of me. My new husband of just a few months was over six feet and very muscular. This man was small and chubby. Weak but determined. It occurred to me that I could get the upper hand. I didn't have to die. I was athletic and fit, a runner and an aerobics instructor, an aging acrobat. But I was a little drunk, and he was on top of me, grabbing, punching, and choking me. Struggling, both of us.

I heard the deep *whirrrr* of the military-grade hundred-mile-an-hour duct tape, and felt his weight shift off my back so he could flip me over. *I hear you, Oprah, I won't go to a second location. That's where he will chop me into a thousand pieces and dump me into the lake. Justice is home waiting for me. She will starve to death before anyone even notices I'm missing.* It must have been the perfect shot with the rock in my right hand, no idea where exactly it landed. Maybe his nose. His weight shifted off me for just a second when the sharp rock hit him, and in that second, I got up, as if someone lifted me, and I ran faster than I'd ever run. I heard his footsteps for just a few seconds behind me, then the loud slam of his truck door. I went around the grass polo field buried in snow; I heard the engine of his vehicle. I was so close to home. Too close to him to run for home. But I didn't know where to go, how to get there. I was disoriented and finally feeling the pulse of pain and blood, from the gravel, from him. There were two fields and a tall tower between me and our empty apartment. Empty but for Justice. I crouched behind a bush and snow bank and listened for the engine. My mother's voice rang in my head. A year or two earlier, there was another unsolved murder of a young woman in our isolated community. Her legs were found on the highway in the spring thaw. Her head in the lake. My mother had warned me about this woman, who was supposedly also a lieutenant's wife.

"Ang, be careful in Sackets all alone. I worry about you. Remember that young wife. No one even knew she was gone, because her husband was deployed."

I don't know how long I waited there, crouched and stunned. Too shocked to be terrified, I wouldn't feel the terror until a few hours later. The reality of what I'd escaped, the possibilities of what I'd escaped. I waited next to my building for silence, for the sound of his engine to fade. I remained motionless until I heard nothing, then I went around the back of my building and into the door with the glass window. My key was under the mat. Justice, my soul mate in the form of a four-legged creature, was waiting there at the door. Normally she slept like a log, but the floor was covered with her drool and she was pacing and whining. How did she know?

I didn't stop to hush her but ran straight for the bathroom, turned on the shower, and vomited. I had enough sense to keep the lights off. I immediately got into the shower, again hearing the voice of the *Oprah* expert warning me that I was destroying evidence. I imagined calling 911, imagined the mayhem of chaos. The uniformed men who would look at me like I was a stupid, irresponsible girl. Would Jack come home? Would his commander just walk slowly into his tent and say, *"Hey, Jack, I have some kind of bad news. It's about Ang. She's okay, but something happened"*?

I didn't give a shit about that man. Who he was and bringing him to justice. I got away. No one needed to know; I didn't need this following me around for the rest of my life. The time I got a little tipsy and decided to sit on a curb and ponder my existence. Over the years, maybe because I never told anyone, the details became less and less clear. Eventually I wasn't sure what of my memory was real. But at MILE 6, it came screaming back.

I stayed in the shower, sobbing through hands that covered my mouth and scrubbing until the hot water ran out. Even my scalp felt sore to the touch. Once I was in my house, I wasn't afraid anymore. Yes, that's weird. But I had Justice with me there. I don't know why I didn't think he might know where I lived. My sense that his choice of me was random and opportunistic was certain. I did not call the police. I did not call my parents. I couldn't explain this to anyone. I hadn't seen him enough to identify anything except the way he felt and how he smelled. I didn't see his truck, just heard the diesel. What I remembered was the sound of the tape and the feel of his pudgy, soft body. I washed him off me and vowed to never tell a soul. Actually, I don't think I decided this then—that I would carry the secret with me for the next fifteen years. Then, I only knew I couldn't call the police. The rest I played by ear.

My physical wounds were painful and sore looking, but superficial. Easily hidden by winter wear. The bruises low on my neck and knees didn't fade for weeks. I covered the few gravel marks around my chin and one side of my cheek with makeup.

The next morning just as dawn hit, I could see enough from a streetlight shining through my bedroom window to pack a small bag. I took the bag and Justice out to my car, which was buried in snow, and I drove away. I didn't even take an extra minute to let the cold car warm up or scrape the snow. I let it fall behind me as I drove away. My neck throbbed as I turned my head to look behind me, just to be sure. I barely stopped, only to refuel and let Justice go to the bathroom in the ten-hour drive to Virginia, to where my parents were living. *Surprise! I missed you guys. No, no reason. Justice and I just got lonely. Sure, Red Lobster sounds great.*

"Oh, Angie. I'm glad you came home." *Like Virginia was "home." That's a very army family thing to say; every place is home, and no place at all.* "I worried about you up there in no-man's-land all by yourself. That place is so desolate in the winter. And that lieutenant's wife. You know, I don't think they ever caught the guy who did that to her."

Did it change me? It changed me. But it didn't fuck me up, at least not much. I think if I'd gone to the police, gone through the process of being labeled a victim, a stupid one at that, it would have fucked me up much more. People would have seen me differently. What he did to me and stole from me was my own private hell. I didn't need to share it. It was my own intimate companion. What it did was change my perspective. It gave me an irreverence and fearlessness that I didn't have before. I beat him. I got away from him. I won. I stopped following rules. I drew on the memory of that night from time to time for strength. That might be fucked up, but it's the truth. What he took from me was my ability to run outside and my tolerance for tight necklaces. With my wedding dress, I was supposed to wear a chic one-piece pearl necklace that would be looped into a double-strand pearl choker. Instead, I wore the pearls as a single strand that hung low below my throat. So in some ways, I gained far more than I lost. I didn't know if I would ever be able to explain this to anyone else, especially Jack. Even though Jack was the one who needed to know.

Over the years, it left me with resolve and determination. The Belinda Becks and Eeyores of my life be damned. The same for deployments. Small potatoes. Like the night I drove myself to the hospital in the middle of a heart attack instead of calling 911; I handled it myself.

MILE 7. The first few years, the memory of the night haunted me, and eventually it faded enough and became irrelevant. Or so I thought. But it defined me in undeniable ways like my fear of running outside, unguarded.

It defined me in good ways, too. And that realization hits me as I see the sign MILE 8. I've used that night to my advantage. The attack has given me my buoyancy. In an odd way, overcoming that horrific experience on my own and keeping the secret all these years have afforded me my feeling of impervious strength.

MILE 9. What is Mira's buoyancy? What is Eeyore's buoyancy? Does Audrey-Jill, the Delicate Cajun, have buoyancy?

I cross the finish line at last; Mira, the perfumed turds, and me. Each of us struggling with demons uglier than the hard pavement pounding under our shoes. Some of us nearing the end of the fifteen months and knowing our normal will again change into another new normal of welcoming strangers back into our homes and beds. Our time together as our own family of just women is winding down, and while we feel relieved to be nearing the end, we are sad to see our routines and our rituals together end.

But this day, all we care about is beating the race, winning against something. We've kicked the ass of that ten-mile race, each of us—a victory when we've had none for so long. Maybe everything else in our days is shades of gray, but this day is black-and-white. We won; it lost.

when i get home i want
to pick up the pieces

*The days leading up to a deployment are ticked off on
a calendar one by one. So are the days leading up to a welcome
home ceremony. The preparations for both days are intense and
filled with anxious anticipation. An eager dread surrounds both days
equally. "Welcome to the jungle; it gets worse here every day."*

A FEW DAYS BEFORE Halloween of 2008, we get our first big
snowfall of the season. I've promised my kids that Daddy will be
home before the snow hits. Another set of words I wish I could take
back. Something else for the kids to be angry at *me* over.

The soldiers finally begin returning in groups of about two hundred at a time. Jack will return in the last group. Leaders bring up
the rear. After fifteen months, the last week seems like an eternity.
We prepare and plan as diligently for redeployment as we did for the
deployment, reminding families that reintegration is not easy and that
patience, understanding, and commitment are the key. More Kool-
Aid. What they don't tell us is that there will be a stranger standing in
our kitchen, awkwardly groping our asses and asking for a reminder of
where we keep the boxes of cereal. We sit through three-hour seminars
where the awkward brigade chaplain lectures us about easing back
into sexual relationships with our spouses. *Snicker, snort, from the*

wives. A chaplain talking about sex. I'm not the only one with a nervous laughter tic.

We are all on each other's nerves, but value our last moments as the family we've become before the soldiers return and we take on yet another battle rhythm. Ben entertains everyone in long briefings by passing around pictures taken of me a year earlier, thirty pounds heavier from my nightly lovemaking rituals with Ben & Jerry's and bags of Cheetos. I barely recognize that girl.

I don't tell the kids that Jack is coming home until I get confirmation that he is "wheels up" from his last layover. The disappointment from the delay of just one day would be crushing. We arrive at the gym, where all the welcome home ceremonies are held. I hear Eeyore Sweeney and Weasel Liesel complain about not having front row reserved seating, and I smile. Some things never change. I feel numb, like I did the day he left. I am there in body, and that's about it. Like I'm watching from the ceiling. The soldiers march in and are held in formation through speeches, songs, and a ceremony. Finally, they release formation, and everyone runs toward the person they've waited all this time for. Luckily, the kids dog-pile Jack with smothering hugs, and I have an excuse to hang a few paces behind. My stomach is in knots. I feel shaky and sick, not elated.

There is no other feeling that compares.

Television portrays the moment that troops come home from battle as pure joy, elation, and relief. An exhale of tension. The day we can't wait to arrive. But in reality it's a day that I dread as much as look forward to. An awful limbo of sorts. From the moment those boots stomp through the heavy steel doors of the auditorium and the crowds of waiting families scream, cry, and whoop over some cheesy, patriotic country song blaring too loudly in the background, I can hear the clock begin to tick down until he leaves again. I can feel his tension emanate toward me from somewhere in the crowd of desert-camo-covered soldiers. They should've chosen to blast "Welcome to the Jungle" instead; it would fit the moment better than "God Bless the USA." I feel it even before he bursts through, leading his exhausted but determined troops home and into the arms of families who are also exhausted but determined. Home for just a second. Just long enough to make us question which is our normal, home or gone. Just time enough to figure out a new battle rhythm.

I teeter on my spike Stuart Weitzman heels, the ones I promised myself I would buy if I survived until today, dressed up for the flashing bulbs of the media and my husband's eager eyes. Inside I'm screaming, staring at the flag with nothing but emptiness and a hint of bitterness in my gut as we are obliged to sing the national anthem one last time before the welcome home ceremony ends and finally they release the formation of haunted soldiers to find their way in the crowd back to what is left of their families and themselves. Standing together and belting out the national anthem as the final hurdle in a long deployment is a subtle but undeniable reminder that duty comes first. Families have to wait. War does not.

Jack called me the night before from Ireland, where his flight stopped to refuel. Instead of both of us overflowing with excitement, we discussed the details of the welcome home ceremony. He told me he would lead the procession of troops into the gym, right in front of where the kids and I would be seated. He asked me to remind the kids to be respectful during the ceremony and not run into the formation of troops. I wanted to roll my eyes. I probably did. I heard the exhaustion in his voice. I braced myself that morning, thinking back to his first welcome home ceremony and how then all I felt was pure relief and happiness. I would be able to sleep peacefully with him home.

Ben saw the stress on my face before the ceremony, a look he has surely become more accustomed to than a look of lightheartedness. He put his hand on my arm and asked rhetorically, "You ready?" Just fifteen months ago, he'd asked almost the same question. Now I see him trying to mask a look of elation and relief. He's almost off the hook.

After the ceremony ends and soldiers are released into the empty and waiting arms of their families, Jack hugs me stiffly and I see his jaw muscle flex. The flexing jaw muscle tells me he's pissed that I hadn't followed the instructions he gave me when he called last night from Ireland. During the ceremony, Greta ran out to the formation to hug him, which took me by complete surprise. After the way she reacted to him when he came home for R&R, I never thought she would do that. I hadn't listened to his warning to keep the kids under control, because I didn't think Greta would recognize him. I hadn't spent the deployment with pictures of Daddy plastered all around the house. My coping style has robbed our kids of a daily reminder of what he looks like.

Greta took off in a dead run toward Jack and he instinctively held the palm of his hand up to stop her. His hand took even me by surprise. I suppose he thought commanders weren't allowed to bend the rules. At the sight of his hand, Greta spun in midair and bolted back into my arms, hot with embarrassment. There was a resounding "Awwwww" from the crowd, and I saw Jack's face flash in anger. *You made me look like a dick in front of all these people, and I warned you to hold the kids back during the ceremony.* I'm not surprised when the eventual hug is stilted, and I know it is my own fault.

war hangover

Jack tries to sleep curled up on the floor now. But I don't think he even sleeps. Not even in the bedroom, a different place each night. He cleans closets while we sleep. Punishment for what he's missed, punishment for what I've failed to do.

A RMY WIVES HAVE a rule of thumb. The bliss of homecoming cannot last for longer than seventy-two hours. Sometime in those three days, we long for our days of solitude, at least once. My time comes within the first twelve hours. The night of the welcome home ceremony, the kids have a Harvest Carnival at their appealing little Catholic school. I can tell the crowd of easygoing people catches Jack off guard. He is jet-lagged, and beyond that, he feels out of place. I don't go out of my way to help him feel content. He stands at the indoor bouncy house and watches the kids play, neither of us quite grasping that he is here. He is physically present.

Standing on the other side of the school auditorium is one of Jack's soldiers, one he barely recognizes. I am well acquainted with his wife, who is infamous with our rear detachment cadre. She has finagled to get her husband home on leave so that she can pass off a new pregnancy as his. Seeing his wife bursting with pregnancy, I wonder if he even suspects and if he will see the baby for the first time and recognize nothing of himself. I never should have pointed them out to Jack. It is my gossipy instinct, to share with him something that has been a huge source of drama and speculation for our rear detachment team. Her very name has sparked fury and outrage from the whole cadre. She epitomizes the image of the bad army wife.

Jack's face blazes red when I gave him the thirty-second rundown of the drama. He reaches into his belted khakis and untucks his shirt, possibly a reaction to unfetter himself and dissuade a rising tantrum. At any rate, I regret pointing the family out. He hisses at me, "Does she not know what her husband went through to get back to his family?"

And as awful as what the woman has done, and as grotesque as I find her very existence, I want to blaze back at him, "*Do you have any idea what we went through to wait for you?*" But I don't. I will pick my battles. This one is not worth it. Our demons are our own.

ABOUT A WEEK before Thanksgiving, when we're up to here with forced family time, I stand in the kitchen alone and cooking dinner on a Friday afternoon when Mira texts and asks if she can borrow an egg. I immediately text back, "Get your Koreana ass over here."

She is at my door within the minute. Looking as relieved as I feel to be in each other's company.

"I have a function tonight," she says. "Some kind of themed Hail and Farewell, and I need to get the kids fed before Mike gets home to pick me up. He'll be here in an hour."

"We have time for wine." I open a bottle and pour us each a glass. The bottle is empty within thirty minutes, and both of us are a little drunk. It isn't even five o'clock.

I won't remember what we talk about, if anything. We just need this time together to unwind from the stiff discomfort of having our husbands home. We need to exhale and let it hang out. Our husbands' presence is like that angry in-law who visits and refuses to take the hint that it's time to leave. These men won't be leaving, well, at least not for another year.

Seeing Mira's rosy cheeks makes me feel at home. "Mike's gonna be so pissed that I'm drunk already." She slurs her words and seems almost proud of herself. That woman needs to learn to hold her booze.

That night, after Mira leaves and after we finish a family dinner, I soak in a long bubble bath. Jack can tell I've been drinking, but he doesn't let on that it bothers him. He walks quietly into the bathroom. "Ang. Please talk to me. I can't sleep. You're different. Cold. What happened? Please tell me what you're hiding," and he turns and walks out. He doesn't even wait for an answer.

Really? I'm the one who has changed? And I thought the "reintegration period" last time was rough. This time he doesn't even sleep with me, ever. Not because he doesn't want to share a bed with me, but because he doesn't sleep at all. Each morning when I've gotten up in the past month since he returned, there's a new set of closets, perfectly rearranged and organized while the rest of us slept.

Just exactly who is the fucked-up one in this scenario?

His words hit me right in the face, and I let them sink in, allow my defense mechanisms to relax, just for a moment. And I've thought I hid it so well. Maybe that race has brought it out again. And I am convinced the issue lies with him, the heavy cross to bear. He's the one who is sleeping only an hour or two at night curled in a ball on the hardwood floorboards, the ones with the taunting gouge from his stupid recliner. He's the one with memories of dead children and of men who will never again sit at their mother's dinner table and the ripples of dealing every day with a bully breathing down his neck. I harbor one little secret in comparison. So I step out of the tub and put pajamas on and walk downstairs and sit next to him.

I tell him the whole story of Sackets and why for years I've screamed when he walks into a room without my expecting it and why I choose to run on a treadmill and why I can't wear anything tight around my neck and why I can't stand being held down and tickled. He takes the news exactly like I expect, at first. That it was a violation of him, a personal affront against him. He can't grasp why I didn't call the police and why I couldn't bring myself to tell him all these years, and I don't really have an easy explanation for that. But at least now it's out there. It feels good to dump something in his lap for a change.

WE STRUGGLE THROUGH the holidays and various welcome home celebrations and military balls as a family and *command team*. Those words piss me off. We feel like anything but a team and barely speak. Both of us still too weary and bruised to indulge in the arduous work our marriage needs. Jack brings the weight and intensity of the Iraqi war zone back with him and dumps it into my previously relaxed living room. I am reminded of lyrics from a favorite song: "When I get home I wanna pick up the pieces. When I get home I wanna believe in Jesus." All of this makes the actual deployment seem like the easy part. Without Helen, our earthy, crunchy, hippy therapist, we probably wouldn't have survived. Each week, she reminds us to *fake it until we make it*, and this advice seems like an attainable goal. We are proficient at glossing over what lies beneath the surface.

hails and farewells

Fake it till you make it. Somehow that's what gets us through.
Too stubborn to give up, somehow we survive those months
of "reintegration." Such a stupid, Kool-Aid-saturated
word for what is really just a domestic battlefield.

JUST BEFORE CHRISTMAS, I attend a volunteer and rear detachment awards ceremony at the Commons, the place where we've had so many events. So many pizza nights and craft parties for the kids. The book nights and holiday parties and steering committee meetings. If these walls could talk. It feels familiar and safe to be in the company of our rear detachment cadre and FRG leaders. I've seen them here and there in the past six weeks, but this is the first time we've all been together. I've missed us. Who we were during those fifteen months. I wonder if they miss it too. I wonder if the rear detachment cadre members have grown to appreciate their time guarding the flock.

Ben is leaving Fort Drum sometime over the holidays, and I might not see him again after today. I don't want to have the wretched good-bye scene that I have with my girlfriends when one of us moves on, so I try to be laid-back at the idea that this could be the last time I might see him. I will miss the light laughter, all the stories and experiences, and the hell we shared over fifteen months. The things Jack experienced in his own way with Kate, but different from my path. While

Jack and Kate were close from their working relationship, they didn't
share the irreverence that Ben and I enjoyed. Jack thinks I let my guard
down with Ben, and he's right. I resent that Jack doesn't know me well
enough to realize that I am incapable of maintaining a guarded relationship for any period. It's against my nature.

Ben smiles and says, "Hey. I gotta tell you something. You guys
must be working through the tough reintegration stuff, and I think
I can make you laugh. I have something in my car. Come out to the
parking lot with me for a sec."

I follow him outside, and the snow and wind take my breath. He
is parked right in front, and I hear the beep-beep of his remote opener,
and the back hatch of his Jeep-type vehicle opens. I spot it right away.
The tattered brown box with the bowling ball in it.

"You suck! You totally lied to me! Why did you tell me you put
that JEANNIE ball in front of Donna's house? Where has it been all
this time?"

He chuckles. "I figured out early on that it's better to tell you what
you want to hear. It was my means of survival. You can be as relentless as your husband, in your own twisted way. I kept it at the office in
a closet. I was going to take it back to the bowling alley and wait for
you to find it on your own, but I couldn't execute that plan. I didn't
have the patience and it's too risky. This *is* stolen government property, after all. I do have some standards." And he laughs again. "It's
yours now. I just transported your stolen property in my POV. I'm sure
that's some kind of horrible offense. So you know where my loyalty
lies. I had your back, and I will after I leave. I missed The Fight this
time, but this was an eye-opening experience. There were days when
I hated your guts, but it was worth it. I'm a better person for it. Take
this damn ball, and clean up your own mess, now."

I am freezing and laughing at the memories of the last fifteen months. If I linger, it will turn to tears. I take the ball and give him a quick hug and say, "See ya, brutha. Thank you for putting up with me."

So let us not talk falsely now, the hour is getting near.

On my way back into the Commons, I duck into the coatroom and stash the box with the JEANNIE ball in the corner. I will never see it again.

IN DREARY JANUARY 2009, Jack takes thirty days' leave, and I travel alone and desperate to my parents' farm in Indiana. I crave but can't find peace in my marriage or my home, and Jack requires time alone with our kids without me hovering or hiding. I look for peace in the winter-dark home of my parents, in my childhood bed. My wounds need coddling, not just his. I blame Jack for not coming home gently, but coming back with his charts, lists, and matrices. No respect for the way I've raised our children in his absence, not just this absence, but also the many before. My life is wrapped up in his career and buying into the notion that I am an invaluable member of our command team. I see now that it is bullshit. None of this translates onto my own résumé. I have no career and thus no way of maintaining a life apart from our marriage. I am left with a deep love for a brimming-to-the-top glass of wine and my list: "Crazy Shit People Said to Me in Fifteen Months." Yet I love army life. I resent him for making me even contemplate an existence apart from a life I love and am invested in.

At my parents' comforting home, I feel as claustrophobic as I did in my own. The change in scenery isn't the quick fix I hoped it would be. The boredom and silence overwhelm me more than the chaos I left behind. I reread my list of Crazy Shit, smile at the memory of Mallory Bond asking if everything in my home is owned by the government, feel sick at the memory of the devoted but weary young mother who wanted to give her son up for adoption. I tear that page from my journal and throw it into the fire. I don't even wad it first. I want to see the words burn. I'll later wish I'd kept that list, but the secrets no longer feel like mine to share. The list resonates too personal and loaded to keep in my custody.

Jack begs me to come home after two weeks, so I do. I miss my life, my kids, and my friends. Miss my army sisters. Miss our pizza Fridays. Miss the rush of adrenaline we are accustomed to. I miss Jack. The memory of the reverberation and cadence of his boots calls me home to our life. Another new normal waits there. He needs me. Like a child who takes out his pent-up anger and tantrums on his parents because they are his safe place, Jack considers me his safe place. He can't direct his gall where it belongs, and I hope he can push through. That we can push through.

As the snow piles up yet again and the holidays and thirty days of leave end, we gather together as a brigade for the last month before we all change commands with the new, bright-eyed, and full-of-energy teams poised to take our places. Just like we were almost three years earlier. I sit through all of the good-bye speeches and presentations and begin to see the deployment through the eyes of everyone around me. Luckily I am wily enough to arrive early for the farewell dinners with seating charts so I can move my seating to avoid the perfumed turds whom I can't stand another moment next to. Caution is long gone. I don't even care if someone from the protocol office sees me. It takes me an army's worth of social lubrication to survive the merry-go-round of mandatory farewell receptions and brouhaha events. Getting liquored up is unavoidable.

Barb Petty looks as haunted as I feel. Her husband is slighted by everyone at his own farewell; not one of the six battalion commanders who served under him stands or speaks on his behalf—which goes against typical farewell protocol and makes it clear how miserable life under him must have been for more than just Roselle Hoffmaster and Jack. Everyone in our brigade is in a reflective mood, sharing intimate stories and anecdotes that make me realize I was not alone. I was so consumed with making it through myself that I hadn't imagined the mutual hardships and also the beauty of the past year and a half. I give Barb a pair of sterling spur earrings, the christening of a cavalry wife. Although she is married to a quintessential schoolyard bully, she has earned her place with me. Barb left me alone and didn't micromanage the way I chose to lead. I can't fault her for her husband. If anything, she deserves her spurs even more.

I glance around at the faces so familiar, the women. I absorb images of the men who are their other half, the half that's much less familiar to me, and likely to them as well. The men look pinched and uncomfortable, like Jack. The women appear strained and exhausted. We all reek of weariness. A room full of the black-soul phenomenon. All of a sudden I don't feel so alone in the recognition of my own mixed feelings mirrored in those faces. In those faces, I see that the seemingly repugnant behavior wasn't so atrocious after all. Everything is forgivable. Everything we said and did and felt was magnified by the presence of something we couldn't control, and that fact definitely brought out the crazy. Each of us will carry a balance of regret and pride for the rest of our lives.

Or until the next deployment.

Our replacements arrive from the Ranger Battalion at Fort Benning, an Italian American man who is barely over five feet tall and his wife, an angry and rough ex-stripper (according to the rumors) who makes her disdain for the army immediately clear. Lovely and so painful that we are leaving the battalion we poured our souls into in these hands. One tiny pair of hands and the other, stripper hands.

The first week of February 2009 brings more farewells and ceremonies as the entire leadership for the brigade makes the transitions to various other positions and schools; many people prepare for yet another deployment. Wondering when and where we might ever rid ourselves of that burden, if ever. All of us stronger and weaker for our experience. Energized and depleted of strength.

In the mass exodus of our team, which is more of a tight-knit family than a team, Ben leaves for Fort Leavenworth, but before he goes, he pulls me aside after a change-of-command ceremony to say good-bye. The good-bye I thought we already had. As with all tough good-byes, I hover somewhere above myself so I can get through the moment. For us in this life, living in the moment is next to impossible. Ben smiles his charming smile and gives me that look of concern one last time with his head cocked to the side. I wouldn't have made it without him kicking my ass and holding me together. He says to me, "Whatever you do, I've got your six. Are you going to be okay? Hey, maybe I complained a lot, but this was worth every second. And you know that's hard for me to admit. Thanks. I'm a better person for it. I don't think I ever want to get married, because you're all a bunch of high-maintenance beeyotch monsters, but it was worth it." I can't answer him, because I don't want to cry and people are watching. War-weary, that's all I can feel anymore. And shit. Haven't we already said good-bye and gritted our teeth through this part? The end is always full of good-byes, and some of them bear repetition.

part five

echoes of chaos

*With a vivid appreciation for each other and what we overcame,
none of us are the same. Not Jack or me. Not Ben. Not my friends.
When young death is just part of the daily rhythm, it takes a piece
of your soul and flushes it. But it adds something else. Maybe jaded,
maybe even a little bitter. But mostly sweeter. Never mediocre.*

—JUNE 2012

◆

The bullets in our firefight is where I'll be hiding, waiting for you

—DAVE MATTHEWS

THREE YEARS SINCE we left Fort Drum. Bin Laden is dead. Iraq is over. Neither of these events is as defining or pivotal in our minds as one might expect. We in the army paid less attention to the big picture; over the years, seeking revenge on bin Laden specifically slid down our list of priorities. Soldiers and their families like Jack and me needed to get through the day intact, with our people intact. That was our success; ridding the world of bin Laden or Saddam Hussein was an afterthought at best.

I questioned whether my marriage would survive, and now that the chaos of war is winding down, we have to figure out a new normal again. The dull weariness remains, but maybe it will never go away. The main reason our marriage survived is more likely because it does take the back burner to the hypervigilance of war for so many years. And because we are both supremely stubborn and refuse to quit anything. There is no time or energy to indulge in the essence of our marriage. We weren't connected then in a traditional sense; during that period we were more like business partners than a married couple. Detached and focused on the mission, time for the touchy-feely shit later. Our souls are forever blackened, but maybe that doesn't have to be a bad thing. Black is the amalgamation of all colors, right? Black is better than gray.

In truth, Jack is more emotional than me but is better at setting his emotions aside when he needs to. Learning to compartmentalize is vital to this lifestyle of constant stress and change. I wonder if everyone's marriage feels as dilapidated and smacked around as mine. Still to this day, Jack doesn't sleep for more than a few hours at a time and can't get comfortable in a bed. Aside from the weight on his spirit, Jack's rigorous combat lifestyle of treating his physical body as another obstacle to overcome has taken its own toll. Jack has endured three complicated shoulder surgeries, both ankles and elbows are forever damaged, and he continues to delay a surgery, which will fuse discs in his back. The surgery will greatly decrease his twisting mobility and possibly take him from the infantry for the rest of his career. On top of that, his hearing is severely impaired as a result of years spent in roaring helicopters surrounded by IED blasts and gunfire.

Those are the kinds of war stories we don't talk about with each other, the wives. I'm not alone in this experience. War doesn't pick and choose the good from the bad, though goodness is the earnest goal of our soldiers and that of the senior wives, to an extent. We are the mentors. We have to keep our shit together, our war faces firmly locked in place, or at least give that appearance.

The fact that it took twelve years of our lives to accomplish killing bin Laden robbed us of time, but blessed us with wisdom. It robbed my children of years with their father, childhood years that Jack will never get back. Years of memories: soccer games and stomach viruses. The kids will be fine. It's Jack who will look back and maybe face regret.

Vick Petty has been forced into retirement, asked to go quietly. He was implicated in contributing to the suicide of Roselle Hoffmaster through his toxic leadership and bullying. There is a slight moment of relief that he finally got his dose of karma, but it comes too late. Roselle's family will never feel justice for her loss.

Jack and I are back in the North Country visiting for the wedding of Ben Black in Sackets Harbor on Lake Ontario. Our first time back since we drove away on a rainy day in 2009. We drive around Fort Drum, past his old battalion, down our old streets. The smell of the pines brings memories flooding back. I can almost see the snow banks piled to the top of the stop signs even though it's a sweltering day in June. This place feels familiar and also very uncomfortable, unfinished. A time of reflection, remembering what we were and what we are now. Remembering the things that we thought had broken us, but just bent us instead. Not long ago I found a date book from that time, completely full of endless and mostly meaningless meetings. Neat to-do lists filling the sides of each page. Visit new mothers in hospitals. Take dinner to so-and-so. Send thank you note. Pick up new army wife handbook for what's-her-face. It was endless, and where was the real meaning in it?

Now that I'm standing back, I see it differently. My importance to the greater machine is meaningless; it goes right along with or without me. The army machine doesn't care about any one individual. Each of us is expendable, but we leave a collective footprint. The deepest meaning is in the sisterhood, how we kept each other from drowning.

Are we as buoyant as Elizabeth and I hoped? Maybe we sank underwater for a while, but we did not drown. Now, how we swim out of the calming waters remains to be seen.

Where will Jack and I be without the mistress to take our focus and energy?

AT BEN'S WEDDING reception, I take a stiff cocktail and walk by myself down to the edge of the water to look out over the now calm lake. The lake that wasn't always so serene. The lake that stood and watched a faceless man try to overpower me and silently stood witness to the fight in the snow-slushy gravel almost twenty years ago. A lake that kept my secret. The lake shares my understanding of what overcoming the attack means: buoyancy. It built my impervious shell that has allowed me to endure the nearly twenty years that have led me here again; it began my journey toward the black-soul syndrome. For the protection those things offered, the horror of that night was a sick blessing. One that Jack might not ever quite understand, and that's okay. I don't understand his demons either, but our love endures beyond the haunting memories we don't share. In spite of them. Our shared path continues, now with a truce between us. Jack is a part of me; he has been from the day I first laid eyes on him in that bar with the dirt floor until now, twenty-one years later. He is the team to my command, as the army saying goes. As much as we don't understand the specifics of what we've each faced, we understand just enough. Just enough to give us peace. Finally. Placing my head in the crook of his neck has always been my safe place, but one where I never allowed myself to feel too vulnerable. I couldn't count on that feeling of safeness then, but now maybe I can. For the first time in a long time, it doesn't feel like we are *faking it until we make it*. We're making it now.

Ben walks up behind me as I take a whopping gulp of my vodka-and-something-I-can't-identify drink. *Hey you.*

"How was the wedding? Did you like it? Sorry you have to sit with people you don't know for dinner. I didn't do the seating chart; Jane's mom did it. I know how you hate small talk with strangers."

"The wedding was magnificent, Ben. Perfect. How is *Town & Country* magazine not here to cover it? I'm just thrilled that Jack and I could make it back, and that so many from the old team are here. We're all the same but different too, still connected. Don't you think? And yeah, there will be a price to pay for you sitting me next to your new in-laws' cousins. Jack is itching for the DJ to start so he can tear up the dance floor. Will you make sure they play Salt-N-Pepa for him, please?"

Laughter. And his familiar squeeze on my arm. Nothing is perfect, but it all feels as it should be. Full circle, or at least full oval. Imperfect but beautiful still. Weary but hopeful.

Images and words spoken from our years here at Fort Drum will from time to time pop into my mind and bring it all back like it was yesterday. Those memories are a part of me as much as the legs that carry me into whatever the next chapter is. My wounded heart will recover. Above everything else, beyond the long hardships, one outcome is the most invaluable. The sisterhoods. The lifelong friends and bonds that will never lessen. Years can go by, and I will pick up with each of those sisters as if a single day hasn't passed. Only we can truly understand one another; not even our husbands can fully grasp what we've been through with each other and how ironclad those bonds are.

This place is radioactive with memories. Sackets isn't a place; it's a person. It sees me, it saved me. It stood by and sacrificed me, knowing in the end it would only give me the resiliency to survive. Instead of feeling afraid here, I am wiser for appreciating Sackets for what it was.

In the end, nothing is good or evil. I am, as we all are, somewhere in between. It is entirely possible that writing this book could turn me into a pariah among my peers in the hard-core, gung-ho combat culture, for discussing our weary, black souls and our secret sisterhood that both embraces us and knocks us off our high horses, but my gut hopes otherwise. If my instincts are off, it's a price I'm willing to pay to get my story out there—the story wives share privately but don't publicly discuss. A tale desperate to slip out of my soul and into the minds and hearts of civilians, readers who often have a skewed and contrived perception of what we've been through. The ones who think we knew what we were getting into when we signed up for this lifestyle.

Memories of how it brought out the best and worst in all of us. How lucky we were to have stood in those shoes and felt what it means to live through wartime. And none of us wants to lose that. Even if I had a heart attack along the way. Every single word and every single day was worth it. Together we found beauty that lies in the center of chaos.

army-speak as
a second language

A NY DECENT, KOOL-AID-DRINKING army wife uses these words fluidly in her everyday conversations and understands that while many of the words appear synonymous, it's all about the context and nuance of usage. For the sake of a comprehensive explanation, I've gone a little heavy-handed in each example. So if anyone tries this at home, use an off-the-books rule of no more than two per sentence, please.

AAR (after-action review): "That bake sale was a disaster. Too many cookies, and the brownies sold out right away. We didn't have enough change, and we have to label the gluten- and peanut-free stuff better. These lessons learned can be written in the AAR, and next time it won't be such a nut roll."

AO (area of operation): "Kids! Police up your AO before Dad gets here. Do you want to be doing pushups until you're old enough to vote? Make it happen! ASAP."

ate up (basically, a mess): "The commissary bagger who loaded my groceries today was all ate up. She packed the canned goods in the same bag with my bread. This is just soup sandwich."

AWOL (absent without leave): "Who last had eyes on the remote control for the TV? It's AWOL from its designated spot right here on the GD table!"

BLUF (bottom line up front): "I don't have time to listen to your long-winded diatribe about the woman who ranted at the last meeting. Just gimme the BLUF; I can get the details later."

break contact (leave a location): "When are we going to break contact? This luncheon is hella lame and I have important shit to get done."

brief (a statement of fact): "The kids have a DONSA today. No school. I briefed you on Sunday. You really need to pull your head out of your ass and establish some SA."

BUB (battle update brief): "Here's the BUB. She fell out of a tree, no broken bones, but she will need stitches and light duty for a few days."

Charlie Foxtrot (abbreviation for *cluster fuck* using the phonetic alphabet): "I knew that the wives' coffee was going to be a Charlie Foxtrot. She didn't even put an RSVP date on the Evite. It was doomed from the word go."

chow (food, of any kind): "You're really going to serve lasagna as the chow for your dinner party?"

combat roll (a way of falling to avoid injury): "Thank God she executed a combat roll when her bike hit that tree. She wasn't even looking. Betcha she doesn't have a mark on her."

DONSA (day of no scheduled activity): "Did you hear some lame dud lost a pair of NODS [night vision goggles] and the guys have work on Friday? It was supposed to be a DONSA. What a brainiac move."

downrange (a dated way of referring to a deployment): "When my husband was downrange, he never got to call. Not once." "Bitch, please. No one says 'downrange' anymore. The nineties called, and they want their lame peacekeeping terminology back."

ETA (estimated time of arrival): "Chow will be ready at 1700, and we are not going to wait for you. What's your ETA from work?"

extract/exfil (depart from an area, usually picking someone up): "My commander is spinning, and I'm in PowerPoint hell. I know you have a coffee scheduled for tonight, but you're going to have to extract the kids from soccer practice. Sorry 'bout that. Mission first, baby."

eyes on (watching closely): "Honey! One of the kids left the gate open and the dog escaped. Oh wait, I have eyes on him. He's sniffing around down the street."

fire & forget (an angry outburst quickly followed by a recovery to normal, calm behavior): "She screamed a stream of four-letter words at the snowplow driver in front of everyone this morning and then came over to borrow an egg fifteen minutes later, like nothing ever happened. Whew. Thank God that woman is fire & forget by nature."

Gold Star (family members of a fallen soldier): "This is just subpar. We are going to have five Gold Star families at this reception, and this crudité plate looks a week old. We can do better than this. Call Sergeant Somebody and square this away!"

got your six/mind your six (I've got your back/watch your back): "You'd better mind your six with that crowd. That bunch of spotlight rangers will do anything to make themselves look better. Don't worry, though. I've got your six."

GTG (good to go): "Are you GTG for the Hail & Farewell tonight?"

head down (watch out): "The colonel's wife is on a rampage. Keep your head down and stay in your lane, and the storm will pass."

high speed (badass): "The new houses have real hardwood floors! This is some high-speed living right here!"

hot wash (quick, mini after-action review): "Kids! Listen up! We conducted PCIs before this hike! Everyone has the gear they need, and no, I am not going to carry any of you back or hump your gear. Pillows and stuffed animals were not on the packing list. What you have there is a personal problem and an inability to follow packing orders. As soon as we get back, we will do a hot wash to make sure we don't have unnecessary gear weighing us down. Then we can update our packing list with lessons learned for the next hike. But for now, shake it off and drive on. Or no cookies when we get home. No more whining, are we clear?"

hump (walk, or carry your own gear): "No way, José. You are three years old now and can hump your own stash of Halloween candy.

Buck up, little man. Mommy is not humping that heavy pillowcase stuffed with crummy candy. Unless I can have the M&Ms. Then we can negotiate."

IRP (immediate response, please!): "Where's the social roster? These phone numbers are all jacked up. I can't disseminate this soup sandwich information to the wives. We have one hour to fix this, IRP!"

JOC (Joint Operations Center): Wife: "Tell me again what the difference is between a JOC and a TOC [Tactical Operations Center]? Is one a building and the other a tent? I don't get it. They seem like pretty much the same damn thing." Husband (eye roll and sigh): "Listen. We don't have tents. This isn't *M*A*S*H*. JOCs are bigger. TOCs are smaller. Anything else?"

Joe (slang term to describe soldiers): "That entire area of bars off of Factory Street is off limits for Joes. Joes need to just stay in the barracks to party."

move out (get moving): "I just vacuumed! Who was eating in here? Get your gear and move out of this AO!"

net call (establish phone contact with entire team): "I just realized I haven't seen any of the kids in over thirty minutes. Let's do a net call to establish SA on everyone's whereabouts, roger?"

no-go (not gonna happen): "Tyler, your sleepover is a no-go tonight. That kid has slept over here every weekend, and I have a coffee tonight. Babysitter coming over, and I'm ordering pizza for chow."

OBE (overcome by events): "Listen, I'm not going to be able to make it to the Whine and Wine this afternoon. The newsletter is jacked up, I have an insubordinate volunteer to deal with, and one of the kids just projectile-vomited. I'm a little OBE right now."

O-Dark (any time before daylight): "I guess the projectile vomiting wasn't food-poisoning-induced. Another kid woke me up at O-Dark puking her guts up."

PCI (precombat inspections): "If you'd conducted proper PCIs before the hike, you wouldn't be asking me for a bite of my sandwich. Sucks to be you."

POV (privately owned vehicle): "I was so distracted when I went to the commissary that I had no clue where I'd parked my POV. Can you believe it? I need to pull my head out of my ass and establish some kind of SA, or I will never survive this deployment."

prepare to copy (grab a pen and paper): "Do you have the number for the child-care reservations line? All right. I'm prepared to copy."

rack out (go to sleep): "Today has been never-ending. I'm going to rack out early tonight and try to forget that this day ever happened."

ranger candy (aka "Vitamin M," 800 mg ibuprofen): "I'm exhausted from trying to keep up, and my damn legs are killing me. Do you have a bottle of ranger candy?"

ranger on/drive on (keep moving forward regardless of how shitty the situation): "This place is soup sandwich. We're going to have to just drive on and push through. Suck it up, buttercup."

RECON (reconnaissance): "How in the hell did you not realize there are no outlets available for all these Crock-Pots? You get a no-go on your RECON mission. No one is going to buy a cold chili dog. Major fail."

roger/roger out (understand/good-bye): "I don't even know how to start the snow blower. If you snow-blow my driveway, I will get your commissary essentials before the next wave of lake effect [snow] hits, roger? GTG. Roger out."

rub the tab (a reference to rubbing, supposedly for a burst of strength and endurance, the gritty RANGER tab worn by army rangers on their left shoulder): "You have no idea what pain is until you give birth. Pop a piece of ranger candy and rub the tab."

SA (situational awareness): "The meeting was Wednesday morning, yesterday. You missed it. Your calendar is all ate up. You'll never survive fifteen months of this bullshit if you can't pull yourself together and maintain a little SA, got it?"

scouts out (first out the door): "Hey! Trick-or-treat started at five, and you know everyone runs out of candy quickly. Do you want to make a candy killing? Then scouts out! Gotta beat the crowds."

Sergeant Somebody (no one has any idea who this elusive character is): "Where are the copies of the social roster for the Hail & Farewell tonight? Sergeant Somebody must have them."

SITREP (situational report): "Sorry I'm late for the unit military ball planning meeting. Gimme a quick SITREP. What did I miss?"

soup sandwich: See *ate up*.

SOP (standard operating procedure): "What's the SOP for the kids' bedtime? Do you give them their baths and then a bedtime snack or the other way around? And who needs a nightlight? We're raising a bunch of soft babies. They need to get hard and sleep in the dark, on the floor! Like the kids in Iraq. Kids in Iraq don't have friggin' blankies."

SP (start point): "You need to bump up SP if you want to be on time for school. Yesterday you almost missed the bus, and I don't have time to drive you."

spotlight ranger (glory hound, only performs when people are looking): "She turns on the charm when the big dogs show up. She brought a damn bag of Chips Ahoy! to the last potluck, and this time she brings a full lasagna because she knows a GO [general officer] wife is going to be here? Bitch puleez. Everybody knows she's a spotlight ranger wife."

squared away (ready): "Those centerpieces for the ball are gorgeous! You guys did a phenomenal job on the tables. Everything is squared away and GTG for tonight."

stay in your lane (stick to what you know): "I am in charge of the roster, got it? You plan the agenda for the steering committee meeting. Mind your own bidness and stay in your lane."

step it out (walk faster): "Step it out, or we're going to be late for the change-of-command ceremony."

suck it up: See *rub the tab*.

tracking (understanding): "I am not tracking what this bitch is talking about. Girl, are you tracking? 'Cause I have no clue."

war face (game face): "This is going to be a three-hour meeting. I just know they're going to read a hundred PowerPoint slides to us, verbatim. Better get our war faces on."

WARNO (warning order): "Ladies, everyone needs to RSVP for events, are we clear? Protocol is important, and this is just good manners. Consider this a WARNO. Next time, heads will roll."

WILCO (will comply): She: "Can you pick up milk en route home tonight?" He: "WILCO. Anything else?"

acknowledgments

FIRST AND FOREMOST, I am grateful to my agent Kim Witherspoon for envisioning a novel behind a three page rambling email with a concept, but not a manuscript. By encouraging me to tell my story you made my childhood and secret lifelong dream of becoming a writer a reality. I am humbled by your wisdom. Many thanks to Allison Hunter for talking me off the ledge throughout the journey. To Jack Shoemaker and his team at Counterpoint, thank you for your passion and commitment to this project and for your patience and kindness. Dan Smetanka, where would I be without you reminding me to keep my mean girl on a leash and for ruthlessly cutting my redundancies? You've been an incredible mentor and partner. Thank you to everyone at Inkwell Management and Counterpoint Press for giving validity and a voice to the journey of "just an army wife."

Without the service and sacrifice of the families of TASK FORCE GHOST, 1-71 Cavalry, and all those who have lost a loved one to war, this book wouldn't have been written. Thank you for allowing me to become part of your lives and for making sure your lost souls are never forgotten. Each war is different and leaves a unique footprint. This is ours.

Many thanks to the Graham family and Roselle Hoffmaster's widower, Gordon Pfeiffer, for allowing me to be a voice. For more information and to help in the crusade against suicide, please refer to the Jeffrey and Kevin Graham Support Services.

To every army sister, even the ones I wanted to shove out of the boat we shared—thank you for giving me a lifetime of rich memories. No doubt that I needed to be shoved out into the deep waters many times, too. In the end our sisterhood was stronger than whatever divided us. Your strong, beautiful and colorful personalities and stories helped fill the pages of my book. There are three sides to every story; mine, yours and what really happened. This is my version, my memory.

A special thanks to Susette Ryan, who didn't make it into this book, but is still the best friend an army wife could have. I've been incredibly blessed with a rich posse of girlfriends who remind me every day that I'm not alone and not as weird as I think.

I am the luckiest daughter in the world for the devoted and engaged parents who gave me the life any kid would envy, and who tirelessly read me the story about Pablo the penguin over and over as a preschooler, though I had it memorized. You taught me the beauty of losing myself in the pages of a book before I learned to read. My mother taught me to always do better and my dad taught me to speak my mind. Both taught me to work my ass off, and good things will come. I hope my children love their life as army brats as much as I've loved mine.

Thank you to my Aunt Lindy and the Fish family in Indiana for giving me a place to call home every summer and whenever I needed respite. The gift of a steadfast home in the whirlwind of nomadic army life is priceless.

My Grandma Kathryn died before I was born, but I've felt her steady hand on my shoulder at every dark or bright moment of my life. I can't wait to meet you in heaven.

I remember so clearly at the age of eight, my librarian cousin Pat brought me piles of books that looked so grown up, thank you Judy

Blume. I hope Pat knows that she shaped my view of the world with those books. To all the teachers who inspired me along the way, I am grateful.

What about all the people in between? If I acknowledge some of them, then surely I will overlook and hurt the feelings of other people I love and adore and who have listened to me whine, procrastinate and obsess for the past two years since I sat down and thought, "Hey, I think I'd like to write a book." Renegades sisters, thanks for reminding me that each of us is unique, but none of us special. Miri Macneilly, Aneice McShan and Leslie Jaworowski, you are incredible friends and tirelessly detailed beta readers. Your support and feedback has been invaluable.

My children. I love each of you to infinity and beyond. I'm lucky to be your mom. Thank you for giving me a reason to move forward everyday, for making sure I laugh out loud, and for giving so much of yourselves to something you couldn't control. The sacrifice of military children is beyond measure. Each day you remind me to slow down and soak up every moment, even the ones I'd like to forget. I am so proud of the independent, strong and kind people you are becoming.

Most of all, to my handsome and loyal husband Darrin. I am grateful for your love and support, for your optimism and for being a devoted, generous and encouraging father to our sweet children. You've made up for what you missed. Most of all, I love being able to say that you are my better half. You have made me a better person for putting up with me all these years. Thank you for allowing me to tell this story and for encouraging me every single day to go like hell. I'm sure you would have written a very different book, but thank you for allowing me to write it my way. We survived the storm and the best is ahead.